School-Based Management as School Reform

Joyce Barksdale
Laraine Caldwell
Ruby Fisher
Cheryl McClure
Ida Reale
With deepest gratitude for all their help

School-Based Management as School Reform

Taking Stock

Joseph Murphy
Lynn G. Beck

CORWIN PRESS, INC.
A Sage Publications Company
Thousand Oaks, California

For information address:

 Corwin Press, Inc.
2455 Teller Road
Thousand Oaks, California 91320

SAGE Publications Ltd.
6 Bonhill Street
London EC2A 4PU
United Kingdom

SAGE Publications India Pvt. Ltd.
M-32 Market
Greater Kailash I
New Delhi 110 048 India

Printed in the United States of America

Library of Congress Cataloging-in-Publication Data

Murphy, Joseph, 1949-
    School-based management as school reform: Taking stock / Joseph
Murphy, Lynn G. Beck.
        p. cm.
    Includes bibliographical references and index.
    ISBN 0-8039-6175-8 (alk. paper).   —   ISBN 0-8039-6176-6 (pbk.:
alk. paper)
    1. School-based management—United States—History. I. Beck,
Lynn G. II. Title.
LB2806.35.M87   1995
371.2'00973—dc20   95-7733

This book is printed on acid-free paper.

95 96 97 98 99 10 9 8 7 6 5 4 3 2 1

Corwin Press Production Editor: Gillian Dickens

Contents

Foreword

The 1983 publication of the National Commission on Excellence in Education report, *A Nation at Risk*, triggered one of the longest sustained periods of school reform in U.S. history. For more than a decade, and probably continuing into the foreseeable future, seemingly endless numbers of education reform reports and proposals have been streaming from U.S. think tanks and policy grinders.

This reform period has witnessed the first ever presidentially convened governors' summit devoted to education, covering new congressional enactments aimed at reforming long-standing federally financed education programs, proposals for national examination systems, construction of vastly new mechanisms for appraising teacher performance, state-initiated efforts to free schools from layers of long-standing regulatory restrictions, local school districts contracting with private sector firms to manage and operate schools, and numerous proposals to privatize schools even further by relying on voucher plans.

These reform initiatives have flowed from federal, state, and local governments; private foundations; intergovernmental commissions; influential candidates for national office; professional associations; and private sector interests. Some suggestions are remarkably naive and overly simple. Others are models of self-interest and short-sightedness. Still others are complicated beyond comprehension. A few are thoughtful and genuinely intended to render education more effective or more efficient. Regardless of the source or the motives, however, the proposals proliferate, and even if no single reform strategy seems yet to be gaining dominance among policy makers and practitioners, the more remarkable phenomenon is the sustained momentum of and the wide range of creativity to be found within the overall effort. Reformers may not agree on the manner in which schools should be changed, but there appears to be imaginative and virtually boundless energy directed at changing them.

School-based management, the subject of this book by Joseph Murphy and Lynn G. Beck, is a prominent and persisting reform proposal. It is an idea widely discussed among reformers and often contained in local, statewide, and even some federal, suggestions for rendering schools more effective. Because school-based management has many different components, indeed, even many different definitions, it is difficult to trace its roots. Almost any reform idea seems to have an infinite regress of predecessors. One has a feeling that Socrates, Hammurabi, or Genghis Khan invented everything and that the remainder of us have only been honing their ideas ever since.

Be that as it may, the first time that school-based management appears as a complete idea was in a New York state education reform report, issued by the so-called Fleischmann Commission in 1973. The idea was not widely embraced in New York. Then-governor Nelson Rockefeller was actually hoping for a recommendation from this blue ribbon body for public aid to nonpublic schools. What he got was a set of thoughtful analyses about school finance and governance. In his disappointment, he ensured that the ideas were buried for New York.

However, the analysts and advocates who framed the complex of notions for New York were subsequently employed in Florida to redo that state's school finance system. In the process of designing a new scheme, they simultaneously put forward school-based management as an accompanying governance reform to counter the heavily centralizing components of the scheme they were advocating for raising and distributing revenue. Florida was then blessed with a particularly farsighted group of state legislators, many of whom went on to even greater prominence as U.S. senator, governor, lieutenant governor, and so forth. The notion of school-based management was attractive to them, and they embedded many of its components in a 1975 Florida education reform statute. The entire idea received another substantial infusion of publicity and energy when the Thatcher government made school-based management a prominent feature of its landmark 1988 Education Reform Act (ERA).

In the two decades since its unsuccessful debut in New York state, school-based management has been a reform component in many prominent settings. It persists as an idea, and a practical reality in selected instances, because it addresses several fundamental criticisms of the existing system of educational management. Depending upon the variant of school-based management under discussion, it promises to reduce mindless bureaucratic regulatory layering, unleash the creative potential of teachers, rebuild the nexus between parents and schools, and restore public school power to the public. These justifications are deserving of greater discussion.

One set of school critics contends that professional performance and accountability are impeded by the present model of school district governance, which often provides central office officials with great authority and grants only limited discretion to administrators, teachers, and others at school sites. The heavy regulatory overlay that tends to accompany such a centralized authority model is said to impede effective accountability because the layers of rules govern process and provide endless excuses for school personnel when student performance is low. A school principal can act like the surgeon who proclaims surprise and regret that the patient died after he performed the operation absolutely by the book. Similarly, education professionals, in a centralized system, can proclaim their innocence of failure because they may have literally volumes of procedural rules behind which they can hide. "I am sorry that Johnny cannot read. We adhered to the state or central office guidelines regarding class size, teacher qualifications, textbook selection, use of drill sheets, deployment of reading specialists, and so on." "We went by the book that you all proscribed. If Johnny doesn't read, then maybe those of you on the school board and at the central office should change the book."

Advocates of school-based management often assert that public education can only be rendered more effective if this central office mode of proscription is disrupted and true operating responsibility is placed close to the point where instruction actually occurs—in schools. By empowering principals, teachers, and perhaps parents, school-based management reformers intend for decisions to be made closer to the children and families affected and believe accountability will be enhanced because one can actually determine if students are learning. If they are not, then the weak link in the system is more evident—it is not some districtwide set of policies and rules, but rather the performance of those at the actual school site.

Yet another observation on the dysfunctional nature of centralized control stems from those who believe "the public" has been frozen out of public schools. These observers contend that excesses of school district and school consolidation, and the tremendous population growth of the past century, have combined to render many school districts overly large and bureaucratized systems in which the will of the citizenry is neglected and only the insistent self-serving demands of special interests are heard. When this analytic viewpoint is heard, the accompanying reform that is frequently called for is parent or citizen empowerment. The solution is seen as decentralization or the establishment of parent advisory councils at school sites.

These are the reforms proposed by those who continue to believe that the school system should continue to be publicly managed and operated. Those of less faith contend that the appropriate reform is continued public management, but reliance upon private provision. More radical yet are those who have lost virtually all faith in public control and call for privatization. Privatization is the next reform category for discussion and will be the focus of a forthcoming book by Joseph Murphy. Here we continue to concentrate on the public hope of decentralized management.

The Role of This Book

This book about school-based management concentrates on a reform at the heart of current change efforts. For those who believe that schools need to change in order to deliver what society needs in the 21st century, but are reluctant to overthrow the entire existing means for governing and managing schools, school-based management is an eminently sensible approach. It retains public control while simultaneously fostering good instructional practice and good management tactics. It also offers the prospect of effective accountability.

However, school-based management is not a self-implementing policy. It can be threatening to many current stakeholders. From a school board member's perspective, school-based management may be designed to reduce micro management, but it holds the potential for restricting political responsiveness. School-based management, if misperceived by superintendents and other central office authorities, appears to erode their central authority. Principals, on the other hand, may fear school-based management precisely because it empowers them and strips away their ability to hide behind procedural rules. Teacher union officials may oppose school-based management if it is perceived as eroding union authority over matters such as transfer and seniority privilege. Teachers themselves may be less than fully enthusiastic, because school-based management may conjure up an image of far greater work, to accompany the far greater professional responsibility. Last, parents and the general public may not care much about the issues involved because the information costs involved in understanding school-based management are high and the entire issue hardly ranks with such current events, however fleeting, as a celebrity murder trial or sports championships.

Almost since its contemporary launch, researchers have poked and probed to determine what about school-based management works and what does not. The definitional thickets, political complexity, and multiple practical challenges involved in implementing school-based management render this book all the more timely and important. Does it—can it—deliver the hoped-for benefits? What components make the most sense? What opposition is unjustified and what is simply self-protective? To begin to sort all of this out, we need a thorough, dispassionate, analytic review of what is known, and not known, about this reform strategy. Such is precisely what Murphy and Beck have constructed, and they provide the added bonus of a readable package.

JAMES W. GUTHRIE
Peabody College, Vanderbilt University

About the Authors

Joseph Murphy is Professor and Chair, Department of Educational Leadership at Vanderbilt University. His primary interest is in school improvement and the role that educational leaders play in that process. His work also focuses on the preparation of school administrators. Recent books include the following: *Restructuring Schools: Capturing and Assessing the Phenomena* (1991), *The Landscape of Leadership Preparation: Reframing the Education of School Administrators* (1992), and *Understanding the Principalship: Metaphorical Themes, 1920s to 1990s* (with Lynn G. Beck, 1993).

Lynn G. Beck is an Assistant Professor of Educational Administration at the University of California, Los Angeles. Her research and teaching focus on administrative ethics, the principalship, and leadership preparation. Recent publications include the following: *Understanding the Principalship: Metaphorical Themes, 1920s to 1990s* (with Joseph Murphy, 1993) and *Reclaiming Educational Administration as a Caring Profession* (1994).

When Americans grow dissatisfied with public schools, they tend to blame the way they are governed. (Tyack, 1993, p. 1)

There is an emerging agreement that the first step in restructuring is the decentralization of the management function. (Rungeling & Glover, 1991, p. 415)

"School-based management" is rapidly becoming the centerpiece of the current wave of reform. (David, 1989, p. 45)

In sum, the resurgence of school based management provides researchers with the opportunity to investigate school based management in a variety of settings and under diverse conditions. If those who are interested in school based management seize this opportunity, then we could generate the knowledge base needed to determine whether school based management operates primarily as a symbolic response or whether it can, under certain conditions, operate as a substantive strategy that achieves its stated objectives and improves the performance of schools. (Malen, Ogawa, & Kranz, 1989, p. 30)

Introduction

Curiously, enthusiasm for SBM [school-based management]
seems to have far outstripped a clear understanding of its
organizational form, operating characteristics, and outcomes.
(E. M. Hanson, 1991, p. 1)

The goal of this volume is to address the shortcomings
noted by Hanson. This introductory chapter first provides an overview of the book. We then examine the current school-based management (SBM) phenomenon in three ways: (a) using a historical lens,
we locate the current round of SBM in the longer cycle of educational
reform; (b) we touch briefly on the extent of SBM activity over the
past decade throughout the United States; and (c) we place SBM within
the larger restructuring movement of which it is a part. We close by
discussing two major concerns about our ability to undertake the
task at hand—the noncompatibility of cases and problems in generating reliable generalizations.

In Chapters 1 and 2, we describe what Hanson refers to as the
organizational form and *operating characteristics* of the current SBM
movement. Our review begins with the *definition* of SBM and shared
or school-based decision making (SBDM). Particular attention is

devoted to teasing out the implicit and explicit *premises* of SBM. From that endeavor, we create a model that captures the central tenets of the argument for decentralization. (Later, in Chapter 6, we test the model by examining the empirical work on SBM completed primarily over the past decade.)

In Chapter 2, we unpack the literature to reveal the three operating *types* of SBM—administrative decentralization, professional decentralization, and community control. Finally, activity in the various *domains* of SBM is examined to develop a picture of the extent of decentralization visible in school districts throughout the country. By using the frameworks presented in the first two chapters, the reader should by this point be able to answer the following question for any SBM school: What and how much is controlled (domains) by whom (types) for what ends (definition)?

The forces that are driving and shaping the current SBM movement occupy our attention in Chapter 3. We begin the chapter with an analysis of the failing health of schooling. We then examine ways in which the larger environment in which education unfolds is fueling demands for SBM. We close by reviewing how the struggle to redefine education supports calls for more participatory forms of organization and governance.

In Chapters 4 and 5, we discuss how the underlying dimensions of SBM have evolved through earlier eras of decentralization—from the teacher council movement of the early 1900s through the community control movement of the 1960s and 1970s. We are thus able to gain some insights into the outcomes of past attempts to devolve decision-making authority to the school level. We also provide background for examining how the current wave of SBM builds upon or diverges from its historical antecedents.

The outcomes of SBM are of central concern in Chapter 6, especially those of the decentralization efforts of the past decade. We start with a brief review of the impact of SBM on four educational stakeholders—students, teachers, principals, and district office administrators. The next section of the chapter examines the validity of the premises embedded in the SBM construct. Our analysis here follows the model of shared decision making established in Chapter 1. The final part of the chapter presents our attempt to explain the findings on SBM—in particular to account for the pattern of less-than-hoped-for effects on schools, the educational process, and students.

In Chapter 7 we analyze the reasons for the outcomes presented in Chapter 6. We focus on both implementation issues and the underlying nature of SBM as a reform strategy.

A companion volume (Beck & Murphy, in press) lays out our plan for reinventing SBM. There, we describe four factors that can enable shared decision making to live up to its promise, factors that we label the educational, community, leadership, and support imperatives. We also look at some sites where SBM has been harnessed in service of school improvement.

The School-Based Management Movement

School-based management has been adopted and implemented by school systems in literally every corner of the nation: from Washington to Florida and from California to Massachusetts. (Ogawa, 1992, p. 1)

A Leitmotif in a Larger Score

Attempts to decentralize decision making in education are hardly new:

Decentralization is one of these recurring elements of educational reform. The history of school decentralization, like that of back to basics or the open classroom, is a history of perpetual motion, rising and falling but never fading away. (Mirel, 1990, p. 40)

Proposals to delegate decisionmaking authority to subunits of school districts or to individual sites and proposals to distribute that authority among various combinations of administrators, teachers, parents and community residents have been enacted, rescinded and reenacted for decades. (Malen, Ogawa, & Kranz, 1989, p. 6)

As we report more fully in Chapter 3, historians chronicle the evolution of the U.S. educational system through successive eras of decentralization[1] and centralization policies (Cuban, 1990; Mirel, 1990; Tyack, 1993; Warren, 1990), with each succeeding set of initiatives designed to correct the flaws of the preceding one (Chapman & Boyd, 1986; Elmore, 1993).[2] Some reviewers employ the pendulum metaphor to describe these alternating periods of decentralization and centralization (Brown, 1992; Lindelow, 1981). Others picture them as successive waves that wash over the educational system, leaving the landscape largely unaltered. Our own reading directs us to a different image. First, the pattern is less neutral and more evolutionary than is sometimes assumed: "Patterns of governance . . . have been more nuanced and complex than the conventional terms of the debate would suggest" (Tyack, 1993, p. 4). Second, it appears to us that over time the forces for centralization have been more vigorous than those for decentralization (Clune & White, 1988). We have witnessed alternating and diametrically opposed sets of policy initiatives, and growth has occurred in a fragmented fashion (Cohen, 1989), but overall the landscape has become increasingly more centralized (Hill & Bonan, 1991; Tyack, 1993; Wise, 1978). Third, the succeeding waves of reform leave behind a good deal of debris, or what Cohen (1989) refers to as "organizational sediment" (p. 6). This process of accretion has led to the development of an educational system characterized by considerable discontinuity (Cohen, 1989).

A Reform Agenda for Today's Schools

From the mid-1980s through the mid-1990s, we have been witnessing yet another movement in the cyclical pattern of centralization and decentralization policies in education—demands for the devolution of authority to local school communities. Fueled by an assortment of forces, which we examine in Chapter 2, and "promoted through a variety of recent commission reports" (Wohlstetter & McCurdy, 1991, p. 391), efforts to improve schooling under the banner of decentralization are taking hold in states, districts, and school communities throughout the United States and through much of the industrialized world as well:[3]

> School based management has resurfaced as a prominent education reform. Numerous commissions, task forces, organizations and individuals are advocating this reform. Numerous states and districts are discussing, instituting or reinstituting a variety of school based management provisions. (Malen et al., 1989, p. 1)

As early as 1989, 14 states had fostered the development of SBM projects (Wohlstetter, 1990) and by 1991 "thousand of districts across the country [were] experimenting with it [SBM] in some form" (Hill & Bonan, 1991, p. v).

In Kentucky, House Bill 940, which was passed in 1990, mandated with a few minor exceptions that all schools in the state employ an SBM model of governance by July 1, 1996, as part of the Kentucky Education Reform Act (KERA). By the end of the 1991-1992 academic year, 420 of the 1350 schools in Kentucky had established school-based councils (Steffy, 1993). Signed into law in 1989, Act 366 of the Hawaii State Legislature "is a major initiative . . . designed to facilitate improved student performance in the public school system through School/Community Based Management" (Pacific Region Educational Laboratory, 1992, p. 1). In Oregon, legislation was passed in 1991 to establish site-based decision-making committees in all public schools in the state by 1995 (Mills, 1992). And in Texas, "Senate Bill 1 [1990] and House Bill 2885 [1991] introduced the term site-based management to schools throughout the state of Texas" (Wagstaff & Reyes, 1993, p. 7) by establishing a "legislative decree for site-based management" (p. ii). Related events are unfolding in Washington, New York, Tennessee, South Carolina, and other states.

At the district level, especially in urban areas such as Dade County, Chicago, Los Angeles, and Rochester, similar efforts to move decision-making authority to the school level have been gaining momentum (Duttweiler & Mutchler, 1990; Marsh, 1992).[4] For example, a provision for the establishment of SBM councils with broad authority over budget, personnel, and curriculum is at the heart of legislation passed by the Illinois General Assembly to improve schooling in Chicago (Hess, 1991). Likewise, in Memphis, reform was launched through an initiative to bring "school based decision making management" (Etheridge, Valesky, Horgan, Nunnery, & Smith, 1992, p. 4) to selected inner-city schools (Diegmueller, 1991). In Detroit, the "cornerstone of the district's approach" is its "empowerment" plan in which "empowered schools receive 92 percent of the district's per-pupil spending of about $4000 and are free to run their own affairs" (Bradley, 1992, p. 10). Similar reforms are occurring in Dallas, Cincinnati, Los Angeles, White Plains (NY), and hundreds of other districts. In South Carolina alone, "at least 50 percent of school districts have recognized the importance of individual school initiative and have implemented some reform of school-based management" (Stevenson & Pellicer, 1992, p. 136). As early as 1988, a nationwide survey sponsored by the American Association of School Administrators (AASA) found that 25% of the superintendents reported that SBM was in effect in their schools and 28% claimed that SBM was in the planning stage (Heller, Woodworth, Jacobson, & Conway, 1989). By 1991, "seven out of the eight largest urban districts in the United States [were] in various stages of implementing school-based management" (Wohlstetter & Buffett, 1991, p. 1). A 1994 study on high school restructuring found that 66% of the schools in the sample had "fully or partially implemented" SBM programs (Viadero, 1994, p. 1).

A Place in the Restructuring Agenda

It is important to note that although SBM is often the "centerpiece" (Sackney & Dibski, 1992, p. 3) or "cornerstone" (Wohlstetter & Buffett, 1991, p. 1) in the current reform edifice (Robertson & Buffett, 1991), it is generally embedded in a larger improvement agenda (Brown, 1991; Murphy, 1990, 1991). As Ogawa (1992) correctly remarks, "school-based management is one of several types of educational reforms that are currently being employed to alter the structure of public education in the United States" (p. 1). Indeed, SBM is only one of "a wide variety of reform proposals" (Elmore, 1991, p. 2) that is finding a home within the "big tent" (Barth, 1991, p. 123), "magic incantation" (Tyack, 1990, p. 170), or "smorgasbord of ideas and programs" (Rowley, 1992, p. 3) known as school restructuring. Chief among these proposals are reform initiatives to (a) expand opportunities for parents to play a more vital role in the education of their children, especially proposals to enhance parental voice and choice; (b) decentralize control over education from the state through the district to the individual school community; (c) professionalize teaching, both at the state and federal levels and at each individual school site; (d) replace the behavioral underpinnings of learning and teaching with constructivist principles; and (e) infuse more market-sensitive measures of accountability into the schooling process, while deemphasizing historically entrenched bureaucratic controls (Murphy, 1991, 1992a, 1993a). This reality in some cases enhances and in other situations dampens the effectiveness of SBM. As we discuss more fully below, the interwoven nature of initiatives in the school restructuring agenda substantially impedes our ability to analyze the effects of this decentralization strategy.

Guiding Concerns

The site management concept has great promise and has proved successful in numerous districts where it has been implemented. (Lindelow, 1981, p. 94)

At least in the schools we studied, SBM is a relatively puny reform. . . . Perhaps changes in other institutional rules would have more potency; this one, without supplementation by other organizational arrangements shows meager promise. (Weiss, 1993, p. 17)

Such divergent claims about the effectiveness of SBM are woven throughout the decentralization literature. They inform us in a rather direct manner that any attempt to understand a phenomenon as complex and contextually grounded as SBM needs to advance with caution. Therefore, throughout this volume, we temper our assessment, based on two sets of related factors that need to be made more explicit: noncompatibility of cases and concerns about causality. In navigating these shoals, we also endeavor to bring greater clarity to issues in these areas.

Any analysis of SBM will be plagued by the issue of noncompatibility of cases. In reality, SBM is less a coherent intervention than variations on a theme (David, 1989; Mojkowski & Fleming, 1988). It materializes in a variety of ways and forms in different settings (Brown, 1990; Hannaway, 1992): (a) stressing different components and strategies to varying degrees (Jenni, 1990); (b) empowering different sets of stakeholders in various communities differently (Malen et al., 1989); (c) meaning quite different things to different groups of stakeholders (Prickett et al., 1990), to different actors at the same school (Brown, 1990), and to similar role occupants throughout the same district (Alexander, 1992); and (d) being packaged in diverse ways with other reform initiatives (Rumbaut, 1992). It is also often less a proactive, coordinated response to a problem than a damnation of the status quo and a celebration of "the virtues of what might be" (Cohen, 1989, p. 2).[5]

At the most basic level, there is a lack of clarity about the meaning of SBM: "The constructs constituting school based management are quite far from being universally understood" (Jenni, 1990, p. 22).[6] What this means, as Lindquist and Mauriel (1989) remind us, is that throughout the United States, "each district has chosen unique approaches to the process of implementing and diffusing SBM" (p. 406). At the school level, even greater variation is evident, meaning that even in the same system, "alternative versions of school-based management [are] being practiced" (Daresh, 1992, p. 110). The overall picture is one in which

> There is no standard version or model of site-based management. Schools operating under the rubric of site-based management have varying degrees of control and make some or all decisions about curriculum, instruction, personnel, and budget. In addition, there is great variation in the way teachers and parents are being involved in planning and decision making. (Wagstaff & Reyes, 1993, p. 1)

As we discuss more fully in Chapter 1, "there is a considerable range in the amount of decentralization" (Brown, 1990, p. 25) at SBM sites and quite diverse patterns of sharing devolved authority by stakeholders at the school level. Even within a specific group at the building level (e.g., teachers), SBM can take on quite divergent meanings, as Brown (1990) discovered: "At one point, half the school staff was 'for' school-based management and the other half was 'against.' School-based management was perceived by some as a vehicle for retrenchment. For others, it was believed to be a path to collegiality" (p. 209).

Compounding the issue of compatibility is the fact that the meaning of SBM is heavily determined by the context within which the school operates. Substantial diversity among communities means that each school is likely to create its own understanding of SBM. This pattern provides a good fit with the school improvement literature (Louis & Miles, 1990; Murphy, 1992a), but it bedevils comprehensive assessment efforts (Bryk, 1993; Malen et al., 1989).

A second set of cautions—ones focused on the issue of generalizability—also guides our analytic work throughout this volume. Unfortunately, even though the body of empirical work on SBM continues to grow, the literature in this area is still "characterized by a preponderance of project descriptions/status reports and position pieces, a paucity of systematic, empirical investigations, and a propensity to focus on exemplary programs" (Malen et al., 1989, p. 5).[7] A host of subproblems complicate the task of assessing SBM as a planned intervention. Much of the work on SBM either assumes that schools are beginning at ground zero—and thus fails to account for preexisting collaborative decision-making processes at the site (Rumbaut, 1992; Rutherford, 1991)—or neglects the matter of baseline data altogether.

The newness of the recent round of decentralization efforts also makes the search for strong conclusions problematic (Bryk, 1993; M. Hanson, 1991; Trestrail, 1992). Malen and her colleagues (1989) articulate three dilemmas that hinder our ability to develop a generalized assessment of SBM. First, because as we noted earlier, SBM means different things in various settings, different studies cannot help but "examine quite different versions of school-based management" (p. 4). Second, SBM studies "focus on quite different dimensions" (p. 4) of shared decision making (e.g., changing roles of stakeholders, effects on students). Third, the "tendency to study model arrangements" (p. 5) tends to skew assessments.[8] Finally, as Rumbaut (1992) correctly notes, in many school communities, SBM is conjoined with an assortment of other reform initiatives. Yet we find little evidence that Rumbaut's (1992) observation is being noted by SBM analysts. In some cases, outcomes attributed to SBM can be linked to other interventions. In all cases, the matching of cause and effect is difficult. The inability—or unwillingness—of researchers to address these issues creates real problems in attempting to draw generalizations about SBM.

With these cautions in mind and using the conceptual scaffolding we discussed earlier, we turn to the body of the text. We begin in the next chapter by examining the form and structure of SBM.

Notes

1. It is important to point out that the various waves of decentralization, although always grounded in opposition to centralization policies, are animated by different purposes (David, 1989; Prickett, Flanigan, Richardson, & Petrie, 1990; Reed, Prickett, Richardson, & Flanigan, 1990). For example, Crosby (1991) notes that although the decentralization policies of the 1960s and 1970s "were adopted to give political power to the local communities and to off-set state authority" (p. 2), the intent of SBM today "is school improvement and organizational change" (pp. 2, 3).

A close reading of the literature lends support to March and Olson's (1983) conception of SBM projects as "garbage cans"—"highly contextualized combinations of people, choice opportunities, problems, and solutions" (p. 286). In particular, SBM often looks like a solution in search of a problem—disenchanted communities at one time, unhappy teachers on another occasion, and inadequate student performance at still a third time. Or as Ogawa (1992) puts it, SBM has "been employed as a strategy to address a variety of issues which have shifted over time" (p. 18).

2. As we describe more fully in Chapter 3, the language of each era is dramatically different. During periods when stakeholders see a need for centralization, "expertise, professionalism, non-political control and efficiency" (Lindelow, 1981, p. 97) are the watchwords. When demands for decentralization arise, such terms as "local control," "ownership," and "democracy" are heard. What this reveals is that "the preferred type of school governance . . . is more a matter of conflicting values and philosophy than of technical feasibility" (Fusarelli & Scribner, 1993, p. 19).

3. "Various forms of SBM have been mandated in England, New Zealand, Australia, Hong Kong, and North America" (Sackney & Dibski, 1992, p. 3). On the topic of the international character of SBM, see, for example, Chapman (1990) and Olson (1992b).

4. Although SBM in urban districts is increasing in dramatic fashion, it is probably still true that "SBM programs are more common . . . in smaller districts" (Clune & White, 1988, p. v).

5. This pattern of building improvement efforts more on condemnations of the status quo than on evidence of beneficial effects of alternative strategies is common in the domain of school reform. For an example in the area of educational leadership, see Murphy (1992b).

6. Although this absence of definitional specificity may be useful (Mitchell & Beach, 1993), as Rutherford (1991) reveals, ambiguity can also "negatively influence development of SBM" (p. 4).

7. This absence of empirical evidence on the effects of SBM is placed in the larger context of organizational reform by March and Olson (1983):

> For the most part, reorganizations have been proposed and understood in instrumental terms, as possible solutions to perceived problems (Mosher, 1967; Olsen, 1976). Nevertheless, there are few attempts by the initiators of reorganizations to discover what really happened as a consequence of their efforts. . . . In those rare cases where information is available, it is not attended to reliably. (p. 289)

8. A similar critique laces analyses of other major recent reform efforts, especially the "effective schools" and "instructional leadership" movements (see Murphy, 1988; Murphy, Hallinger, & Mesa, 1985).

1

School-Based Management (SBM): Definitions and Assumptions

To understand the results of participation in the decision making of educational organizations, the concept must first be delimited and defined. (Conway, 1984, p. 17)

An important issue in the implementation of SBM is the definition of the concept. (Lindquist & Mauriel, 1989, p. 404)

For reasons described throughout the next two chapters, developing an understanding of SBM is not an easy task. Therefore, our effort to bring some clarity to this reform initiative requires us to observe the issue with a variety of lenses. In the first section of this chapter, we review definitions of SBM and extract from them the essential elements of this strategy for school improvement. We then examine the ambiguity associated with shared decision making, taking pains to explain why SBM often means quite different things to different stakeholders. Both conceptual and operational causes are treated. The third section is devoted to an analysis of the "logic in operation" (Bryk, 1993, p. 2) embedded in SBM. Based on these explicit and implicit "theories of action" (Malen et al., 1989, p. 2), we construct a model of the expected effects of shared governance—a model that we test against the empirical work on SBM in Chapter 4. In Chapter 2, we finish unpacking SBM in three ways. We examine the context of shared governance and the three major forms of SBM— administrative, professional, and community control. We also describe the domains of shared governance and, in so doing, provide a vehicle for judging the effectiveness of various SBM initiatives.

SBM Defined

Although the public media, professional literature, and school practice have focussed extensive attention on school-based management in recent years, there is neither clarity nor agreement on its definition. (E. M. Hanson, 1991, p. 1)

School-site management is a complex set of concepts and processes described by a virtual cornucopia of new terms. (Mojkowski & Fleming, 1988, p. 2)

In their 1988 review, Clune and White reveal that "school-based management goes by many different names including school-site autonomy, school-site management, school-centered management, decentralized management, school-based budgeting, school-site lump sum budgeting, responsible autonomy, shared governance, the autonomous school concept, school-based curriculum development and administrative decentralization" (p. 3). It is an "abbreviated catch phrase" (Weiss, Cambone, & Wyeth, 1991, p. 1)—a "relative" (Hill & Bonan, 1991, p. 4; Wagstaff & Reyes, 1993, p. 23), "generic" (Malen et al., 1989, p. 7), or "umbrella" term (Conley & Bacharach, 1990, p. 540; S. B. Lawton, 1991, p. 2) that covers considerable territory, both in meaning and approaches. The "vagueness and ambiguity" (Jenni & Mauriel, 1990, p. 3) associated with "the lack of a mutually agreed upon definition of school-based management" (Stevenson & Pellicer, 1992, p. 127) means, not surprisingly, that SBM gets defined and operationalized differently in different locales (Fusarelli & Scribner, 1993; Sirotnik & Clark, 1988).[1] There are "different perceptions about the role and function of SBM in schools" (Jenni & Mauriel, 1990, p. 3); there is no standard operating model of shared governance (Wagstaff & Reyes, 1993). For example, "under the Chicago Reform Act, Local School Councils were to become the primary site of school governance in Chicago. There has been considerable disagreement in the city, however, about what that entails" (Hess, 1992, p. 8). As we discuss more fully below, the elusiveness of "decentralized participation as a construct" (Taylor & Bogotch, 1992, p. 2) also often "creates problems for the implementation process" (Rutherford, 1991, p. 12).[2]

Emerging Definitions

SBM remains empirically and conceptually elusive (Malen et al., 1989) and somewhat abstract, but definitions are beginning to pile up. For example, for Marsh (1992), the "operational definition of SBM . . . is decentralizing power, knowledge, information and rewards within school organizations" (p. 10). For Etheridge and her colleagues (1992), SBM "is a formal inclusionary process whereby principals, teachers, parents, students, and community residents (the people closest to the school and student) participate in decisions" (p. 10). Short and Greer (1989), in their definition, spotlight empowerment: "School-site management systems is a strategy which promotes the concepts of empowerment and of empowering individuals in schools" (p. 8). Candoli (1991), in turn, addresses the balance of authority in the system: "Site-based management (responsible autonomy) means achieving a balance between accountability and freedom in all parts of the educational system" (p. 34). Wohlstetter and Mohrman (1993) label SBM an "organizational approach" (p. 9) to reform. Smith (1993) presents SBM as a "form of school governance" (p. 1). Nearly all definitions highlight "a major shift in the locus of decision-making responsibilities" (Garms, Guthrie, & Pierce, 1978, p. 278) and alterations in the "members of the decision making cast" (Weiss, 1993, p. 1).

Central Elements

An examination of these and other definitions of SBM leads to a number of conclusions, including the following: Although "definitions of SBM differ" (D. L. Taylor, 1992, p. 3) and there is wide variation in how SBM plays out in practice, "the philosophy of SBM is surprisingly coherent" (Clune & White, 1988, p. 11). Two central tenets—"school-level autonomy plus participatory decision making" (David, 1989, p. 50)—form the heart of this approach to educational reform. Numerous scholars discuss the essential nature of autonomy in SBM:

> The fundamental feature of SBM theory is delegation. (Lindquist & Mauriel, 1989, p. 404)
>
> The essence of school site management is a shift of decision-making responsibility from the school district to the individual school. (Garms et al., 1978, p. 278)
>
> The foundation of school-based management is shared decision-making. (Crosby, 1991, p. 3)
>
> The backbone of school-based management is delegation of authority from district to schools. (David, 1989, p. 46)

At its core, school-site management is about decision making and decision makers. It is a process for devolving decision-making responsibility to the stakeholders at the school building level. (Mojkowski & Fleming, 1988, p. 3)

Other analysts describe the importance of an inclusionary process for using delegated autonomy, generally involving some formal structure comprising a "broad group of stakeholders" (Lindquist & Mauriel, 1989, p. 404; see also Designs for Change, 1991; Mills, 1992):

The key issue in site-based management is . . . management through the participation of the school system's professional staff. (Wagstaff & Reyes, 1993, p. 1)

A second central feature of SBM theory is the site council. (Lindquist & Mauriel, 1989, p. 404)

In school-based management, creating and empowering the site council often has been the main change intervention. (Wohlstetter & Mohrman, 1993, p. 6)

As in the American models, a key component to SBM was the formation of a Local School Council. (E. M. Hanson, 1991, p. 18)

Essentially the approach [SBM] involves creating formal structures . . . composed of building administrators, teachers, and parents at each school. (Malen & Ogawa, 1988, p. 251)

Variations on a Theme

The organization and operation of SBM programs is extremely diverse. Programs operate in different ways and in different local contexts with no discernable common model. (Clune & White, 1988, p. 11)

Despite the presence of common elements and some agreement on the broad philosophical infrastructure of SBM, variation remains the norm in the operation of this approach to decentralization. Conley and Bacharach (1990) even raise the possibility that "school-site management [may] simply be an umbrella of such vast size as to be operationally irrelevant" (p. 540). In analyzing the reasons for this phenomenon, we are able to develop a better understanding of shared governance in education.

Conceptual Variation

> *SBM is a proposal to decentralize and debureaucratize school control. For some of its advocates, it is also a proposal for shared decision making within schools. And for some, it is a method of increasing the influence of parents in school decision making. (Sackney & Dibski, 1992, p. 3)*

"SBM is a complex innovation" (Rutherford, 1991, p. 4). In many ways, it resembles a black hole: A lot of material—some of it pulled in without much thought—is collapsed into a very small space, or very terse descriptors. SBM is being asked to do considerable work by its supporters. At the most fundamental level, SBM is a vehicle designed to meet four different objectives, objectives that do not always mesh well together and that have the potential to pull this reform strategy in diverse directions. To many, SBM is a "political issue" (Wohlstetter, 1990, p. 2). Analysts in this group subscribe to Kaufman's (cited in Chapman & Boyd, 1986) adage that "the calculus of reorganization is essentially the calculus of politics itself" (p. 51). They see SBM "largely as a political phenomenon involving the transfer of power to local councils" (Wohlstetter & Mohrman, 1993, p. 9). The spotlight is on "politics as a lever" (Bryk, 1993, p. 5) for school change. Viewed through the political lens, "SBM is a form of school governance" (Smith, 1993, p. 1) and the focus is on "formal alteration[s] of governance structures" (Malen et al., 1989, p. 1).

Looking at the issue from a slightly different angle, a second group of analysts sees SBM as an issue in democracy, an attempt to open "up school systems to involve . . . groups previously not involved in school governance" (Wohlstetter, 1990, p. 2). To these reformers, "participatory decision making is a collaborative approach in which superordinate and subordinates [and community members] work together as equals in an attempt to identify, analyze, and solve problems that face the organization" (Wood, 1984, p. 63). Two lines of reasoning are underscored by analysts in this group. One holds that grassroots democracy offers the most hope for improving schooling. The second holds that only by living in democratic institutions will students learn the meaning of democracy in society (Murphy, 1991).

Others observe SBM from leadership and organizational perspectives. To those in the former group, "site-based management can be described as a management concept" (Wagstaff & Reyes, 1993, p. i) or as "a system of educational administration" (Lindelow, 1981, p. 94) in which "the individual school becomes the fundamental decision-making unit within the educational system and, subsequently, authority is redefined through the system" (Duttweiler & Mutchler, 1990, p. 44). To the SBM as "an organizational arrangement" (Sackney & Dibski, 1992, p. 44) group, shared decision making is defined as a "mode of organizational operations" (Conway, 1984, p. 12), more specifically as a "decentralized organizational structure" (Lindquist & Mauriel, 1989, p. 404).

Finally, although "school-based management is chiefly instrumental in its orientation" (Brown, 1992, p. 258) and most analysts choose to "defend the process on practical grounds" such as organizational efficiency, responsiveness, effectiveness, and so forth, there are those who cling to the belief that SBM is "a *value position* as well as a *process* designed to achieve certain purposes" (Burke, 1992, p. 36). These authors see SBM as a moral issue. They tend to hold three beliefs about shared decision making. First, meaningful involvement of stakeholders is appropriate regardless of instrumental outcome. Second, teaching is a moral activity and as such should be subject to the control of teachers themselves (Bolin, 1989). Third, "site-based management/shared decision making can also serve as a moral doctrine by which students can regulate their behavior" (Fusarelli & Scribner, 1993, p. 8).

Operational Variation

There is considerable variation in the way SBM is operationalized in districts and individual schools. In this section, we cluster the reasons for this variation into the following categories: variation in focus, elements with multiple meanings, and contextual differences.

Variation in Focus. At one level, variation exists because "many districts consider SBM more as a frame of mind or orientation than a structured, technical system" (Clune & White, 1988, p. 16). As Malen and her colleagues (1989) remind us, "the emphasis is more on the spirit of the approach than the details of the arrangements" (p. 8). What this often means in practice is that districts establish "some basic parameters regarding SBM" (Hill & Bonan, 1991, p. 91), but leave "the specific details of the governance process up to the individual school" (p. 91). For example, in one of the more thorough studies of SBM completed to date, Smith (1993) concludes that "beyond a statement of broad goals, the districts provided little clarification of teachers' decision domains or authority and little guidance about how to enact SDM [shared decision making]" (p. 29). "The district's ambiguity about SDM left teachers to construct their own definitions of SDM, and these varied greatly" (p. 29). In his investigation of school reform in Chicago, Hess (1992) reveals that the first 2 years of SBM were a "time of informal negotiations" (p. 8) during which shared decision making began to take on meaning.

At another level, variability arises because districts employ different implementation strategies. Some rely on pilot sites (Clune & White, 1988) and "gradual implementation" (Hill & Bonan, 1991, p. 77) strategies. Others move to establish "advisory" relations before evolving to more shared arrangements. In some districts, schools volunteer to participate; in others involvement is mandated. "The number of schools per district also varies [—for example] only one of a few schools in Rosemount, Minnesota, and Eugene, Oregon; approximately half of the schools in Tulsa, Oklahoma; the majority of schools in St. Louis, Missouri, and Charleston County, South Carolina; and all of the schools in Duval County, Florida; Monroe County, Florida; Cleveland, Ohio; and Edmonton, Alberta" (Clune & White, 1988, p. 12).

In addition, participatory decision making differs across districts because some local education agencies (LEAs) stress one link in the SBM chain—for example, the management piece or "decentralizing control from central district offices to individual school sites" (Wohlstetter & Mohrman, 1993, p. 1)—whereas others underscore other links—for example, the professionalization piece or "a shift in the locus of initiative from individuals who have responsibility for the entire organization to individuals who have responsibility only for particular areas or functions" (Hill & Bonan, 1991, p. 7).

Elements With Multiple Meanings. Variability is also caused by the complexity of shared governance. As shown in Figure 1.1, SBM comprises a considerable number of key elements.[3] Almost all of these components are continuous variables that are subject to diverse interpretations. School districts can "define" each of these elements in a multitude of ways. Take, for example, the issue of *decision actors* (see Conway, 1984). In some districts, the major focus of SBM is internal—"restructuring the teacher/administrator relationship" (Marsh, 1992, p. 1) by creating more equitable influence relationships between the principal and the teachers.[4] In others, external agents are a major part of shared governance. In some systems, the external spotlight highlights the role of parents. In others, both parents and general community members occupy key roles. Even when all relevant decision actors are in the equation, representation varies across sites. In systems such as Chicago's, for instance, parents occupy 6 of the 11 seats on school site councils; there are also 2 community members on the council. In other plans, "professionals and patrons are 'full partners,' on parity through numerical representation requirements or equal vote stipulations" (Wagstaff & Reyes, 1993, p. 11).

As a second example of variability in the meaning of the components of SBM, look at "scope" of "involvement" under *decision process* in Figure 1.1. To begin with, involvement "can range from the mere presentation of an opinion, where the locus of authority rests elsewhere, to membership in the group which exercises final authority over the issue" (Wagstaff & Reyes, 1993, p. 8). Given this reality, the "scope" of that involvement—the stage of the decision process (Conway, 1984)—can vary considerably, from defining the problem at the outset, to assessing alternatives provided by others, to selecting from an array of final options (Imber & Duke, 1984). LEAs will arrive at different resolutions to this issue. Even when they develop a common understanding, the actual meaning of that understanding is still likely to vary. For example, in one school that decided to govern by consensus, the "term 'consensus' meant different things to different individuals. Although one person understood that the Leadership Team would have the final word, another understood that the Leadership Team would make the final decision only after a faculty vote. Still others defined consensus as 100% agreement and therefore impossible to reach" (Rumbaut, 1992, p. 18). And what is true for "scope" of the decision process is equally true for the other elements of the model. When one aggregates the interpretations or definitions of the components of SBM, the model taking form in one place is likely to be quite different from one emerging elsewhere. As a consequence,

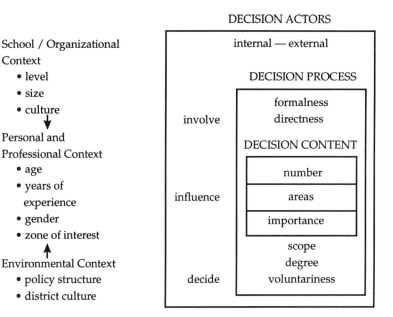

Figure 1.1. Elements of Site-Based Management

there is no standard version or model of site-based management. Schools operating under the rubric of site-based
management have varying degrees of control and make some
or all decisions about curriculum, instruction, personnel,
and budget. In addition, there is great variation in the way
teachers and parents are being involved in planning and
decision making. (Wagstaff & Reyes, 1993, p. 1)[5]

Contextual Differences. An examination of Figure 1.1 also reveals
that the context in which decentralization initiatives unfold can
shape the meaning of SBM in important ways. Take, for example,
"environmental context." As Hill and Bonan (1991) note, "in many
nominally site-managed school systems, school staffs are encouraged to operate democratically, but their actions are still tightly
constrained by policies, regulations, and contracts; waivers may be
technically available but hard to obtain, and teachers and principals
know that they must not interfere in certain aspects of school
policy" (p. 7). Clearly SBM will not look the same in these systems

as it will in those where the policy context and culture are more supportive of change (see Chapter 2).

In a similar vein, the same district model of SBM implemented in different "School/Organizational Contexts" will result in fairly distinct patterns of participatory governance at the school level. Small school communities[6] in which teachers and parents are already involved in significant ways in school decisions—what Alutto and Belasco (1972) refer to as decision equilibrium—are likely to implement shared decision making quite differently from those schools where teachers are experiencing decisional deprivation.

Finally, analysts have shown that several personal and professional conditions "moderate the effects of participation" (Wagstaff & Reyes, 1993, p. 8) and produce variety in the operationalization of SBM. Although the data on such variables as years of experience and academic qualifications are mixed (Riley, 1984), the health of shared decision making does appear dependent on how stakeholders perceive the relevance of decisions.

The Logic of SBM

School-based management may be seen as grounded on certain assumptions. (Brown, 1991, p. 21)

Consequently, it is important to define clearly the central concepts of SBM that have been driving many of the implementation efforts. Either implicitly or explicitly, these definitions provide a bench mark against which the success or failure of a school's SBM effort may be partially evaluated. (Lindquist & Mauriel, 1989, p. 404)

Throughout most of these writings there seems to be an unstated assumption that there is a direct relationship between participation and increased morale, productivity, and the general effectiveness of the organizations. (Conway, 1976, p. 130)

Unpacking and reordering the central concepts of SBM lead to the development of the model shown in Figure 1.2. The glue that holds the model together is a set of assumptions or premises about the relationships between and among the various elements. Mojkowski and Fleming (1988) and Bryk (1993) do particularly nice jobs of teasing out the logic inherent in the model:

> An assumption of school-site management is that those persons closest to the students should make decisions about the educational programs (that is, curriculum, instruction, and the organization of time, people, facilities, and other resources) for those students. The hypothesis of school-site management is that such a practice will result in increased student performance through a more effective organization. (Mojkowski & Fleming, 1988, p. 3)

> Reformers hoped that these new arrangements would create a political force for improvement in school communities. It was argued that such a politics could leverage the organizational changes needed to make schools more responsive to the communities, families, and students they serve and ultimately boost educational achievement. (Bryk, 1993, p. 2)

Embedded Premises

This definition of SBM contains several embedded assumptions that are not often discussed in the material advocating decentralized decision making. (Lindquist & Mauriel, 1989, p. 405)

The focus of this section is Burke's (1992) admonition to be certain that SBM policy is "based on assumptions that are clearly specified" (p. 37). At the heart of the entire model is one central premise: Those closest to a situation are uniquely positioned to address their needs and the needs of their clients. Embedded in this belief that "decisions should be made at the lowest possible level" (David, 1989, p. 46)—that "activities that directly impact the students on a day-to-day basis must be determined as close to the student as possible" (Candoli, 1991, p. 40)—are six assumptions:[7] (a) "that those most closely *affected by* school-level decisions—teachers, students and parents—ought to play a significant role in making decisions" (Wohlstetter & Buffett, 1991, p. 1, emphasis added)[8] about school affairs; (b) that "stakeholders in the school system . . . have the right and *responsibility to be involved* in the decision making" (Burke, 1992,

p. 38) process; (c) that "students, parents, school staffs and communities have *unique needs*, and that these needs can best be identified and addressed by them" (Jewell & Rosen, 1993, p. 1); (d) that because the school "is the fundamental decision making unit within the educational system" (Guthrie, 1986, p. 306), "schools have to [be given] the capacity to identify and respond to student needs" (Stevenson, 1990, p. 1); (e) that "imposed educational decisions disempower certain categories of stakeholders" (Burke, 1992, p. 39); and (f) that "those actors with the best information about a particular subject should have the discretion to make decisions about that subject" (Hannaway, 1992, p. 2) and that "schools often know best" (Brown, 1991, p. 3)—"the people in closest contact with students are the ones most likely to make good decisions" (Hill & Bonan, 1991, p. 6).[9]

Turning to the model itself (see Figure 1.2), we can cull out a host of premises that draw meaning from the assumptions noted above. The basic chain of logic is as follows: SBM empowers local stakeholders; empowerment promotes ownership, which in turn increases professionalism and enhances organizational health; and changes in these two variables result in improved organizational performance. One issue demands attention before we proceed: Although much of the work on SBM assumes fairly linear relationships among components, the model in Figure 1.2 acknowledges the recursive nature of the linkages.

Empowerment

A term popular today is "empowerment." Though we are not exactly sure what this term means to those who use it, we know that one of the arguments for introducing site management is that it is believed to bestow more "power" on the people in the local school, especially on the site council members, and therefore it is believed to be a "good" thing. (Jenni & Mauriel, 1990, p. 4)

The initial step in the SBM process is the enhancement of authority at the local level: "School-based management (SBM) is a system designed to improve education by increasing the authority of actors at the school site" (Clune & White, 1988, p. 1); "and that is the point— the goal is to empower school staff by providing authority" (David, 1989, p. 52). Authority, in turn, leads to descriptions of:

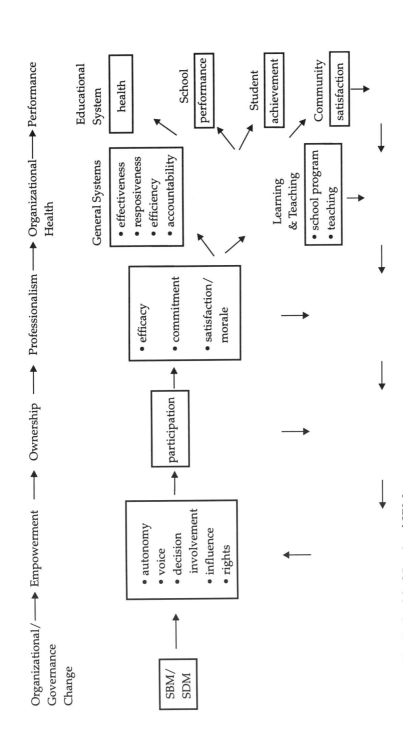

Figure 1.2. The Embedded Logic of SBM

autonomy—
> SBM facilitates local autonomy . . . (Sackney & Dibski, 1992, p. 15)
>
> School-based management permitted school staff and community representatives to exercise more autonomy over decisions . . . (Dellar, 1992, p. 4)

decision involvement—
> Central to the concept of school-based management is involving the . . . key players in making decisions. (Prickett et al., 1990, p. 5)
>
> Empowerment would result in increased meaningful involvement of teachers in decision-making in areas of substantial importance in schools. (High, Achilles, & High, 1989, p. 1)

influence—
> School based management should enable teachers and parents to exert considerable influence on school policy decisions. (Malen et al., 1989, p. 10)
>
> One of the main effects of reorganization is to redistribute influence. (Chapman, 1990, p. 226)

voice—
> School site management would offer consumers a greater voice in school affairs. (Garms et al., 1978, p. 278)

rights—
> Scholars have predicted that SDM will increase teachers' rights. (Smith, 1993, p. 6)

The base premise here—often unstated and untested—is what Malen and her associates (1989) refer to as the governance theory of SBM, the assumption that formal alterations in decision-making structures will lead to *real* changes in the involvement, voice, and autonomy of local stakeholders. Or more specifically, that "decentralized schools alter the educational power structure" (Wohlstetter & McCurdy, 1991, p. 391).

A second premise is that this augmented autonomy and authority provide the requisite context for change, "that school autonomy is a prerequisite for a school to be effective" (Robertson & Buffett,

1991, p. 3; see also Chubb, 1988). "With adequate authority at the school level, many important decisions affecting personnel, curriculum and the use of resources can be made by the people who are in the best position to make them (those who are most aware of problems and needs)" (Clune & White, 1988, p. 3). The final premise at work here is "the assumption that change in the venue of decisions will alter one or more of the major components that determine the kind of decision that emerges from the decision-making process" (Weiss, 1993, p. 2). More specifically, "there is a significant relationship between providing authority to employees at the work site and achieving the organization's ultimate goal" (Duttweiler & Mutchler, 1990, p. 30)—"if schools have greater autonomy, students will learn more" (Wohlstetter, 1990, p. 2):

> If the community (meaning the people who lived near the school) and the parents of school-age children had more voice in the schooling enterprise, then there would be more parental satisfaction with the schools and more commitment to the educational process. The result would be improved educational attainment. The democratization of the governance process and the representation of parental and community interests would lead to improved schooling. (Lewis, 1993, p. 91)

Ownership

> *First and foremost is the notion that participation in decision making by a site council representing school constituents will lead to a feeling of ownership by those constituents. (Lindquist & Mauriel, 1989, p. 405)*

> *The . . . argument is psychologically based. It holds that people who are involved in making decisions will have a greater stake in those decisions than those who are not. (Imber, 1983, p. 36)*

In the logic of SBM, empowerment, or the opportunity to wield significant influence over school-level decisions, is supposed to enhance widespread participation of local stakeholders in the activities of the school (Clune & White, 1988; Garms et al., 1978). This "broad-based involvement in decision making" (Conley, 1991, p. 37)—what Burke (1992) refers to as the "participation in the formulation

of collective viewpoints" (p. 39)—promotes a general "sense of ownership" (Etheridge et al., 1992, p. 10; Lindelow, 1981, p. 126) by members of the school community, a "greater personal stake in seeing those
decisions succeed" (Rothstein, 1990, p. 22), and staff ownership for
the results of those decisions (Short & Greer, 1989).

The ownership piece of the SBM model is critical due to the widely
held belief that "change requires ownership" (David, 1989, p. 46).
Thus, ownership is the fulcrum for school improvement efforts.[10]
The influence of ownership on organizational climate and outcomes
in turn is mediated through professionalism.

Professionalism

> Advocates also claim that participation advanced professionalism. (Weiss et al.,
> 1991, p. 1)

> Our review of the literature suggested that decentralization might lead to . . . in-
> creased professionalism of the staff. (Harrison, Killion, & Mitchell, 1989, p. 55)

Woven throughout the literature on SBM is the premise that
empowerment and ownership work to improve organizational processes and outcomes through their influence on three important
bridging variables—commitment, efficacy, and satisfaction/moti-
vation. It is widely held that "members of the school community
(teachers, parents and school employees) should be more committed to decisions if they participate in making them" (Rothstein, 1990,
p. 6)—that "people will show a greater level of support . . . for educational decisions in which they have meaningfully participated"
(Burke, 1992, p. 39). Participation reduces alienation (Carnoy &
MacDonell, 1990) and promotes a sense of connectedness (Short &
Greer, 1989), which, in turn, nurtures commitment to organizational
decisions (Duttweiler & Mutchler, 1990; Weiss et al., 1991). Reyes
and Laible (1993) argue, in fact, that "shared decision-making is a
form of empowerment that enhances the commitment of teachers
toward the goals of the school" (p. 4). Commitment, in turn, leads
stakeholders to work harder to implement decisions (Imber, 1983;
Rothstein, 1990) and to take greater responsibility for activities
(Burke, 1992).

Stated less explicitly is the embedded belief in some of the SBM
literature that "involvement in decision making may also enhance

teachers' sense of efficacy" (Smith, 1993, p. 6) or "professional confidence" (Duttweiler & Mutchler, 1990, p. 35), both of which are expected to enhance school performance (Burke, 1992).

Finally, it is generally assumed in the literature on participatory management in education that autonomy and ownership will "improve the morale of schools and their communities" (Pacific Region Educational Laboratory, 1992, p. 1): "One of the key arguments frequently offered in favor of site-based management is that it may help increase teachers' satisfaction" (Levine & Eubanks, 1992, p. 74). Analysts of SBM maintain that participation will help all stakeholders feel better about their school (Wagstaff & Reyes, 1993) and enhance motivation (Malen et al., 1989): "The belief seems to be that people who have more influence over decisions will be more satisfied with those decisions" (Jenni & Mauriel, 1990, p. 4).

Organizational Health

> The assumption underlying school-based management/shared decision making is that greater decision-making authority at the school level will enable the school to respond more efficiently, effectively, and flexibly to the needs of its unique student population. (Duttweiler, 1990, p. 1)

> By altering decisionmaking relationships, site-based governance could make schools more responsive to their clients and constituents, more receptive to innovation. (Malen & Ogawa, 1988, p. 251)

An array of indicators is often used to assess the health of organizations, for example, the efficiency of resource use, the density of leadership, responsiveness, and goal attainment (Hoy & Ferguson, 1985). Interlaced throughout the literature on SBM is the belief that participatory management improves nearly all of these indicators. For purposes of analysis, we divide these premises about SBM into two groups, those that address organizational processes in general and those that focus specifically on the core technology of schooling—teaching and learning. We examine outcome measures of health in the final section of the chapter.

General Organizational Processes. Burke (1992) observes that participation serves to broaden dialogue, establish a "more diverse information base" (p. 39) for decision making, and produces "more informed stakeholders through shared experience of people with a range of perspectives and expertise" (p. 39). Proponents argue that these conditions, which are at the core of SBM, result in *higher-quality decisions* (Conley & Bacharach, 1990; Smith, 1993; Wagstaff & Reyes, 1993), with quality being determined by the match of decisions to the needs of students (Weiss et al., 1991), creativity (Burke, 1992), acceptability (Wagstaff & Reyes, 1993), and relevance and workability (Burke, 1992).

SBM advocates also contend that decisions made in a more participatory manner will be *more responsive* to the needs of local constituents than is the case under centralized management (Epps, 1992; Garms et al., 1978). As S. B. Lawton (1991) informs us, "the key indictment here is that bureaucracy's lack of response, its commitment to uniformity and standardization, and its susceptibility to political rather than economic forces result in an inability to respond appropriately" (p. 7). Bryk (1993), in turn, argues that "enhanced democratic activity at the local level can be an effective antidote to unresponsive societal institutions like urban public schools" (p. 5). The idea is "to debureaucratize school system control" (Sackney & Dibski, 1992, p. 4). "The shift to a school-based focus enables increased attention to targeted instructional strategies and conditions, promoting a higher degree of responsiveness than can be accomplished at the district level" (Mojkowski & Fleming, 1988, p. 4). As schools become "more responsive to community and student needs" (Lindelow, 1981, p. 126), as they "focus attention on issues central to improving the performance of . . . particular student population[s]" (Duttweiler & Mutchler, 1990, p. 42), flexibility moves center stage (Garms et al., 1978) and diversity and variety become the norms (Sackney & Dibski, 1992). Thus, it is the contention of many that SBM will "enable school communities to shape distinctive forms of school life" (Bryk, 1993, p. 14). They reason that SBM "will ultimately produce a drastically new kind of public school system. Instead of a group of virtually identical schools, each adhering to standard mandates on policy and practice, a site-based managed school system will offer a variety of schools, each based on a definite mission and approach to instruction" (Hill & Bonan, 1991, p. 67).

In addition to believing that SBM will produce more effective and responsive decisions, advocates of shared governance also hold that "site-specific decision making will produce *more . . . efficient decisions*" (Fusarelli & Scribner, 1993, p. 1, emphasis added), that under

SBM, local stakeholders will both "define and solve problems more efficiently" (Conley, 1991, p. 36). On one side of the ledger, efficiency focuses on the expenditure of financial resources. A basic assumption of the model is that SBM increases "the efficiency of resource allocation" (Lindelow, 1981, p. 124). This "allocative efficiency" (S. B. Lawton, 1991, p. 6) results from a reduction in welfare loss due to forced collective consumption (Carnoy & MacDonell, 1990; Oates, 1972).[11] Stated alternatively, efficiency "results from the decisions of more knowledgeable agents" (Hannaway, 1992, p. 3), stakeholders who are closest to the action (Caldwell, 1990; Wohlstetter & Buffett, 1991). There is a "better match of the educational program with local needs" (Clune & White, 1988, p. 14):

> With political and administrative decentralization, communities and collectivities can affect, through voice or choice, the values promulgated, services delivered, and staff employed by a government agency. In the case of school-based management, locals can be empowered to ensure that their values, and not those of some other group, are reinforced by the flow of public funds. (S. B. Lawton, 1991, pp. 17-18)

On the other side of the ledger, it is assumed that SBM will make more efficient use of human resources. It is expected to do a better job of meshing the energy of "all who engage in renewal at the building level" (Candoli, 1991, p. 34): "Shared decision making in the district and at school site can harness the energy currently expended by students (to underachieve, tune out, rebel, or drop out), teachers (to circumvent the system), parents and community members (to flee the system), and principals (to try to keep the lid on)" (Mutchler & Duttweiler, 1990, p. 12).

SBM is also supposed to promote "the selective utilization of available expertise in the community" (Burke, 1992, p. 42). And as with all the embedded premises in the model, there is an assumption that efficiency will improve productivity (Hanson, 1991).

Malen and her colleagues (1989) remind us that "school based management is advanced as a robust remedy for a wide range of problems" (p. 10). "There are many benefits ascribed to participatory decision making" (Duttweiler & Mutchler, 1990, p. 47). These remedies and benefits are also predicated on certain logical assumptions. One of the most important in the area of general organizational processes is that SBM will *facilitate change* (Hess, 1992)—by encouraging action when performance declines (Garms et al., 1978), by reducing resistance to improvement efforts (Duttweiler & Mutchler, 1990), and by making implementation of decisions more probable (Short & Greer, 1989). Another premise is that "SBM will reduce the traditional isolation of teaching and will *increase* teacher *collegiality*" (Smith, 1993, p. 6). Third, it is proposed that team management "will ensure frequent and continuing communication and interaction between the school and the community" (Burke, 1992, p. 36), that overall the *quality of communications will be enhanced.* Finally, decentralized management is expected to "promote *increased attention to important equity* requirements" (Mojkowski & Fleming, 1988, p. 3) in schools.[12] The underlying premises of the equity agenda are that the downward shift in power to local communities will (a) "decrease alienation between school and community" (Epps, 1992, p. 144), (b) make "schools more responsive to the needs of minority children" (p. 144), and (c) "provide more equal educational opportunit[ies]" (Garms et al., 1978, p. 294).

A central tenet of SBM is that it "provides a mechanism for making professional educators more accountable for their performance" (Garms et al., 1978, p. 293): "The purpose of site-based management, like the movement toward participatory management in business, is to improve performance by making those closest to the delivery of services—teachers and principals—more independent and therefore more responsible for the results of their school's operations" (Hill & Bonan, 1991, p. v). *Accountability is enhanced* under models of shared governance in three distinct but related ways. To begin with, there is a shift in the locus of responsibility from the district to the individual school (Clune & White, 1988). SBM is designed to "focus accountability within each school" (Pacific Region Educational Laboratory, 1992, p. 1); accountability is pushed closer to parents and communities (Bryk, 1993; Epps, 1992). Second, it is anticipated that, under SBM, there will be a change in the clientele to whom schools are responsible (David, 1989), a movement away from the hierarchical model of accountability. In its stead, two alternatives take root—professional accountability and market accountability. In both cases, there is a reduced reliance on responsibility to the system and its managers. In the former case, professional norms rise to prominence in the control system. In the latter case, SBM represents a shift to a "grass roots approach to the control of schools" (Chapman, 1990, p. 222) in which the spotlight is on responsiveness to clients. Third, many predict that SBM will alter the focus of accountability, from a preoccupation with inputs and process to an emphasis on outcomes (Lindelow, 1981), especially student outcomes (Duttweiler & Mutchler, 1990).

Learning and Teaching. There are a host of suppositions in the work on SBM about the effects of decentralized governance on the core technology of schooling. They all draw strength from the basic assumption that participatory decision making "affects the conditions of . . . teaching and learning" (Duttweiler & Mutchler, 1990, p. 31), "that teaching and learning at the school level will improve when sites are given control over decision making" (Wohlstetter & Odden, 1992, p. 2). As Bryk (1993) notes in discussing school reform in Chicago, "the major premise of PA 85 1418 is that enhanced participation at the school community level will leverage the systemic restructuring needed to sustain improvements in teaching and learning" (p. 37). It is argued that SBM will professionalize teaching (Malen et al., 1989) and "strengthen the role of the teacher in the classroom" (Garms et al., 1978, p. 290). "Proponents of SBM have posited that it will change [existing] teachers' roles" (Smith, 1993, p. 1) and will facilitate the development of new roles (McCarthey & Peterson, 1989; Murphy, 1991, in press a). These changes, which encourage teachers to "do things differently and better" (Hannaway, 1992, p. 3), are expected to "lead to *better teaching*" (Wohlstetter, 1990, p. 2, emphasis added) and to improved teacher performance and effectiveness (Sokoloff & Fagan, 1991) by helping teachers make "more innovative, progressive decisions about instruction" (Weiss, 1993, p. 1), especially "teaching strategies that promote active involvement in complex learning tasks" (Taylor & Bogotch, 1992, p. 3).

It is also widely accepted that participatory decision-making efforts will obtain an *improved educational program* (Daresh, 1992) and promote "lasting school improvement" (Rice & Schneider, 1992, p. 2) by directing "attention to issues of curriculum and students" (Weiss, 1993, p. 1). Advocates of SBM claim that "greater involvement of all stakeholders will result in improved school program practices and climate" (Stevenson, 1990, p. 1). "School improvement efforts, contend proponents, will flourish and prosper" (Mojkowski & Fleming, 1988, p. 1). Thus, reformers see widespread participation as a lever to restructure education and improve schools (Bryk, 1993; Hess, 1992). Burke (1992), in turn, entertains the possibility that shared governance may lead to even more comprehensive improvement:

> Decentralization of control could raise the consciousness of individuals and groups in the community such that they come to perceive themselves as able to take informed initiatives and become proactive about the nature, purposes and processes of their schools. (p. 42)

> Collective school community responsibility for education could lead to the sharing of information, knowledge and skills which, in turn, could make for more informed and broader debate about the policies and processes of education. (p. 42)

Performance

> *Typically, the rationale for attempts to promote increased educational decision making opportunities for teachers has rested on the notion that ultimately, such a course would have a positive effect on the productivity of schools. (Imber, 1983, p. 36)*

> *The SBDM model was seen as a way to stimulate the initiation of additional school reforms that would result in better education. (Etheridge, Hall, & Brown, 1990, p. 10)*

The conviction that SBM will improve school performance is fairly well ingrained in the literature on shared governance. At the macro level, proponents claim that SBM can propel to the forefront market solutions to the woes besetting education (Carnoy & MacDonell, 1990). As Garms and his colleagues (1978) conclude, "site based management . . . rest[s] on the assumption that public schooling will be improved if consumers are given greater responsibility for deciding what educational services are provided" (p. 278). What we see here is a macro-level analog to the organizational health issue discussed earlier. There the concern was with the health of the individual school or school district. Here the spotlight is on the entire system of education. Advocates insist that because decentralized decision structures help foster competition, the overall well-being of the system—using the variables examined above (responsiveness, efficiency, accountability, and so forth)—will be improved.

At a more micro level, there are numerous references to the presumed outcome benefits of SBM on particular schools. Some describe SBM "as a vehicle for improving the performance of schools" (Ogawa, 1992, p. 12). Others write about school productivity (Imber, 1983; Wohlstetter & Buffett, 1991): "By shifting formal decision making authority away from central administration to a smaller decision making arena, the school, advocates argue that school productivity will increase because decisions regarding the educational program will be made by those most closely affected by them (teachers, students and parents)" (Robertson & Buffett, 1991, p. 1). Still others talk of progress (Guthrie, 1986), of serving students better (Hill & Bonan, 1991), and of school effectiveness (Duttweiler & Mutchler, 1990; Malen et al., 1989).

Also central to discussions about SBM is the belief that "student outcomes will improve as the principal, teachers, and parents collaboratively decide upon needed programs and practices" (Wagstaff & Reyes, 1993, p. iii). These "significant improvements in student outcomes" (Bredeson, 1992, p. 2) are anticipated in two areas—student social responsibility (Clune & White, 1988) and student achievement (Brown, 1992; Hannaway, 1992).

We have already chronicled the link that proponents have forged between SBM and the morale and satisfaction of the professionals who operate schools. A number of analysts assert that this decentralized form of government will also "produce greater satisfaction for constituents" (Lindquist & Mauriel, 1989, p. 405)—students, parents, and community members. Burke (1992) also proposes that the "realization of self-direction . . . could enable school communities to frame educational goals which promise to enhance the quality of community life" (p. 42).

Looking Ahead

In this first chapter, we started the task of cultivating a deeper understanding of SBM by dismantling the concept and repackaging it in different ways. We began with the definition and some of the central elements of shared decision making. Next, we explored the variability associated with this reform strategy. We closed the chapter by scrutinizing the logic inherent in SBM, following a chain of premises from empowerment through performance. In Chapter 2, we continue the work we initiated here. Our focus is threefold: We discuss the context of SBM; we delineate the three forms or models of shared governance—administrative, professional, and community control; and we portray the domains of SBM.

Notes

1. It is important to note that a lack of definitional specificity also characterizes most of the other major reform initiatives (e.g., decentralization [Bimber, 1993] and choice [Elmore, 1988a]) as well as the larger construct—restructuring—in which these initiatives are embedded (Mitchell & Beach, 1993; Rowley, 1992).

2. Abstractness or vagueness of definition serves the objective of permitting a variety of diverse perspectives to find a home within participatory management, but implementation forces the various stakeholders to explicate more clearly the meaning of SBM. It is at this level that perceived agreement often unravels.

3. The model presented herein draws heavily on the scholarship of Conway (1984). We acknowledge our debt to that work.

4. As Marsh (1992) points out, even within the issue of creating more equitable authority relations between teachers and administrators, the resolution will vary among schools.

5. In examining an array of SBM projects, Wagstaff and Reyes (1993) have developed

> four distinct models or patterns of site-based decision making. These patterns or models include: 1) site-based management/shared decision making; 2) site-based management/shared decision making with principal veto; 3) site-based management/loose central office control; 4) site-based management/tight central office control. Each of these models evokes a different pattern of behavior from site-based management participants, especially principals. (p. 1)

6. Bachus's (1991) study on SBM apprises us that although there may be a correlation between size and decisional state, one cannot assume that teachers in small schools are automatically more pleased with their decisional status than are their colleagues in larger schools (Riley, 1984).

7. There is, of course, no a priori reason to accept these assumptions. E. M. Hanson (1991), for example, challenges the belief that those closest to students are in the best position to make key decisions when he asks, "Are individual school staff in a better position than state education agencies, school boards, and central office administrators to decide which policies and regulations are important and which have outlived their usefulness?" (p. 1). It is also worth noting that decisions imposed on a teacher by colleagues at the school level are likely to be every bit as onerous as those mandated by the district—perhaps even more so if perceived degrees of freedom to ignore decisions are reduced as they are made closer to home.

8. Emphasis in each of these points in this section has been added.

9. The idea that each school knows what is best for its students assumes that "variety, not uniformity" (Hill & Bonan, 1991, p. vi) is the coin of the realm (Brown, 1991, 1992).

10. The issue may not be as tidy as many believe, however—that is, although there is a connection between ownership and improvement efforts, the relationship

is not unidirectional. It is quite likely that ownership can emerge from involvement in change efforts (e.g., see Guskey, 1986; Murphy et al., 1985).

11. It is important to report that there are also welfare gains—economies of scale—associated with collective consumption (Oates, 1972). For the organization in its entirety, there are also "increased coordination and monitoring costs produced by decentralization" (Hannaway, 1992, p. 3). The point here is that at the conceptual level the issue of allocative efficiency is more complex than SBM proponents often acknowledge.

12. For a theoretical analysis of the effects of SBM on equity, see Murphy (1993b).

2

Unpacking a Reform Strategy: Context, Models, and Domains

School-site management addresses both the kinds of decisions that are made at the school building level and the manner in which those decisions are made. (Mojkowski & Fleming, 1988, p. 3)

This literature review indicates that school based management ventures could be described and compared along several dimensions, notably the authority that is delegated in the domains of budget, personnel and program, [and] the manner in which that authority is distributed among combinations of stakeholders at the school site. (Malen et al., 1989, p. 29)

In the previous chapter, we examined the definition and premises of SBM. Here we analyze the context of SBM as well as the manner in which decisions are made—the models of SBM—and the kind of decisions that are made—the domains of SBM.

Context of SBM

A number of large metropolitan school systems, such as New York, Chicago, Detroit, Philadelphia, Cincinnati, and others have attempted decentralization by creating subdistricts based on task-area concepts that do, in fact, provide a hierarchy of school administration at a level closer to the citizens. (Candoli, 1991, p. 31)

State→District/School

The amount of autonomy that can be decentralized from the district to the school is heavily dependent on the degree of freedom enjoyed by the school system. This in turn is determined to a considerable extent by the state regulatory framework under which schools operate (see Carnoy & MacDonell, 1990). The amount of authority that districts can push downward to the school level will be minimal if school systems are ensnarled in an ever-expanding web of regulations and prescriptions. Thus, central to the SBM agenda are efforts to enhance the authority enjoyed by school systems that can be used to empower stakeholders at the school-site level (Murphy, 1991).

A three-pronged strategy is being used to address the restrictions that state regulations impose on school-based decision making. The most far-reaching of these—full deregulation—involves promoting SBM by pulling back the entire regulatory framework. Under this model, schools are provided (or asked to provide) goals and are held accountable for results. In turn, they are given considerable discretion in selecting the processes, strategies, and activities they will use to reach objectives. North Carolina's 1989 School Improvement and Accountability Act is a good example of statewide deregulation. Under the provisions of this law, school districts volunteer to participate and those that do "receive money for instructional materials, supplies and equipment, textbooks, testing support, and driver education in a lump sum, to be spent as each wishes" (Bradley, 1989, p. 16). In return, they are held accountable for reaching 75% of their goals. A more widely accepted version of this model, employed in South Carolina and Maryland, involves deregulating only the top-performing districts. For example, in South Carolina, "schools with a history of superior academic achievement [about 10%] will automatically be released from numerous state regulations governing staffing, class scheduling, and class structure" (Flax, 1989a, p. 1), as well as from a variety of restrictions in the deployment of personnel (Flax, 1989a, 1989b). North Carolina frees all schools from a variety of regulations, but South Carolina and Maryland focus on those that have already proven themselves.

Reducing the number of prescriptions and rules promulgated by government units—enhanced flexibility—is the second avenue being pursued to increase district and school autonomy. Agencies

employing this strategy examine their regulatory framework to identify where they can cut back on rules and eliminate some of the over-
regulation in education. The goal is to hasten the pace of innovation
by providing additional flexibility to districts.

Third, granting schools and districts exemptions, or waivers, to
existing regulations is the newest and most widely used tool in the
state arsenal of strategies to facilitate local control.[1] Waivers at this
level operate in a fashion parallel to those between management and
unions at the district level. Under enabling legislation passed in many
states in the late 1980s, schools and districts can "request waivers
from state law and regulation that they see as constraining their
ability to accomplish their objectives" (Elmore, 1988b, p. 16).

District→School[2]

> *In searching for a way to decentralize the district's organizational structure,
> the central office sought to devise a mechanism that would at the same time equally
> distribute the district's resources and allow individual school sites to partici-
> pate actively in the resource-allocation process. The central office's solution
> reorganized the district along feeder patterns into six self-directing commu-
> nities of schools. (Hill & Bonan, 1991, p. 78)*

Structural Change.[3] SBM districts are undergoing four types of
structural change. In some cases, most often in large, heavily centralized districts, there has been a dismantling of the larger bureaucracy into "smaller field units" (Wohlstetter & McCurdy, 1991,
p. 393), "subdistricts" (Candoli, 1991, p. 31), "community school
districts" (Epps, 1992, p. 144), or "pilot district[s]" (Olson, 1991a,
p. 13). For example, in the late 1980s the superintendent of Milwaukee "decentralized the school bureaucracy by dividing the
district into six 'service delivery areas' " (Olson, 1990, p. 15). To
"increase broad-based representation in decision-making at the
school level," the Dade County public school system restructured
from four administrative offices into six regional ones (Fernandez,
1989, pp. 26-27). In Cincinnati, "the district's 80 schools [were
reorganized] into nine 'mini-districts' consisting of a high school,
middle school, and six or seven elementary schools" (Gursky, 1992,
p. 13). In Dallas, the district's schools were divided into eight K-12
zones at the start of the 1992-1993 school year (Olson, 1991a).[4]

A reduction in size of central office staff is a second type of structural change sometimes found in SBM districts, often accompanied by the elimination of entire layers of the central hierarchy. For example, in the ABC Unified District in California, "the goal was to reduce the number of management levels between the superintendent and the principals to one" (Sickler, 1988, p. 355). Over a 5-year period, "22 district management and secretarial positions" (p. 355) were eliminated. The first year of the Chicago Reform Act (1988-1989) saw a 20% reduction in central office staff, from 3300 positions to 2660 positions (Designs for Change, 1991). By 1992, the Chicago Board of Education was "forced to reduce staff in its administrative units by 840 positions" (Hess, 1992, p. 31). In Dallas, two layers of the bureaucracy were removed when one deputy superintendent replaced two associate superintendents as well as the assistant superintendents for elementary and secondary education (Olson, 1991a). In May 1992, the superintendent of Cincinnati, J. Michael Brandt, in order "to improve direct services to children," reduced "the number of central office administrators from 127 to 62. In addition, 27 non-administrative support-staff positions [were] eliminated, as were 50 clerical jobs" (Gursky, 1992, p. 1). This streamlining was accompanied by a flattening of the organizational structure. "Several layers of the bureaucracy, including the district's area superintendents and the entire department of administration, curriculum, and instruction" (Gursky, 1992, p. 13) were eliminated. In Chaska, Minnesota, district decentralization also produced a "flattened-out" model of organizational structure (King & Ericson, 1992, p. 119). In Milwaukee, all associate superintendent positions were eliminated (Clear, 1990) and in Dade County, the transformation of the educational system resulted in "fewer middle-management positions and the reassignment of area personnel to feeder patterns" (Dreyfuss, Cistone, & Divita, 1992, p. 91). In Jefferson County, Kentucky, "the implementation of participatory management resulted in a . . . dramatic reduction in the number of associate superintendents" (Hill & Bonan, 1991, p. 89).[5]

Third, employees who previously occupied middle-management roles at the district office are sometimes reassigned to support activities in individual schools (Lindelow, 1981). In other cases, the money used to fund these positions is freed up to support new initiatives at the site level (Sickler, 1988).[6] In Chicago, in the first year of reform, "the redirection in central office staff [340 positions] generated $40 million, which was shifted to the schools" (Designs for Change, 1991, p. 4). "Whereas, in December of 1988 88.5 percent of [Chicago's] staff was budgeted to schools, by the midway point in reform implementation, the proportion had grown to 92.4 percent" (Hess, 1992, p. 31). "In FY 1989, 68.0 percent of the staff had direct contact with students; by FY 1992, 70.9 percent did" (p. 32). The streamlining of staff in Cincinnati was expected to save $16 million over the 1992-1993 and 1993-1994 school years, all of which was targeted to flow "directly to schools" (Gursky, 1992, p. 1). In addition, many of the former Cincinnati central office administrators who do not retire "will move to school-based positions" (p. 13).

Finally, as this "flattening of the hierarchical structure" (Zwyine, Stoll, Adam, Fullan, & Bennett, 1991, p. 10) occurs, responsibilities and tasks historically housed at the district office level are often transferred to schools (Lindelow, 1981) and "functions that are currently centralized [are] spread over a larger number of people" (Thompson, 1988, p. 15). As we discuss below, the job of "middle managers becomes more focused on providing services directly to schools" (David, 1989, p. 49).

Function. Carlson (1989) describes the prevailing change in district work under SBM as follows: "The central office must come to see itself not as a regulator or initiator but as a service provider. The primary function of the central office must be to assure that individual schools have what they need to be successful" (p. 3). Under some decentralized plans, central office departments are becoming service centers for schools (Hirsh & Sparks, 1991), what Wohlstetter and Odden (1992) refer to as "help giver organiza-tion[s]" (p. 538). For example, in the Halton School Board, decen-tralization has required central office support staff "to think and behave as service providers to teachers in schools, as opposed to deliverers of policy and procedure" (Stoll & Fink, 1992, p. 34). In Milwaukee, the central focus of district managers became "devel-opmental assistance" (Clear, 1990, p. 4). This movement from a bureaucratic management style to a service orientation is also occur-ring in restructuring districts in Kentucky (Murphy, in press b). In helping support local decision making, the function of central office personnel changes from attempting to ensure uniformity across schools to "orchestrat[ing] diversity to ensure that the common educational goals of the system are met, even if in many different ways" (Schneider, cited in Clinchy, 1989, p. 293; see also Wardzala, 1993)—a change that one superintendent describes as moving from managing a school system to developing a system of schools (Murphy, in press b).

Central office personnel in districts implementing SBM are spending less time "initiating projects in schools" and are "respond[ing] to school requests most of the time" (Brown, 1991, p. 78). They are serving as "liaisons between the building and central office and act[ing] as 'brokers' of central-office services" (Hirsh & Sparks, 1991, p. 16). In one sample of SBM districts in Kentucky, the central office facilitative role—the "new role of supporting school decision making" (Wohlstetter & Odden, 1992, p. 545)—has meant less emphasis on telling, more advisory work and consultation, additional legwork in securing information for schools, and becoming more of a transmitter of information rather than a developer of strategies (Murphy, in press a, in press b). In Riverside, California, decentralization "as it involved central office changed communications patterns inside and outside the office to one of listening; changed decision-making to consensus; [and] changed workstyle to facilitation" (Wissler & Ortiz, 1988, pp. 94-95). In a third district in the Midwest, SBM caused central administrators to begin managing and leading in more of a partnership arrangement with teachers, rather than as initiators or directors (Smylie, 1991): There was "a shift from unilateral to shared decision making for district administrators" (p. 17); "district administrators' interests shift[ed] from controlling information to ensuring that it was available to everyone" (p. 14). Not surprising, there was a "leveling of work roles" (p. 16) throughout the district.

Models of SBM

Across school districts, approaches to decentralization reform vary considerably. Although all plans decentralize decision making by shifting responsibility from a big, centralized bureaucracy to some other level, new decision makers—some combination of school and community groups—differ across districts. (Wohlstetter, 1990, p. 1)

School reform through decentralization is plagued by one important problem: Education reformers disagree fundamentally over what decentralization really entails. For some, decentralization means making principals the new locus of authority in schools; for others, it means allowing teachers to play the dominant role in managing the school; and for still others, decentralization points chiefly to increased parent and community participation. (Bimber, 1993, p. ix)

In Chapter 1, we reported that there is considerable confusion about the meaning of SBM. In particular, we saw that "the organization and operation of [SBM] programs is extremely diverse" (Clune & White, 1988, p. v). In this section, we create a typology to classify various shared governance initiatives. Central to the discussion is our effort to address Elmore's (1993) caveat:

> To say that authority and responsibility for key decisions should be "decentralized" in an educational system is to say very little, in the absence of some set of beliefs about who are the objects or beneficiaries of decentralization, whose interests are to be served by decentralization, and how decentralization is supposed to serve those interests. (pp. 40-41)

The metric we employ is the locus of decentralized authority. Our typology is grounded in the knowledge that "school based management plans distribute authority differently" (Malen et al., 1989, p. 9), that "there are a variety of patterns of authority distribution among school-site participants" (Duttweiler & Mutchler, 1990, p. 40). Our goal is to create categories that are representative of a variety of shared governance initiatives.

In forging our classification system, we rely heavily on the work of others who preceded us, especially Ornstein (1983) and Brown (1990, 1991, 1992). Ornstein (1983) describes two models of SBM. "Administrative decentralization is a process whereby the system is divided into smaller units; the locus of power and authority remain with a single, central administration and board of education" (p. 3). Alternatively, community participation and control result in the distribution of authority to stakeholders outside the hierarchy, or "*out* of the administrative structure of the school system" (Bimber, 1993, p. 8). Brown (1992) also outlines two models of SBM—organizational and political decentralization. He asserts that "organizational decentralization stems from representative democracy, wherein an elected school board governs via its administrators with clear lines of authority" (p. 291). Political decentralization,[7] he contends, "demonstrates participative democracy, wherein those who work inside the system and those the structure is intended to serve are invited to have a direct and deciding vote" (p. 291).

These scholars have laid an impressive foundation, but additional clarity can be gained if we revisit Elmore's (1993) advice and focus specifically on the issue of whose interests are to be served by SBM. The interests of five different groups can be highlighted—students, administrators, teachers, parents, and community members. As we are aware of no SBM plans that place the interests of students or community members (other than parents) on center stage, we drop them from our analysis here.[8] That leaves us with three pure models—*administrative control*, in which principals assume decentralized authority; *professional control*, in which influence pushed down to the school level resides primarily in the hands of teachers; and *community control*, in which parents (and members of the larger community) hold the balance of power[9]—as well as a variety of hybrids. An added benefit of this framework is that it matches quite nicely with the three key accountability systems in schools—bureaucratic, professional, and consumer (Kogan, cited in Brown, 1990).

Administrative Control

> *It is possible, as noted earlier, to shift power from the central office to the school site without decentralizing it further. (Lindelow, 1981, p. 125)*

> *In a school-based management system, the principal becomes the central actor. (Lindelow, 1981, p. 116)*

The starting point in SBM is "decentralized policy making and administration from the district offices to the individual school building" (Goldman et al., 1991, p. 2), a "shift [in] decision making from one level of hierarchy to another" (Mutchler & Duttweiler, 1990, p. 1), or "the granting of increased authority to the principals of schools" (Chapman, 1990, p. 223). An important consideration here is that the transfer of power from the district to the school tells us little about the nature of participatory decision-making arrangements in the school (Murphy, 1991). Equally important, the "literature on bureaucracy does not support the view that decentralization must entail the diffusion of power among workers or the combining of arrangements for representation and administration in local units" (Bimber, 1993, p. 13). Rather, "decentralization means only that discretion over decisions rests with managers or leaders who are present where the tasks are being performed" (p. 14).

The administrative control model of SBM is more widespread—and the professional control model less prevalent—than is generally assumed in the literature on SBM. Many incarnations of school-based management "center authority, and consequently power, with the building principal; teachers and parents serve in an advisory capacity under such plans" (Fusarelli & Scribner, 1993, p. 15). For example, based on his extensive work on decentralization, Brown (1992) reports that "teachers are not usually given a controlling vote over school decisions. Rather the usual model for school governance is consultative, where principals lean heavily on the input of teachers but make final decisions and take responsibility for those actions, right or wrong" (p. 8). "In Texas, Senate Bill 1, 1990, has provided that principals are to have primary authority for campus staff appointments, after consultation with faculty regarding the desired qualifications for the position" (Wagstaff & Reyes, 1993, p. ii). And in "Edmonton, Canada, . . . district policy stipulates that principals are responsible for constructing the school budget 'in consultation' with staff, parents and community members; but the principals are not required to establish site councils and much of the consultation is conducted informally or ad hoc basis" (Wohlstetter & Odden, 1992, p. 4).[10]

Professional Control

> A second SBM model features teacher control by delegating decision making down the ranks of the professional hierarchy to building-level educators. Thus, individual schools, typically through site councils where teachers have the majority, are empowered to make some decisions formerly made by the central administration. (Wohlstetter & Odden, 1992, p. 4)

As noted above, initiative can be decentralized to the school level with little alteration in the balance of power between principal and teachers. However, "when schools shift to a system of shared decision making (SDM), some of the principal's authority is transferred to the teacher-administrator decision making group" (Weiss & Cambone, 1993, p. 1). Therefore, professional control "represents a shift in the balance, in an individual school, from control of all important issues by the principal to some degree of open discussion with the staff. Under shared decision making, all decisions are to be made by vote or consensus" (Wagstaff & Reyes, 1993, p. 23). SDM "refers generally to the involvement of teachers in determining how the budget is spent, who is hired, and whatever other authority has been delegated to the school" (David, 1989, p. 50). One of its major thrusts is "to reduce the domains in which the principal holds unilateral sway" (Weiss & Cambone, 1993, p. 1). Another is to give "those who work inside a system . . . a direct and deciding vote" (Brown, 1990, p. 229).

School-site councils are nearly always the formal vehicle used to operationalize professionally controlled or "teacher-driven" (E. M. Hanson, 1991, p. 25) models of SBM. What counts is the balance of representation on the council. For example, in Los Angeles, because "half of the council seats are reserved for teachers" (Wohlstetter & McCurdy, 1991, p. 408), they "will almost assuredly have the votes to control the actions of this governing body" (M. Hanson, 1991, p. 12).[11]

Community Control

> Site-based management often takes the form of political decentralization, involving parents and citizens in the making of decision. (Bimber, 1993, p. 15)

In contrast to the teacher-driven model of SBM, community control "shifts power from professionals and the central board to community groups not previously involved in school governance. Thus, lay persons, not the professional hierarchy, are in control and accountability is directed outward toward the community" (Wohlstetter, 1990, p. 6).

> *Community control* connotes a legal provision for an elected community school board functioning under specific guidelines and in conjunction with the central school board. It means a sharing of decision-making authority and power between the local and central school boards; it also means that the powers of the professionals and central school board members are partially abridged and transferred to community groups. (Ornstein, 1983, p. 3)

Community control permits "parents or citizens in general to control school districts or schools directly via a voting process" (Brown, 1990, p. 229).

As with professional control, local councils provide the framework for community control. Nowhere is this more clearly evident than in Chicago, where "real voice for parents and community members" (Bryk, 1993, p. 1) results from the facts that they (a) control 8 of the 11 council seats, (b) hold the position of council chair, and (c) send one of their own (as opposed to a teacher or the principal) to the subdistrict council (Epps, 1992; E. M. Hanson, 1991; Wohlstetter & McCurdy, 1991). In Chicago, perhaps more than in any other district, "it is clear that power has shifted formally from professionals to the lay members of the LSC [local site council]" (Epps, 1992, p. 152).

Before moving on to analyze the extent of devolved authority that school sites enjoy—the domains of SBM—we should underscore two points. First, the three models of SBM presented represent theoretical categories of decentralization. In practice, they give birth to an extensive array of permutations. Many advocates of SBM advocate the emergence of a model in which the principal, the faculty, and the parents and community members "each become a significant 'site of power' to advance school improvement" (Bryk, 1993, p. 4). Second, there is a good deal of variety in the nature and functioning of the local school councils: "Councils vary from those composed only of the school-site administrator and teacher representatives to those composed of parents, business or community representatives, and district staff as well as various school staff" (Duttweiler & Mutchler, 1990, p. 39);[12] "Students normally serve as members only at the high school level" (Clune & White, 1988, p. 18); "the selection and responsibilities of the council [also] vary from district to district" (Clune & White, 1988, p. 5); "while in some programs, membership on the council is decided on the basis of election, in most instances membership is on a voluntary basis" (p. 5).[13] In addition, there is little consistency in the ways in which council chairpersons are selected.

Domains of SBM

Characteristically three broad areas of decision making fall within the purview of school based management: personnel selection, budgeting priorities, and curriculum/instruction. (Taylor, 1992, p. 4)

In the last section, we studied the issue of whose interests are served by SBM or who receives the devolved influence in the model of decentralized governance. Here the focus is on assessing the extent of the power pushed down to the local school site. This measure of local autonomy can be determined by evaluating both the number of areas or functions that schools control and the level of autonomy enjoyed in each of those domains, what Sackney and Dibski (1992) refer to as "types of decisions and extent of authority" (p. 5; see also Malen & Ogawa, 1988).[14]

On the topic of functions, analysts conclude that "common dimensions of decentralization can be identified (decisions on budget, curriculum, and hiring); but programs differ on which dimension is decentralized" (Clune & White, 1988, p. 11). "In some districts, site-based management has afforded individual schools a significant degree of control over three broad areas related to day-to-day operations: budget, personnel, and curriculum" (Hill & Bonan, 1991, p. 75). "Some SBM programs limit control to only one or two of these areas" (Wohlstetter & Mohrman, 1993, p. 3). "Districts seem to decentralize budget most readily, followed by hiring, then curriculum" (Clune & White, 1988, p. 11). Data from a nationwide survey of school districts on areas included in SBM plans reveal that

> individual schools are the locus for decisions about scheduling in 91 percent of the cases, purchases (85 percent), budget (74 percent), and staffing (62 percent). Maintenance, curriculum, and textbooks are matters slightly more than half the schools decide. Only 37 percent make hiring decisions at the building level, and 22 percent do teacher evaluation. Fewer than 10 percent determine the school calendar, length of day, starting salaries, and raises. (Heller et al., 1989, p. 16)

On the issue of "degree of decentralization" (Wohlstetter & McCurdy, 1991, p. 393) within domains, results confirm "that districts vary in the selection or scope of decision making accorded to schools. There is something of a continuum of delegated decisions" (Brown, 1990, p. 226). The overall picture is one in which there are "few consistent patterns in the scope of decisions given to schools under school-based management" (Wohlstetter & Buffett, 1991, p. 2).

By focusing on the domains, we signal our agreement with Bimber (1993) that "thinking about school governance as a process by which decisions are made about personnel, instruction, budgets, and administration provides a concrete framework for understanding . . . decentralization" (p. x). We also agree with Wohlstetter (1990) that "decentralization at the extreme implies governance by the field subunit over personnel, curriculum, student policy, and financing" (p. 8).

Domain analysis rests on the development of a typology of functional areas in which authority can be exercised. To date, a variety of helpful classification systems have been created. Most commonly, investigators delineate three broad domains of SBM—budget, personnel, and curriculum (Clune & White, 1988; Gips & Wilkes, 1993; Lindelow, 1981). This basic listing is sometimes augmented by adding instructional strategies (Wagstaff & Reyes, 1993), institutional activities and school organization (Hill & Bonan, 1991; Murphy, 1991), and values and mission (Murphy, 1991). More detailed classifications of decision domains are outlined by Collins and Hanson (1991); Duke, Showers, and Imber (1980); Imber and Duke (1984); *Notes From the Field* (1991); and Rice and Schneider (1992). For our purposes here, we draw on the listing of domains developed by Murphy (1991) that incorporates, in condensed form, much of the work noted above. We discuss five areas: goals, budget, personnel, curriculum, and organizational structure.

Goals

> The goal is to help schools develop their own guiding philosophies. (Hill & Bonan, 1991, p. 30)

Perhaps the most important area of local control for self-managing schools is the freedom to determine the purpose and goals of the institution. This is the case because well-developed goals contain the values on which collective action can be taken (Clark & Meloy, 1989). They also represent "agreement on principles" (Hill & Bonan, 1991, p. 29) that assist in the resolution of day-to-day issues. Finally, control of its mission permits each school to forge a unique culture that meets the needs of the local community (Dade County Public Schools, 1989).

Although it is difficult to gainsay the significance of local control over goals, values, and mission, no area of SBM has received so little attention—either in the scholarship of SBM reformers or in descriptions of operational models of shared governance: "Most SBM programs restrict teacher decision making narrowly to operational issues . . . little attention [is] given to subjects such as overall vision and direction" (Wohlstetter & Odden, 1992, p. 5). In addition to difficulties in moving from the status quo of district and state control of goals, two other factors may account for the failure to attend adequately to this key domain of SBM. First, there is a widely held feeling that because, under SBM, "the school board continues to formulate and define the district's *general* policies and educational objectives" (Lindelow, 1981, p. 94, emphasis added), local schools either need not or should not focus on goals. To many, variety under SBM means alternative ways of reaching a common mission. Goals are a given; the new influence enjoyed at the local level becomes evident in choosing different pathways to reach them. Second, a major plank of SBM is the construction of what Trestrail (1992) labels "the School Development Plan" (p. 6). Many educators believe that school missions will emerge from the building and implementation of these plans. The evidence to date suggests that this is an overly optimistic assumption.

It is clear that if mission is the foundation of successful SBM efforts, then reformers need to devote considerably more attention to it than they have to date.

Budget

> Budget control is at the heart of school-based management. Control of the curricula and of personnel are largely dependent on the control of the budget. (*Lindelow, 1981, p. 123*)

> If authority is to devolve to the schools, the schools must have the resources to exercise it. Authority without money to buy the time and services of people at the school level is a cruel joke. (*Sizer, 1992, p. 187*)[15]

The usual practice in the area of school finance has been that "local school management and budgeting are dominated by district superintendents and central office staff. Typically, resources are allocated by norms, which give local schools little flexibility of resource use at the school building or site" (Garms et al., 1978, p. 293). "While traditional schools have always maintained control over some pool of discretionary resources, the school's span of influence

over the education program offered to students remain[ed] marginal" (Wohlstetter & Buffett, 1991, p. 5). Under these circumstances,
"principals had two budgetary functions: They maintained records
for a small amount of restricted money given them by the district,
and they learned and used persuasive techniques in obtaining additional 'special money' that a district administrator controlled to use
for a local school project" (Lindelow, 1981, p. 108).

School-site management, on the other hand, is designed to overhaul existing budgeting systems. Under SBM, "the school site is
responsible for budgeting" (Garms et al., 1978, p. 293). Autonomy
in the finance domain is effected in a variety of ways. To begin with,
there is a change in "resource allocation whereby resources in the
form of dollars are distributed to schools" (Brown, 1990, p. 232). "In
the first step of the [SBM] budgeting process, the central office allocates
lump sums to the individual schools" (Lindelow, 1981, p. 124). Thus,
"the principal budgeting function of the district [becomes] the allocation of funds to each school" (Clune & White, 1988, p. 4), not the
determination of how resources can be consumed. This allows stakeholders at the school site to decide how money will be deployed.
The larger the "school grant" (Trestrail, 1992, p. 6), or "discretionary
lump sum annual budget" (Hannaway, 1992, p. 10), the greater the
amount of decentralization. Some examples: In Dade County, SBM
sites have decision-making authority over 70%-90% of the budget
(Wohlstetter & Buffett, 1991; Wohlstetter & McCurdy, 1991). "The
district office in Edmonton allocates 80% of the total budget to
schools" (Wohlstetter & Buffett, 1991, p. 7). Under Detroit's School
Empowerment Plan, SBM sites control 92% of the budget (Olson,
1992c).

> The second major step of the budgeting process is for the
> school site to actually budget its lump sum. This is the most
> critical process in school-based management, for it is from
> this process that most of the advantages of decentralized
> management stem, in particular the flexibility of the school
> to meet students' needs, and the feelings of "ownership" that
> people derive from making decisions at the school site.
> (Lindelow, 1981, p. 124)

Devolution of authority here rests primarily on the extent to which
schools can "allocate funds according to priorities set at the school

level" (Clune & White, 1988, p. 14) and shift funds among categories. This "ability to exchange dollars across accounts is a significant way to increase the ability of schools to meet the range of student needs" (Brown, 1990, p. 20).

The final budget issue concerns the degree of freedom afforded schools in how they spend their money. A key subissue is the extent to which schools are permitted to use funds to purchase goods and services from outside the district, that is, from nondistrict vendors (Guthrie, 1986): "In traditional schools, the range of services available to schools is limited to what the central office can provide. Schools under school-based budgeting generally have more flexibility and can make purchases from non-district employees" (Wohlstetter & Buffett, 1991, p. 8). For example, "some districts under SBM, such as Chicago, Illinois, and Edmonton, Canada, allow schools to purchase staff development services from experts outside the district" (Wohlstetter & Mohrman, 1993, p. 4). In some of these cases, "central support functions would no longer be cost centers within the district, but would be enterprise funds, expected to finance their own operations" (Wohlstetter & Odden, 1992, p. 10). The more empowered "site-managed schools [are] to buy the help they need on the open market" (Hill & Bonan, 1991, p. 17), the greater the amount of decentralization present in the district.

The second "spending" issue deals with the autonomy schools enjoy to "carry over funds from one year to the next" (Guthrie, 1986, p. 308). In conventional accounting practice in school districts, fund balances revert to the central office. The more budget authority is decentralized, the more schools are able to carry forward budget surpluses (and deficits). Again, we find a range of decentralization in SBM districts. For example, on one end of the continuum are Detroit, where no funds can be carried over, and Los Angeles, where "the only resources that can be carried over, with the exception of a few state textbook accounts, are unspent funds in the substitute teacher account" (Wohlstetter & Buffett, 1991, p. 9). On the other end of the continuum is Edmonton, where nearly all fund balances roll over from one year to the next (Wohlstetter & Buffett, 1991).

Personnel

If principals are to tailor their schools' educational programs to the needs and desires of the community, they must have control of their major resource—teachers. (Lindelow, 1981, p. 122)

Closely connected to budgetary discretion is control over the defining of roles and the hiring and development of staff. As in the fiscal area, there are various levels of local influence. In the least aggressive model of decentralization, the allocation of teaching positions is determined at the district level. Within this constraint, and subject to state regulations, members of the local school community exercise nearly full control over who will fill these slots—that is, although "the central office maintains a pool of qualified applicants" (Lindelow, 1981, p. 102), teachers are no longer sent to the school from the district office. Teachers and administrators select candidates to interview, make the final choice, and pass their selection back to the district. In some places, the shift of "interviewing and hiring of teachers . . . to the school site" (Carnoy & MacDonell, 1990, p. 54) has been accompanied by a reduction in district office personnel staff. For example, in Santa Fe, "a director of personnel is conspicuously absent from the district office" (p. 54).

Under more nearly comprehensive models of local control, the allocation of professional positions is not predetermined—"authority over the mix of professionals" (Wohlstetter & Buffett, 1991, p. 7) (and the mix of staff and other resources) is decentralized. Although schools are still free to select personnel, they also have the option of using funds budgeted for teachers for other purposes.[16] They can take money allocated in principle for a teacher and use it to purchase books and materials or to hire two or three paraprofessionals (Fernandez, 1989; Lindelow, 1981; Moore-Johnson, 1989). In Kentucky, for example,

> while councils may not transfer or dismiss present school employees, when a vacancy occurs, the council members can decide whether they want to fill the vacancy as it is currently defined or whether they want to fill the position with someone with a different certification to perform different functions. Councils can decide to use the money to acquire additional instructional materials and supplies, or to hire teacher aides. (Steffy, 1993, p. 82)

David (1993) reports that, in one district in Kentucky, "council members at a small rural school had the opportunity to hire a counselor or assistant principal. Instead, they decided to hire an extra primary teacher as a resource teacher to provide planning time, professional development, and information to the primary teachers" (p. 36).

In the most advanced cases of decentralization, authority—either full or partial—for the employment of the principal is held by members of the local school community.[17] For example, in Dade County (Fernandez, 1989) and Santa Fe (Carnoy & MacDonell, 1990), teachers are partners in the process established to select new principals. In Chicago (Bryk, 1993; Finn & Clements, 1989); in many British communities (Brown, 1991); in Victoria, Australia (Chapman, 1990; Moyle, 1989); and in Spain (E. M. Hanson, 1991), local school councils are empowered to make final decisions about who will be hired to administer the school.

Curriculum

> *Indeed, school level personnel and budget decisions appear to be framed largely by the demands of the district curriculum. (Hannaway, 1992, p. 23)*

> *In a school-based management system, the school site has near total autonomy over curriculum matters. Within broad outlines defined by the board, the individual schools are free to teach in any manner they see fit. (Lindelow, 1981, p. 122)*

Autonomy at the school site in the area of curriculum means that "the board and central office establish an outline of educational objectives and leave the schools free to meet those objectives in any way they see fit" (Lindelow, 1981, p. 122). Within a broad framework of "goals, objectives, and expected outcomes . . . the method of producing results is . . . left in the hands of the building staff" (Clune & White, 1988, p. 14). School-based curriculum allows the local communities to "determine which instructional materials shall be provided" (Steffy, 1993, p. 82). "School staff make decisions regarding the selection of textbooks, the selection of learning activities and supplemental instructional materials to be used, and determine the nature of alternative programs to be offered in the school" (Clune & White, 1988, pp. 14-15).

The more expansive the decentralization, the greater are the opportunities afforded local communities to (a) select specific pedagogical approaches (Watkins & Lusi, 1989)—including the assignment and grouping of students (Steffy, 1993); (b) "customize staff development to meet the school's unique needs" (Duttweiler & Mutchler,

1990, p. 45)—to "determine which . . . staff development activities best meet the needs of their particular school" (Guthrie, 1986, p. 308); and (c) monitor and evaluate learning and teaching locally.

Organizational Structure

> *The schooling redesign often involves early-on shifts in the organizational structure of the school; in turn, the new organizational unit represents a vital new decision-making arrangement at the school. (Marsh, 1992, p. 16)*

Structures within which the educational process plays out represent a final area of control for teachers, administrators, and parents in decentralized school systems. Where SBM focuses on the "structure of the school day" (Short & Greer, 1989, p. 19), groups are free to alter the basic delivery structure in schools, to develop alternatives to the model of the individual teacher working with groups of 25 to 35 students in 50-minute time blocks. At the elementary level, schools are creating educational programs that dramatically change the practices of grouping children by age for classes and by ability for instruction. At the secondary level, a number of decentralized schools are experimenting with alternative programs, core curricula, and outcome-based education (Murphy, 1991).

SUMMARY

In this chapter, our goal has been to develop a comprehensive understanding of SBM as a reform initiative. We began by surveying the district and state landscapes against which shared governance at the local level unfolds. We then turned our attention directly to participatory decision making. We examined three models of SBM—administrative, professional, and community—models forged on the anvil of stakeholder interest. In the concluding section, the focus was on the amount of influence devolved to the school site. We reported that decentralization can be measured by examining the number of domains controlled at the school site and the amount of authority enjoyed within each of those domains—goals, budget, personnel, curriculum, and organizational structure.

Notes

1. Elsewhere we have discussed the likelihood of success of the waiver approach to facilitating SBM, concluding that it is not a particularly robust strategy (Murphy, 1991).

2. The material in this section is adapted from Murphy (in press c).

3. Here we are reviewing the context around school-level shared governance. There are analogs to these structural issues at the school and classroom level. For example, some schools are dividing into smaller units such as houses or mini-schools and participants in these new units are being given control over what transpires therein.

4. A number of analysts have expressed concern that this pattern of decentralization may just place "another bureaucratic step in the processes between the school and the center" (Chapman & Boyd, 1986, p. 40; see also Candoli, 1991). For example, Moyle (1989) reports that

> ultimately this structure was found to have imperfections with the transfer of operational functions to the regions being partial and incomplete. The centre was continuing to maintain a direct involvement in the administration and management of schools and the school system. In many instances the regions were but an intervening level of authority between schools and the centre. There was duplication and division of functions at central and regional levels. (pp. 14-15)

Part of the issue is in the mind-set of these new regional or area superintendents. In places where the concept works well, superintendents (a) are thought of "not so much as a part of the central office, but as an extension of the school-level administration" (Hill & Bonan, 1991, p. 82); (b) "have very small staffs; their offices are usually in school buildings, and they do not reproduce the administrative or regulatory structure of the central office" (p. 18); and (c) "build personal relationships with all principals and lead teachers in their schools" (p. 18).

5. For a variety of reasons grouped under what Spring (1988) labels the "politics of bureaucracy" (p. 6; see also Downs, 1967; Finn, 1991), streamlining is often more easily accomplished on paper than it is in reality, as Washington, D.C., school officials discovered recently when they attempted to downsize central office operations (Olson, 1991b).

6. This is not always the case, however (Brown, 1990). For example, in Milwaukee, "the reorganization did not result in a cost savings. It actually resulted in a net increase" (Clear, 1990, p. 4).

7. One reason that we are not able simply to borrow the frameworks developed by Ornstein and Brown is that their treatment of political decentralization is not as helpful as it could be. In particular, because any redistribution of authority is wrapped in politics, we believe that all SBM is political—regardless of whose influence is augmented. In a similar vein, we argue that including the expanded influence of teachers in categories with bureaucratic labels, such as administration and organization, masks, somewhat, the idea of professional control.

8. It is worth acknowledging that conceptually models in which the interests of students and community members are paramount can be envisioned and developed. The fact that we are silent on these issues here means only that such models are not available, not that they should not exist.

9. Here we are examining the distribution of augmented authority at the school site. It is also possible, in the absence of efforts to push additional influence to

schools, to redistribute existing authority (Goldman, Dunlap, & Conley, 1991; Rothstein, 1990).

10. Discussions of the value of administrative decentralization are informative. The majority viewpoint is that this model of SBM is not appropriate or desirable— that models reflecting the spirit of collegial exchanges are to be preferred. Some analysts take a fairly strident position on the issue, claiming that this type of "SBM may become just another bureaucratic mode of control" (Conley & Bacharach, 1990, p. 540). Others, however, see some merit in this model of decentralized managerial decision making. Bimber (1993), for example, contends that

> strong, local management is likely to lead to more decisiveness than can be achieved through participatory schemes and the absence of professional management. Discussion, voting, and the reaching of group consensus are more cumbersome and prone to internal tension and division than is managerial decisionmaking. Strong leadership can also enhance accountability, since a single leader can more easily be held responsible for an organization's performance than can a committee or panel of decisionmakers, each of whom can represent a different constituency and none of whom shoulders all the responsibility for a given decision. (p. 15)

11. The question of accountability under the professional model has proven to be somewhat of an intractable problem. The bottom line is that although decision making becomes more participatory, responsibility for those decisions usually remains with the principal (Alexander, 1992; Hallinger, Murphy, & Hausman, 1992; Hess & Easton, 1991).

12. One of the most thoughtful analysts of SBM, James Guthrie (1986) of Vanderbilt, suggests that the employment of community representatives at the site level may not be the most effective use of their time. He suggests that, in general, "membership on an advisory council should be restricted to parents of students currently enrolled in the school. Clearly, other citizens also have a stake in the performance of the public schools, but their interests are more appropriately represented at the district level. The same is true of employee unions" (p. 307).

13. On this issue, there is diversity of opinion, but many educators would agree with Garms and his colleagues (1978) that "members of parent advisory councils would best be selected by an election" (p. 280). They contend that "although the electoral process never guarantees 'true' representation and is cumbersome and time-consuming, it is better than any other procedure" (p. 280).

14. Our earlier discussion of context is relevant here. For example, Wohlstetter (1990) maintains that the "extremeness of the change also may be related to the condition of the school district, with the most radical change occurring when a school district is in crisis" (p. 8).

15. Although it is true that SBM "works best when those being empowered actually have discretionary resources about which they can make decisions" (Rothstein, 1990, p. 22), David (1989) reminds us not to be overly sanguine simply because schools gain more influence over their budgets:

> Because money usually equals authority, budgetary authority sounds like the most important manifestation of granting authority to schools. But this is misleading because whether or not school-site budgeting equals autonomy depends on how much freedom from restrictions is allowed. For example, a school can receive a lump-sum budget for all expenditures including staff, yet have no decision-making authority because of rules governing class size, tenure, hiring, firing, assignment, curriculum objectives, and textbooks. (p. 47)

16. Brown's (1990) finding is worthy of note, however: "Contrarily, the evidence from this study would suggest that schools are in no rush to replace teachers with other resources" (p. 237).

17. The power of this control mechanism is often underscored in the reform literature:

> In Victoria, Australia, the provision for local school-based committees to select their principals and deputy principals has represented at a most practical and vitally significant level the effective devolution of decision-making from the central offices of the Education Department to the school. (Chapman, 1990, p. 230)

> Arguably, the single most important activity of the LSC has been to decide whether to retain the original principal or to select a new one. In each of the six Experiences of Actively Restructuring Schools (EARS), the LSC endorsed a person committed to students and parents in their community. The LSC's effective exercise of its responsibility to evaluate and select a school principal has played a central role in catalyzing the improvement efforts underway at these schools. (Bryk, 1993, p. 24)

3

Forces Fueling
the SBM Movement

The nation's children were poorer, more diverse, and more likely to have fallen behind in school in 1990 than they were 10 years earlier. (Schmidt, 1992, p. 1)

Existing structures for schooling cannot produce the kind of changes necessary to make a substantial difference. (Mojkowski & Fleming, 1988, p. 1)

The concept of self-management has had wide appeal across the political spectrum, with parties of the left being comfortable with initiatives which address the issues of equity and empowerment while those of the right are attracted in particular by the issues of choice and the economy. (Caldwell, 1990, p. 18)

Calls for decentralized approaches to the reform of education emanate from a variety of quarters. Those demands in turn draw strength from conditions that define the environment of schooling and from the efforts of an assortment of stakeholders to radically overhaul the existing educational system. In this chapter, we study these forces in some detail. We begin our analysis with perhaps the most critical issue—the failing health of education and pleas for improvement. We then examine three trends dominating the environment in which schools are embedded—the perceived crisis in the economy, the changing social fabric of the nation, and the evolution to postindustrial perspectives on politics and organizations—that have created a particularly hospitable climate for school decentralization efforts. In the final section, we chronicle how the struggle to reinvent schooling is also propelling communities toward models of shared governance.

The Failing Health of Schooling

Public education consumes nearly 7% of our gross national product. Its expenditures have doubled or tripled in every postwar decade, even when enrollments declined. I can't think of any other single sector of American society that has absorbed more money by serving fewer people with steadily declining service. (Kearnes, 1988b, p. 566)

Current interest in SBM is simply a response to the overwhelming evidence that our educational system is not working effectively. (Reed et al., 1990, p. 9)

Supporting nearly all the proposals for decentralization and SBM are strident critiques of the overall effectiveness of the educational system, as well as of the particular dimensions and elements of schooling that have contributed to this failure. Reformers have generally used seven outcome measures to document unsatisfactory school effectiveness: (a) academic achievement in basic subject areas—compared to historical data about the United States and to student performance in other countries; (b) functional literacy; (c) preparation for employment; (d) the holding power of schools (dropout rates); (e) knowledge of specific subject areas such as geography and economics; (f) mastery of higher-order skills; and (g) initiative, responsibility, and citizenship (Murphy, 1990). Indices in each of these performance dimensions are contained in Table 3.1.[1] Collectively, the data provide a not-very-reassuring portrait of the health of the U.S. educational system.

From our perspective here, the important issue is that reformers contend that these results are traceable to a series of causes—political disenfranchisement, the depersonalization of schooling, hierarchical management systems, a moribund production function, and an absence of accountability—that can be addressed by decentralization-based reform initiatives. It is this belief in the efficacy of participatory forms of organization and governance that is pushing SBM to the forefront as a solution to the problems confronting schooling.

(Text continued on page 68)

Table 3.1   Indices of School Failure

Area	Source
Student Achievement (historical and cross-national comparisons)	
"The National Assessment of Educational Progress (NAEP) revealed a dismal record for 17-year-olds between 1971 and 1982. Test scores reported by the NAEP showed steady declines in vocabulary, reading, and mathematics."	Association for Supervision and Curriculum Development (1986, p. 19)
"International comparisons of student achievement, completed a decade ago, reveal that on 19 academic tests American students were never first or second and were last seven times."	National Commission on Excellence in Education (1983, p. 8)
"U.S. eighth graders' math skills rank ninth among twelve major industrialized countries of the world."	National Governors' Association (1986, p. 5)
"United States 13-year-olds finished last in a six nation study of math and science skills."	*USA Today* (1 February 1989, p. 1)
"Average achievement of high school students on most standardized tests is now lower than 26 years ago when Sputnik was launched."	National Commission on Excellence in Education (1983, p. 8)
"America's top high school science students ranked below those of nearly all other countries in a new comparison of scores from an international test released here last week.	*Education Week* (19 March 1988, p. 4)
"American 12th graders studying biology scored below students from the 16 other countries included in the analysis, which examined data from a 24-nation science assessment administered in 1986.	
"In chemistry, the study found students from all other countries except Canada and Finland out-scored their U.S. counterparts.	
"And in physics, only those two countries and Sweden ranked below the United States.	
"The achievement levels are particularly 'discouraging,' the study's authors note, since the American students in the comparison were drawn from the small proportion of the nation's high-school students enrolled in advanced science courses."	
"At a time when economic growth is increasingly dependent on mastery of science and technology, U.S. eighth graders' knowledge and understanding of mathematics is below that of most of their counterparts in other industrialized countries (12 out of 14)."	Carnegie Forum on Education and the Economy (1986, p. 16)

Table 3.1 Continued

Area	Source
"Despite achievement gains over the past decade, particularly among minority students, American high-school students display a 'dismal' level of mathematics proficiency, the National Assessment of Educational Progress reported last week.	*Education Week* (15 June 1988, p. 1)
"About half of all 17-year-olds tested in 1986 were unable to perform 'moderately complex' procedures usually taught in junior high school, such as finding averages and interpreting graphs, the assessment found. Only 6 percent were able to solve multi-step problems.	
"In addition, NAEP's report says, an 'alarming' number of 13-year-olds lack the skills in whole-number computation needed for everyday tasks, and approximately 7,000,000 of the 3rd and 4th graders who took the test 'have not yet acquired an understanding of rudimentary mathematical skills and concepts.'	
"These results, which federal officials last week called 'tragic' and 'sobering,' are consistent with those of a 1982 international mathematics assessment, which found that U.S. students lagged far behind those of other industrialized nations.	
"The data suggest, according to the report, that students'—and the nation's—economic future may be in jeopardy."	
"Moreover, contrary to widespread opinion, it isn't clear that our top students compare well with the top students of other nations. As Magnet (1988, p. 86) notes, 'the top 5% of the U.S. 12th-graders who took international calculus and algebra tests in 1982 came in dead last among the top 12th-graders of nine developed countries.'"	Boyd & Hartman (1987)
Literacy	
"It is not unusual for one-third of college freshman in the U.S. to read below a seventh grade level."	National Governors' Association (1986, p. 5)
"As we move into another Presidential election year, it's sobering to note that America's public schools graduate 700,000 functionally illiterate kids every year—and that 700,000 more drop out. Four out of five young adults	Kearns (1988b, p. 566)

(continued)

Table 3.1   Continued

Area	Source
in a recent survey couldn't summarize the main point of a newspaper article, read a bus schedule, or figure their change from a restaurant bill."	
"The NAEP reading assessment . . . measured progress at three achievement levels: advanced, proficient, and basic. . . . Only 25, 28, and 37 percent of America's students in grades 4, 8, and 12, respectively met or exceeded the proficient level for reading."	*Network News and Views* (November 1991, p. iii)
"More than two-thirds of the nation's 4th-, 8th-, and 12th-grade students—including one-quarter of high school seniors—are not proficient readers, according to the latest results from the National Assessment of Educational Progress."	*Education Week* (22 September 1992, p. 1)
"Nationwide, more than a quarter of the 4th graders failed to demonstrate the ability to perform simple arithmetic reasoning with whole numbers."	*Education Week* (12 June 1991, p. 1)
"Results from the recent National Adult Literacy Survey suggest that 47 percent of America's adult population possesses low literacy levels."	*Network News and Views* (November 1993, p. 1)

Preparation for Employment

"The business community blamed the schools for failing to prepare students adequately in basic skills. In fact, business leaders charged that the decline in achievement paralleled the decline in performance of American workers."	Association for Supervision and Curriculum Development (1986, p. 20)
"I believe the success of that second wave of reform is critical, because public education has put this country at a terrible competitive disadvantage. The American workforce is running out of qualified people. If current demographic and economic trends continue, American business will have to hire a million new workers a year who can't read, write, or count. Teaching them how—and absorbing the lost productivity while they're learning—will cost industry $25 billion a year for as long as it takes. And nobody I know can say how long that will be. Teaching new workers basic skills is doing the schools' product-recall work for them. And frankly, I resent it."	Kearns (1988b, p. 566)
"While American business has no place telling educators how to run schools, we have two very legitimate roles: The first is to say that	Gerstner, cited in *Education Week* (18 May 1994, p. 6)

Table 3.1 Continued

Area	Source
the output of your schools is not good enough to do the work we need done."	
"Up to 40 percent of the nation's manufacturing firms say their efforts to upgrade workplace technology and increase productivity have been stymied by the low level of education of their workforce, according to a new study by the National Association of Manufacturers.	*Education Week* (11 December 1991, p. 5)
"Because of employee-skill deficiency, the survey indicates, 40 percent of firms are having serious problems upgrading technology, 37 percent are having difficulty raising productivity, and 30 percent have not been able to reorganize into a high-performance workplace by giving employees more responsibility.	
"Businesses also said they reject five out of six job candidates and have found shortages of skilled and semiskilled workers throughout the country, with shortages expected to become severe by 1996."	
"The study, based on Carnegie's first international survey of higher-education faculties, found only about 20 percent of U.S. professors agreeing with the statement, 'Undergraduates are adequately prepared in written- and oral-communication skills.' Just 15 percent of U.S. faculty members agreed with a similar statement about mathematics and quantitative reasoning."	*Education Week* (22 June 1993, p. 12)
"Unfortunately, the vast majority of the schools are about the same as they were 10 years ago. The return on investment in education is minimal when one applies real quality-control measurements to the public school system."	Bowsher, cited in *Education Week* (13 October 1993, p. 8)
"More than half of small businesses have problems finding applicants for entry-level positions who possess the basic skills needed for the jobs, according to a survey by the National Alliance of Business.	*Education Week* (20 May 1992, p. 2)
"The survey of 233 companies with 500 or fewer employees found that 70 percent reported difficulty finding applicants with sufficient writing skills to handle an entry-level job.	
"About 62 percent of those responding had trouble finding applicants with the necessary math skills, and 59 percent reported problems	

(continued)

Table 3.1 Continued

Area	Source
finding potential employees with sufficient reading skills."	
"The USA's most powerful business leaders today tackle a crisis that threatens everyone's future: a near-total breakdown in our public schools.	*USA Today* (3 February 1989, p. 1B)
" 'We simply don't have any more time to wait,' says Owen 'Brad' Butler, retired chairman of Procter & Gamble Co.	
"U.S. corporations spend $25 billion a year teaching employees skills they should have learned at school. Motorola spends $50 million a year teaching seventh-grade math and English to 12,500 factory workers—half its hourly employees. Kodak is teaching 2,500 how to read and write."	

Holding Power

"Large numbers of American children are in limbo—ignorant of the past and unprepared for the future. Many are dropping out—not just out of school but out of productive society."	Carnegie Forum on Education and the Economy (1986, p. 2)
"Large numbers of drop-outs have become a serious problem."	Association for Supervision and Curriculum Development (1986, p. 9)
"The percentage of Hispanics ages 25 and older who have completed high school . . . remains just 51 percent."	*Education Week* (12 February 1992, p. 11)

Knowledge of Specific Subject Areas

Geography: "A 1987 survey of 5,000 high school seniors in eight major cities produced equally dismal results. In Boston, 39% of the students couldn't name the six New England states; in Minneapolis-St. Paul, 63% couldn't name all seven continents; in Dallas, 25% couldn't identify the country that borders the U.S. to the south."	Kearns (1988b, p. 566)
Economics: "A new survey by the Gallup Organization has found high rates of 'economic illiteracy' among 12th-grade students, college seniors, and the general public.	*Education Week* (16 September 1992, p. 10)
"According to the results of the poll, which were released last week by a national economics-education group, the general population could correctly answer only 39 percent, and high school seniors only 35 percent, of 19 multiple-	

Table 3.1 Continued

Area	Source
choice and open-ended questions about fundamental economics issues."	
History: "Results of the history test were, in Mr. Finn's words, 'accurate but reprehensible.' Overall, public-school students answered 54 percent of all questions correctly, with college-bound public-school students answering 60 percent correctly.	*Education Week* (9 March 1988, p. 7)
"For nonpublic schools, the results were only slightly better, he said, with an overall average of 60 percent and an average for independent-school students of 63 percent."	
Literature: "On the literature assessment, public-school students answered an average of 51 percent of the questions correctly, with college-bound public-school students averaging 57 percent. The average score for students in nonpublic schools was 58 percent, and for those in independent schools 60 percent.	*Education Week* (9 March 1988, p. 7)
" 'I consider a score in the low 60's on this a D minus,' Mr. Finn said."	
Writing: "Most American students have trouble getting their ideas across in writing, according to a new National Assessment of Educational Progress report.	"Educational Testing Service" (1994, p. 1)
"The results from the *NAEP 1992 Writing Report Card* show that even the best students who are able to write informative and narrative pieces have trouble preparing arguments and evidence in persuasive writing tasks. In general, fewer than 20 percent of the students wrote 'elaborated' (well-developed and detailed) responses."	
Science: "There was a steady decline in science achievement scores of U.S. 17-year-olds as measured by national assessments of science in 1969, 1973, and 1977."	National Commission on Excellence in Education (1983, p. 9)
"Only about 1 in 20 American adults is 'scientifically literate' and can answer such basic questions as whether the earth revolves around the sun, whether antibiotics kill viruses, and whether astrology is scientific, a federally funded study has found.	*Education Week* (25 January 1989, p. 25)
"The findings, released here last week at the annual meeting of the American Association for the Advancement of Science, are similar to those of two previous U.S. studies, in 1979 and 1985."	

(continued)

Table 3.1 Continued

Area	Source
"American students' 'distressingly low' levels of achievement in science may signal the need for fundamental changes in the way the subject is taught, according to a study released last week by the National Assessment of Educational Progress.	*Education Week* (28 September 1989, p. 1)

"The study showed that, despite gains over the past four years, particularly among minorities, a majority of high-school students 'are poorly equipped for informed citizenship and productive performance in the workplace.'

"And, it said, only 7 percent have the knowledge and skills necessary to perform well in college level science courses.

"In addition, the study found that almost half of the 13-year-olds tested lacked a grasp of the basic elements of science, and that nearly 30 percent of the 9-year-olds—representing 1 million students—'have not yet developed some understanding of scientific principles and a rudimentary knowledge of plants and animals.'

" 'The data in this report present a situation that can only be described as a national disgrace,' said Bassam Z. Shakhashiri, director of the science- and engineering-education directorate of the National Science Foundation, at a press conference here."

| *Science and Mathematics:* "American 13-year-olds performed at or near the bottom on a new six-nation international mathematics and science assessment, according to a federally funded study released here last week. | *Education Week* (8 February 1989, p. 5) |

"Their performance on the math assessment was the poorest recorded, and on the science assessment narrowly surpassed only that of test takers from Ireland and the French-speaking portions of Ontario and New Brunswick."

Mastery of Higher-Order Skills

| "The Nation that dramatically and boldly led the world into the age of technology is failing to provide its own children with the intellectual tools needed for the 21st century." | National Science Board (1983, p. v) |

| "As jobs requiring little skill are automated or go offshore, and demands increase for the highly skilled, the pool of educated and skilled | Carnegie Forum on Education and the Economy (1986, p. 2) |

Table 3.1 Continued

Area	Source
people grows smaller and smaller and the backwater of the unemployable rises."	
"Between 1971 and 1982, there was a net loss of 9-, 13-, and 17-year-olds' knowledge about and ability to use scientific principles. And there has been no improvement in advanced mathematical problem-solving ability."	National Governors' Association (1986, p. 5)
"Only 5 percent of the high-school seniors demonstrated the skills needed for high-technology or college-level work, officials noted."	*Education Week* (12 June 1991, p. 1)
"Between one-third and two-thirds of students perform poorly on mathematics questions that require them to take time to reason and to explain their answers, a new analysis of data from the 1992 National Assessment of Educational Progress suggests."	*Education Week* (8 September 1993, p. 16)
"Fewer than 20 percent of our fourth and twelfth graders understand complex mathematical problems."	*Network News and Views* (November 1993, p. i)
"Only 11 percent of high school seniors who took the American College Testing Program test this year are prepared for college-level calculus, and one in four will need remedial mathematics in college, a study released last week by the testing firm indicates.	*Education Week* (16 September 1992, p. 11)
"Even many of those intending to pursue math and science degrees lack the necessary math background, the study found. Among seniors who said they planned to major in subjects such as engineering, computer science, and physical sciences, only a fourth earned A.C.T. scores that indicated they could enter calculus, while 14 percent would need remedial math."	
" 'On the other hand, in the K-12 system,' he [Paul E. Barton] added, 'there are so few students at the top of achievement levels, and this top itself is unremarkable. And where we do have talent in the pipeline, it leaks as it flows to the higher-education system.'	*Education Week* (5 June 1991, p. 4)
" 'Six-and-one-half percent of our 17-year-olds can solve multi-step problems and algebra,' Mr. Barton said. 'That's not calculus and trigonometry.' "	

(continued)

Table 3.1 Continued

Area	Source
Initiative, Responsibility, Citizenship	
"Too many young people are leaving the schools without . . . self-discipline or purpose."	Twentieth Century Fund (1983, p. 3)
"An 'unacceptably high' number of 15- to 30-year-olds are willing to lie, cheat, and steal, a new survey involving nearly 9,000 teenagers and adults nationwide suggests.	*Education Week* (25 November 1992, p. 5)
"The survey found that 33 percent of the high school students questioned and 16 percent of the college students said they had stolen merchandise from a store within the past year.	
"About one-third of the students in each group said they were willing to lie on a résumé, a job application, or during a job interview to get a job they want. And 16 percent of the high school students said they had already done so at least once.	
"Such unethical behaviors also apparently extend to school; 61 percent of the high school students and 32 percent of college students admitted having cheated on an examination once in the past year."	
"Student behavior and attitudes, ranging from lack of motivation to large number of drop-outs, became a serious problem."	Association for Supervision and Curriculum Development (1986, p. 9)

SOURCE: Excerpts from *Education Week* and *USA Today* (© copyright 1989) are reprinted with permission.

A Changing Environment

A turbulent environment generates a host of highly salient demands and the system is pressed to search for solutions to a cluster of seemingly intractable problems. (Malen et al., 1989, p. 6)

We have truly reached a crisis moment in the social and economic history of this country. (Ramsey, interview in Education Week, *1992a, p. 6)*

As we remarked in the last section, SBM has appeared on the landscape as an alternative to existing political and managerial systems that define—and appear to be failing—education. Concomitantly, pressure to adopt more decentralized modes of operating schools draws considerable energy from movements in the larger environment surrounding education. Three of these forces have particular relevance for schools: the perceived crisis in the economy, the changing social fabric of the nation, and the movement to a postindustrial world. All three conditions lend momentum to the demand for educational reform in general (Murphy, 1990, 1991) and all three are regularly referenced by analysts of the shared governance movement that is sweeping over schooling.[2] We treat each in turn below.

The Perceived Crisis in the Economy

In many countries the most recent educational debate has been conducted in a context of alarm regarding the state of the economy and national competitiveness. (Chapman, 1990, p. 241)

School-based management was viewed by some actors as a means for improving schools and, thereby, enhancing America's position in world markets. (Ogawa, 1992, p. 19)

No aspect of the environment has molded education over the past 15 years more than the economy, more specifically, the perceived deterioration of our economic well-being as a nation. There is a pervasive feeling afoot that the United States is losing, and perhaps has already lost, its foremost position in the world economy—that its "once unchallenged preeminence in commerce, industry, science, and technological innovation" (National Commission on Excellence in Education, 1983, p. 5) has taken a terrible battering. Evidence of this belief is omnipresent in the reform documents that fueled the educational reform movement of the 1980s:

Today, however, our faith in change—and our faith in ourselves as the world's supreme innovators—is being shaken. Japan, West Germany and other relatively new industrial powers have challenged America's position on the leading edge of change and technical invention. In the seventies, productivity in manufacturing industries grew nearly four times as fast in Japan, and twice as fast in West Germany and France, as in the United States.

The possibility that other nations may outstage us in inventiveness and productivity is suddenly troubling Americans. (Education Commission of the States, 1983, p. 13)

Already the quality of our manufactured products, the viability of our trade, our leadership in research and development, and our standards of living are strongly challenged. Our children could be stragglers in a world of technology. We must not let this happen; America must not become an industrial dinosaur. (National Science Board, 1983, p. v)

America's ability to compete in world markets is eroding. The productivity growth of our competitors outdistances our own. The capacity of our economy to provide a high standard of living is increasingly in doubt. (Carnegie Forum on Education and the Economy, 1986, p. 2)

"Whilst there has been no proven relationship between educational achievement measured by specific tests and international productivity comparisons" (Chapman, 1990, p. 241), "underlying much current policy talk about school governance is an assumption that ineffective schools are to blame for the perceived lack of competitiveness of the U.S. economy" (Tyack, 1993, p. 24).[3]

The 1980s will be remembered for two developments: the beginning of a sweeping reassessment of the basis of the nation's economic strength and an outpouring of concern for the quality of American education. The connection between these two streams of thought is strong and growing. (Carnegie Forum on Education and the Economy, 1986, p. 11)

If only to keep and improve on the slim competitive edge we still retain in world markets, we must dedicate ourselves to the reform of our educational system. (National Commission on Excellence in Education, 1983, p. 7)

This assumption of a tight, and causal, linkage between schooling and the economy has helped produce three outcomes. First, blame has been heaped on schools. The economy is failing and schools are held responsible—the "educational systems [are] providing neither an adequate nor relevant education" (S. B. Lawton, 1991, p. 6). As we reported earlier, considerable evidence has been amassed to document both sides of the equation—a deteriorating economy on the one side and a failing educational system on the other.

Second, a rationale for the failure has been constructed. Analyses show that teachers and administrators are drawn from the bottom of the intellectual barrel and then poorly trained for their roles. Conditions of employment for teachers are unprofessional and stifling. The basic operating structure of schools is inadequate. The management of the enterprise has been found to be wanting, especially in providing leadership. The curriculum is a mess, lacking both rigor and coherence. Instruction is poor; materials (textbooks) worse. Students are allowed to drift through school unchallenged and uneducated. And as bad as school is for almost everyone, it is even worse for less advantaged and minority pupils. Everywhere there are intellectual softness, a lack of expectations and standards, and the absence of accountability. In short, it is not difficult to figure out why students subjected to these conditions should fare so poorly in comparison to (a) students from other nations, (b) their peers from other eras, and (c) acceptable standards of performance.

Finally, "in the face of [this] rising national concern for school productivity" (Guthrie, 1986, p. 305), reformers have turned their attention to the very institutions they chastise, asking them to jump start the faltering economy:

> Many reforms reflect the assumption that quality education is a key element in the development of a stable national economy, which in turn is a critical factor in our national security. American productivity has become a political issue, and education is seen as a major factor in improving productivity. (Association for Supervision and Curriculum Development, 1986, p. 2)

Although reformers originally placed their bets on state-developed and mandated requirements, over the past decade decentralization strategies that "reflect the utilitarian assumptions of human capital theory" (S. B. Lawton, 1991, p. 19) and a political and managerial algorithm "that views participation in terms of productivity" (Conway, 1984, p. 13) have gained increasing acceptance in the reform arena. As economic problems continue to plague society, and as

educational responses appear less effective than hoped, more radical types of decentralization initiatives are being weighed and demands for greater voice and participation are expanding (Murphy,
1993a).

Changing Social Fabric

> *These data have implications for educators, Ms. Weitz said, noting that, "if
> we're serious about education reform, we have to also deal with other risks
> children experience, because in the end it will affect the performance of
> students." (Cohen, 1992b, p. 14)*

The fabric of U.S. society is being rewoven in some places and
is unraveling in others, resulting in changes that promise to have a
significant impact on schooling. At the macro level, schools operate
in an environment where social capital for increasing numbers of
students and their families is limited:

Nearly four million American children are growing up in communities that jeopardize their safety and decrease their
  chances of success in school, family life, and the workplace.
  (Cohen, 1994, p. 5)

The economic status of America's children has declined significantly in comparison with that of adults over the past
  three decades, a new study suggests.

Moreover, the social condition of children, as measured by such
  markers as standardized test scores and homicide and
  suicide rates, has deteriorated sharply as well.

American children are in trouble. (*Education Week*, 1992c, p. 11)

The nation's overall social well-being has fallen to its lowest point
  since 1970, according to a Fordham University professor.

Marc L. Miringoff, the director of the Fordham Institute for Innovation in Social Policy, has conducted the annual survey since 1970. He tracks a wide range of federal data on
  16 key social problems, including poverty, infant mortality,
  unemployment, child abuse, teenage suicide, school dropouts, and unemployment, and distills his findings into a
  single measure for each year on a scale of zero to 100.
  Lower scores indicate lower well-being.

For 1990, the latest year for which complete data are available, the index stood at 42, down three points from 1989. The index stood at 75 in 1970 and hit its peak at 79 in 1972. The figure has declined fairly steadily since then.

A subsection on children's health and well-being showed a decline for the fifth year in a row to a record low of 44 in 1990. That index hit its peak, 78, in 1976.

Skyrocketing increases in reported child abuse, the number of children living in poverty, and the number of teenage deaths by homicide fueled the falling index. (*Education Week*, 1992b, p. 3)

One thread of these environmental phenomena is comprised of demographic shifts that threaten "our national standard of living and democratic foundations" (Carnegie Council on Adolescent Development, 1989, p. 27) and promise to overwhelm schools as they are now constituted. Minority enrollment in U.S. schools is rising, as is the proportion of less advantaged youngsters. There is a rapid increase in the number of students whose primary language is other than English. The traditional two-parent family, with one parent employed and the other at home to care for the children, has become an anomaly, constituting only one quarter of U.S. families (Cohen, 1992a). A few citations from educational literature convey the extent of these demographic changes:

Overall, more than 30 percent of students in public schools— some 12 million—are now minority. (Quality Education for Minorities Project, 1990, p. 11)

By the year 2000, . . . nearly half of all school-aged children will be non-white. (Carnegie Council on Adolescent Development, 1989, p. 27)

Forty-six percent of children live in homes where both or the only parent is working . . . about one half of all children and youth will live in a single parent family for some period of their lives. (Kirst, McLaughlin, & Massell, 1989, p. 4)

The report of the 1990 Census also documented that immigration has had a greater impact on the nation during the 1980's than in any other decade since the turn of the century. (Schmidt, 1992, p. 9)

> The share of children with mothers in the workplace rose from 39 percent in 1970 to 61 percent in 1990, and that one in five children—almost 13 million—live in a single-parent home, more than twice the share 20 years ago.
>
> About 10 percent of children under 18 live with other relatives, neighbors, friends, or in institutions. (Cohen, 1992b, p. 14)
>
> Between 1960 and 1987, the number of families headed by females with children under 18 tripled. (Wagstaff & Gallagher, 1990, p. 103)

At the same time that these new threads are being woven into the tapestry of U.S. society, a serious unraveling of other parts of that fabric is occurring. The number of youngsters affected by the ills of the world in which they live—for example, poverty, unemployment, crime, drug addiction, malnutrition—is increasing, as is the need for a variety of more intensive and extended services from societal organizations, especially schools:

> The percentage of children living in poverty in the United States is more than double that of other major industrialized nations. (*Education Week*, 1993, p. 3)
>
> The 20.6 percent poverty rate reported for children under age 18 in 1990—up from 19.6 percent in 1989—"remains higher than that for any other age group," the Census Bureau noted.
>
> The report showed that children under age 18 in 1990 accounted for 40 percent of the poor. (Cohen, 1991, p. 4)
>
> Between 1979 and 1990, the report says, the real median income of families with children fell by 5 percent. The average income for those in the lowest bracket fell by 12.6 percent, to $9,190. Children were the poorest group, it says, with one in five, or 12.7 million, living in poverty in 1990. (Cohen, 1992b, p. 14)
>
> 30% of children in metropolitan areas live in poverty; that will increase by a third by the year 2000. Twice as high a percentage of children aged 0-6 live in poverty as do adults aged 18-64. (Clark, 1990, p. 1)
>
> In 1980, 2.5 million people (labeled the underclass) or 3.1 percent of all households lived in 880 urban census-tract neigh-

borhoods where more than half of the men had worked less than 26 weeks. (Wagstaff & Gallagher, 1990, p. 105)

92 percent of the high school class of 1987 had begun drinking before graduating; of those, 56 percent had begun drinking in the 6th to 9th grades. (Carnegie Council on Adolescent Development, 1989, p. 22)

8 million, or about 40 percent, of junior- and senior-high school students drink weekly, and together consume approximately 35 percent of all the wine coolers sold in the country.

More than 3 million students say they drink alone, more than 4 million drink when they are upset, and nearly 3 million drink because they are bored. (Flax, 1991, p. 13)

Nearly 60 percent of all high school students have used alcohol during the past month, and almost 4 in 10 have had more than five drinks on a single occasion, the U.S. Centers for Disease Control reports. (*Education Week*, 1991, p. 12)

More than half of the high school class of 1985 had tried marijuana, one in six had used cocaine, and one in eight had used hallucinogens like LSD. (Wagstaff & Gallagher, 1990, p. 107)

About half of the teenagers in the United States are sexually active by the time they leave school. . . . One out of four teenage [girls] has experienced a pregnancy. (Wagstaff & Gallagher, 1990, p. 108)

One-fifth of all deaths among U.S. teenagers in 1988 were due to gunshots, while nearly half of all deaths among black male teens that year were by firearms. (M. Lawton, 1991, p. 4)

Nearly two-thirds of elementary school teachers responding to a recent national survey believe that more of their students have health problems today than in the past, according to a report released here last week by the American Academy of Pediatrics and the National PTA.

The 500 survey respondents estimated that, on average, 12 percent of their students last year had a problem that seriously affected their learning. Urban teachers said that fully 18 percent of their students had such problems. (Sommerfeld, 1992b, p. 8)

Indicators that worsened during the 1980's, according to the study, included child poverty, births to unmarried teenagers, numbers of children living in single-parent homes, and percentage of low-birthweight babies. More youths were also required by juvenile courts to spend "formative years" away from their families, and the likelihood of a teenager's death as a result of an accident, suicide, or murder rose. (Cohen, 1992b, p. 14)

A particularly troublesome aspect of this situation is the fact that, by and large, these are the students—low-income, minority, and disadvantaged youngsters—with whom schools have historically been the least successful (Carnegie Council on Adolescent Development, 1989).

Another harsh statistical conclusion is that poverty has increasingly become a black, female, [urban], and youthful condition. (Wagstaff & Gallagher, 1990, p. 104)

The Census Bureau report found that more than 40 percent of Hispanic children live in poverty, compared with just 13 percent of non-Hispanic whites. Puerto Rican children fared the worst, with nearly 58 percent falling below the poverty line. (Schmidt, 1993, p. 22)

African-American and Latino children make up 80 percent of the children living in distressed neighborhoods—a rate 12 times higher than their nonminority peers. (Cohen, 1994, p. 5)

If current trends continue, half of all black and Hispanic children will be poor by 2010, a Tufts University study concludes.

"Poverty will be the rule rather than the exception for the two largest racial and ethnic minorities in the country—and it will grow significantly among white children as well," said J. Larry Brown, the director of the Center on Hunger, Poverty, and Nutrition Policy at Tufts University. (Cohen, 1993, p. 11)

Forty-seven percent of Black and 56% of Hispanic adults are classified as functionally illiterate or marginal readers. (Astuto, 1990, p. 1)

The gap between White and minority achievement remains unbridged. . . . By third or fourth grade, minority and non-minority achievement levels begin to diverge. . . . By the middle school years, test scores show on average that minority children are a year or more behind. By the end of high school, a three-to-four year achievement gap between minority and nonminority youth has opened on tests such as the National Assessment of Educational Progress. (Quality Education for Minorities Project, 1990, pp. 17-18)

In 1989, . . . the combined SAT verbal and mathematics score for White students was still 27 percent higher than combined scores of Black students, 22 percent higher than scores of Puerto Rican students, and 15 percent higher than scores of American Indian and Mexican American students. (Quality Education for Minorities Project, 1990, p. 19)

While the problem of school violence is significant across the country, it tends to disproportionately affect low-achieving schools, and those with large minority populations, according to a survey of teachers also released last month. (Portner, 1994, p. 9)

In 1988, . . . about 15 percent of Black youth aged 15-24 had not graduated and were out of school . . . for Hispanic youth, the similar rate was nearly 36 percent, about three times the rate for White youth. (Quality Education for Minority Project, 1990, p. 18)

60% of prison inmates are dropouts. 58% of all dropouts are unemployed or receiving welfare. (Hutchins, 1988, p. 76)

The job rate for high school dropouts is dismal; of the 562,000 dropouts in 1985, 54 percent were unemployed and likely to remain so. (Wagstaff & Gallagher, 1990, p. 108)

The changing demographics of the United States—what Tom Joe, the director of the Center for the Study of Social Policy, calls "the many new realities of family life" (cited in Cohen, 1992a, p. 5)—are placing tremendous strains on the country's educational system. More and more of the types of students whom educators have failed to help in the past are entering our schools. Not only are educators being asked to educate them successfully, but the definition of success has been dramatically expanded and higher levels of achievement are expected. Most critics see little hope that the ever-widening goals of education can be reached in the current system of schooling. Reformers are attempting to accommodate to these demographic shifts by developing a new model of the educational enterprise—a decentralized model that empowers teachers and parents at the school site to address these problems.[4] In particular, many reformers maintain that SBM can be an effective strategy for tackling this significant challenge to education.

Move to a Postindustrial Society

> We are in the midst of a revolution in the organization of human services. . . . The reliance, in the nineteenth century, on institutions is being replaced by a new service ideology, which emphasizes community programs and client choice. The monopoly of the state on service provision has been broken. The revolution is fueled by a critique of bureaucratic institutions that legitimizes the privatization of care, control, and now education. (Lewis, 1993, p. 84)

Economic Dynamics. There is widespread agreement that the evolution of society from an industrial to postindustrial era is helping fuel the move toward decentralized models of schooling. Three postindustrial dynamics in particular reinforce the relevance of shared models of governance: economic, political, and organizational forces. On the economic front, there is a shift from an industrial to a service economy. "With the development of a service economy [comes] the need for new markets, as well as the need to break the state's monopoly on the delivery of human services so that private enterprises [can] expand. Enter deinstitutionalization," (Lewis, 1993, p. 4), "deregulation and privatization" (Caldwell, 1990, p. 17), and a more direct role, that is, more voice, for stakeholders in shaping the reforming institutions.

Political Dynamics. Reinforcing the dynamics of the shift toward an information-based economy are important alterations in the political infrastructure of our society. At the broadest level, the evolution to the information age has fostered a renewed interest in political—as opposed to administrative—solutions to problems: "to the emphasis on managerial control, it juxtaposes an emphasis on political control" (March & Olson, 1983, p. 283). Equally important is the fact that the politics of tomorrow's world look increasingly democratic in form (Barber, 1994). There is a growing acceptance of the right of affected stakeholders to participate meaningfully in relevant decisions (Blumberg, 1985; Imber, 1983), as well as a renewed belief in the power of "democratic activity" (Bryk, 1993, p. 5) to pull societal institutions from the bureaucratic quagmire of professional control. It is also argued that "more democracy transforms the institution and creates a better educational system" (Lewis, 1993, p. 92).[5]

What this augurs for education is the birth, or rebirth, of democratic principles across an array of dimensions. It means restructuring the internal workings of classrooms and of the school so that children learn about democracy first hand. For those who manage schools, it means acknowledging that their schools

> must recognize their society's commitment to the democratic ideal as its chief organizing principle and must strive to organize and structure their respective institutions in a manner that does not routinely sacrifice the democratic ideal to the ideals of efficiency and power, which as organizing principles themselves, always compete with the democratic ideal. (Slater, 1994, p. 100)

Most important for our purposes here, it means that "school-based management may be an idea whose time has come politically" (Prickett et al., 1990, p. 6). There is both a recognition that teachers "should be directly involved in making work-related decisions" (Imber, 1983, p. 41) and a "demand . . . by individuals and by communities of various sorts to have greater control over the education of their children" (S. B. Lawton, 1991, p. 12).

Organizational Dynamics. Very closely aligned with the democratic forces noted above are serious efforts to overhaul the basic operating structure of our society's institutions—bureaucracy:

> The attack on bureaucracy has come from many angles, philosophical, social, technological, and practical. Perhaps practical difficulties [are] paramount: bureaucracies came to be seen as inefficient institutions unable to achieve their mandated purposes. Critiques suggest bureaucracies, especially

> those involving public monopolies, [are] perverse in their
> rewards, benefiting their own members more than those
> they were meant to serve. (S. B. Lawton, 1991, p. 10)

> The *problem*, so the argument goes—in mental health, correc-
> tions, and now education—is the very institutions we have
> built to handle the situation. The *solution* to our policy
> problems is to do away with the state hospital, the prison,
> and now the public school. It is the *institution* that causes
> the problem and must be transformed. (Lewis, 1993, p. 84)

There seems no longer to be any use for the core correlates of
bureaucracy: Hierarchy of authority is often viewed as detrimental;
impersonality is found to be incompatible with cooperative work
efforts; specialization and division of labor are no longer considered
to be assets; scientific management based on controlling the efforts
of subordinates is judged to be inappropriate; and the distinct
separation of management and labor is seen as counterproductive.

"Decentralized management and shared-decision making [are]
then seen as the likely antidote to such dysfunctions" (Wagstaff &
Reyes, 1993, p. 24). Also coming into focus is the understanding that
schools are and will continue to be increasingly shaped by the need
to organize collective efforts consistent with the evolution of organizational structures in the larger environment. Just as schools have
mirrored the industrial age's bureaucratic model during the 20th
century, so must they adopt a more heterarchical model as society
moves into the information age.

The Struggle to Reinvent Education

> *What has come into question, it would seem, is the very legitimacy of existing
> educational systems. . . . There are doubts that the "technology" of teaching
> and school administration is adequate to meet current challenges. (S. B.
> Lawton, 1991, p. 3)*

In addition to the environmental forces noted earlier, demands
for the implementation of self-managing schools are forming closer
to the educational sector as well. There is a widespread feeling afoot
that a significant restructuring of education is in order, that major

changes are needed in the systems employed to govern and manage schools, and in the way we think about teaching and learning. It is also widely held that the implementation of more participatory arrangements in education—especially SBM—will greatly facilitate this transformational work. Thus, a number of school-related dynamics are pushing educators to experiment with more collaborative methods of conducting business. In the remainder of this section, we examine these school-related forces for reform. We begin by reporting how centralized responses to the environmental forces described earlier were judged to be inadequate. We then review how the search for alternative answers led reformers to examine the more decentralized solutions found in the school improvement literature and in studies of successful restructuring in the corporate sector. We close by chronicling how important dimensions of the struggle to transform education are pushing us toward a more democratic system of schooling.

The Perceived Failure of Earlier
Centralized Reform Initiatives

> *Clearly, the current concern with school-site management developed largely in reaction to the centralized spirit of the first wave of reform. (Conley & Bacharach, 1990, p. 540)*

> *School-site management is a reaction to the highly centralized (state-level) role in reform efforts following A Nation at Risk. (Mojkowski & Fleming, 1988, p. 2)*

In the early and mid-1980s, proposals to improve education focused primarily on raising standards by expanding centralized controls. A state-centered, top-down model of change was employed. Prescriptions and performance measurements were emphasized. Piecemeal efforts were undertaken to repair the existing educational system (Murphy, 1990). A variety of stakeholders found these approaches to be philosophically misguided and conceptually limited (Boyd, 1987; Combs, 1988; Cuban, 1984; Passow, 1984). A number of these critics maintained that the standards-raising movement enhanced the site (and district) bureaucracy while diminishing the morale of school-site personnel, thereby crippling efforts at real improvement (Davidson, 1992). Others argued that the standards-raising

movement failed to take "into account the most fundamental variables in the educational process: the nature of the relationship
between educators and their students and the extent to which students
are actively engaged in the learning process" (Sedlak, Wheeler, Pullin,
& Cusick, 1986, p. ix).

"As a result, many believe the educational reform movement of
the 1980s has been a dismal failure" (Stevenson & Pellicer, 1992, p. 125)
at worst, or has "resulted in disappointing outcomes" (Wagstaff &
Reyes, 1993, p. 7) at best.[6] Whatever benefits did accrue, "these exter-
nally imposed changes often made teachers' work more difficult and
less effective" (Bryk, 1993, p. 13) and, Davidson (1992) contends,
"have bypassed the children of urban poverty[7] and have excluded
teachers from the decision making process" (p. 4). "Thus the move
to greater centralization of control of schools has proven to be costly
according to claims made by both policymakers and scholars. Alternative ways have been sought to improve the quality of education
students receive; one such alternative is the decentralization of control
to the school level or site-based management" (Wagstaff & Reyes,
1993, p. 25).

The Search for Alternative Solutions

The search for alternative solutions to the problems confronting
education led analysts to two sources of information—to lessons
about improving schools and knowledge about restructuring in the
corporate sector.

Lessons From School Improvement

Findings from studies of school effectiveness and school improvement have been
mentioned as justification of decentralization. (Caldwell, 1990, p. 17)

Support for school-based management also has come from studies that found
education reform was most effective and sustained when implemented by people
who felt a sense of ownership and responsibility for the reform. (Wohlstetter
& Buffett, 1991, p. 1)

The importance attributed to school-based management by (a)
the research on effective schools (Murphy et al., 1985; Purkey & Smith,
1983), (b) work in the area of school improvement (Goodlad, 1984;

Louis & Miles, 1990; Sizer, 1984, 1992), (c) the literature on school restructuring (Murphy, 1991; Murphy & Hallinger, 1993), and (d) studies on the school change process (Fullan, 1991) has contributed considerable support and pressure for education to adopt decentralized systems of governance, organization, and management. Three of the major conclusions from these lines of work (see Clark, Lotto, & Astuto, 1984, and Murphy, 1992a, for comparative analyses) are (a) there is considerable school staff involvement in the design of successful reforms—or stated alternatively, "the absence of teacher input in decisions that shape teaching practice often cause . . . innovations to fail to achieve the results that were intended" (Davidson, 1992, p. 5); (b) improvement occurs on a school-by-school basis, and the individual "school is the most appropriate level at which to focus educational reform efforts" (Murphy et al., 1985, p. 626); and (c) the most effective reforms are integrated, comprehensive, or systemic in nature—"improvement efforts must unfold so that changes become woven into the basic fabric of the organization" (Murphy & Hallinger, 1993, p. 257).

The collective message here is that "the school must become largely self-directing" (Goodlad, 1984, p. 276); schools should be provided with substantial autonomy[8] (Chubb, 1988; Purkey & Smith, 1983); and the development of collective decision making at the site level should be nurtured. As Caldwell (1990) informs us:

> The essence of these recommendations and findings is that highly effective schools or schools that have shown outstanding improvement have been given a high level of responsibility and authority to make decisions about staffing and the allocation of resources and, within these schools, teachers have been empowered in a variety of ways to make a contribution to planning and decision-making processes. (p. 17)

The message, or impetus, for SBM in this work is quite clear:

> Because both the effective schools literature and the implementation literature show that a collaborative process is central to successful school reform, it appears that American educators need to give greater attention to the democratic quality of the management process, and particularly so in light of the centralizing trends in many states. (Chapman & Boyd, 1986, p. 54)

Lessons From the Corporate World

Reformers have been fond of arguing by analogy, and copying business has periodically been fashionable. . . . Today they urge "restructuring" or decentralization, citing business practice in each case as a guide to reform in schooling. (Tyack, 1993, pp. 1-2)

Probably the strongest impetus toward decentralization grew out of the business sector of the American social order. (Candoli, 1991, pp. 33-34)

Advocates for decentralizing schools have found support for fundamentally different methods of operation from modern management theory and from activities in the corporate sector (Association for Supervision and Curriculum Development, 1986; Schlechty, 1990; Thompson, 1988). Faced with a series of problems not unlike those confronting schools—diminished product quality, low employee morale, unhappy consumers—businesses looked inward to see how the most successful of their group were operating. By and large, it was discovered that the most effective corporations had transformed their businesses by decentralizing operations—by pushing decisions down to the level of the organization in closest contact with the consumer, by reorienting their management philosophy from control to empowerment, by establishing scrupulous reputations for attention to quality, and by changing their views of workers—from property of the company to partners in the corporate undertaking (Beare, 1989; Maccoby, 1989). In short, they had restructured themselves from more hierarchically organized units to more fluid and organic systems. These lessons are now being held up to schools (Bernas, 1992), especially by corporate managers (Gerstner, 1994; Kearnes, 1988a, 1988b), as blueprints for educational reform. Not surprising, given our long history of infatuation with the corporate world (Callahan, 1962; Tyack, 1993) and the severity of the crisis confronting education, there is considerable "pressure for education to adapt and incorporate current business practices" (Goldman et al., 1991, p. 1), "to emulate leading corporations that have decentralized decision making" (Ogawa, 1992, p. 19), and to reinvent schooling consistent with these "innovative management theories that stress the importance of decentralization" (Short & Greer, 1989, p. 8). Thus, "many of the principles of site-based management are borrowed directly from business and industry" (Reed et al., 1990, p. 8).[9]

The Struggle to Transform Schooling

> *Around the middle of the twentieth century, we entered the post-industrial information age, a new stage in the human evolution. This new age requires new thinking, new perspectives, and a new vision of education. Improving our educational system, which is still grounded in the industrial revolution of the late nineteenth century, will not do in this post-industrial information society. What we need is a new image of education attained by a broad sweep of a comprehensive transformation—a metamorphosis. (Banathy, 1988, p. 51)*

As is the case with other organizations, schools are currently fighting to transform the way they think and act. From the collective effort of those who describe this change, a new vision of education quite unlike the "center of production" (Barth, 1986, p. 295) image that has shaped schooling throughout the industrial age is being portrayed. Embedded in this emerging view of tomorrow's schools are three central alterations: (a) at the institutional level, a change from professional to lay/professional control; (b) at the managerial level, a change from a bureaucratic operational system to more communal views of schooling; and (c) at the technical level, a change from behavioral to constructivist views of learning and teaching (Murphy, 1991, 1992a, 1992b). Each of these fundamental shifts pushes schools to adopt more localized and more participatory methods of operating. Each change is adding fuel to the drive for self-managing schools and shared decision making.

Reinventing Governance

> *From a political perspective, decentralization enables groups heretofore excluded to be in power. (Wohlstetter, 1990, p. 2)*

Most analysts of the institutional level of schooling—the interface of the school with its larger (generally immediate) environment—argue that the centralized approach to education led to "the belief in almost complete separation of schools from the community and, in turn, discouragement of local community involvement in decision making related to the administration of schools" (Burke, 1992, p. 33). Indeed a considerable body of literature suggests that one of the major functions of bureaucracy is the buffering of the school from the environment, especially from parents and community members (Meyer & Rowan, 1975).

Most chroniclers of the changing governance structures in re-structuring schools envision the demise of schooling as a sheltered government monopoly heavily controlled by professionals. In its stead, they forecast the emergence of a system of schooling, and more important for our purposes here, improvement designs driven by economic and political forces that substantially increase the saliency of SBM. Embedded in this conception are a number of interesting dynamics, all of which gain force from a realignment of power and influence between professional educators and lay members of the community. To begin with, the traditional dominant relationship—with professional educators on the playing field and parents on the sidelines acting as cheerleaders or agitators, or more likely passive spectators—is replaced by a more equal distribution of influence. Partnerships begin to emerge (Seeley, 1981). At the same time, the number of stakeholders in the schooling game increases, their legitimate influence expands, and the roles they play are broadened. All of this, of course, reinforces the importance of democratic principles in schools and the vehicles by which these principles find expression—self-management and participatory governance.

Four elements of this emerging portrait of transformed governance for parents are most prevalent: choice in selecting a school, voice in school governance, partnership in the education of their children, and enhanced membership in the school community. Central to all four is a blurring of the boundaries between the home and the school, between the school and the community, and between professional staff and lay constituents (Goldring, 1992). Collectively, these components support decentralized conceptions of schooling (e.g., site-based decision making) and the grassroots political and competitive economic arguments that support the calls for smaller and more locally controlled organizations (Murphy, 1991).

Reinventing Systems of Administration

A commitment to improved education demanded more democracy and less bureaucracy. The problem had been that the institution was insulated from democracy and thus pathological. (Lewis, 1993, p. 91)

School-based management is in large part a reaction to what many educators perceive as an overcentralization of power within school districts. (Lindelow, 1981, p. 94)

"In recent years, critics have argued that the reforms of the Progressive Era produced bureaucratic arteriosclerosis, insulation from parents and patrons, and the low productivity of a declining industry protected as a quasi monopoly" (Tyack, 1993, p. 3). There is growing sentiment that the existing structure of administration is "obsolete and unsustainable" (Rungeling & Glover, 1991, p. 415), that the "bureaucratic structure is failing in a manner so critical that adaptations will not forestall its collapse" (Clark & Meloy, 1989, p. 293).[10] Behind this basic critique lie several beliefs: that central office staff are too numerous (Viadero, 1993) and too "far removed from the schools to know and understand children and their needs" (Wagstaff & Reyes, 1993, p. 25)—beliefs often "emphasizing the incompetence of district administrators" (Garms et al., 1978, p. 290)— and that "bureaucracies are set up to serve the adults that run them and in the end, the kids get lost in the process" (Daly, cited in Olson, 1992a, p. 10; also Diegmueller, 1994; Harp, 1993a). It is increasingly being concluded that the existing bureaucratic system of administration is "incapable of addressing the technical and structural shortcomings of the public educational system" (S. B. Lawton, 1991, p. 4).

More finely grained criticism of the bureaucratic infrastructure of schooling comes from a variety of quarters. There are those who contend that schools are so paralyzed by the "bureaucratic arteriosclerosis" noted above by Tyack (1993, p. 3) that "professional judgment" (Hill & Bonan, 1991, p. 65), "innovation and creativity" (Lindelow, 1981, p. 98), "morale" (David, 1989, p. 45), and responsibility have all been paralyzed (Bolin, 1989; Conley, 1989; Frymier, 1987; Sizer, 1984). Other reformers maintain "that school bureaucracies, as currently constituted could [never] manage to provide high-quality education" (Elmore, 1993, p. 37) and that, even worse, "bureaucratic management practices have been causing unacceptable distortions in educational process" (Wise, 1989, p. 301), that they are "paralyzing American education . . . [and] getting in the way of children's learning" (Sizer, 1984, p. 206; also Cuban, 1989; McNeil, 1988; Wise, 1978). Some analysts believe that bureaucracy is counterproductive to the needs and interests of educators within the school— "it is impractical, and it does not fit the psychological and personal needs of the workforce" (Clark & Meloy, 1989, p. 293); it "undermine[s] the authority of teachers" (Sackney & Dibski, 1992, p. 2); and it is "incompatible with the professional organization" (p. 4). Still other critics suggest that bureaucratic management is inconsistent with

the sacred values and purposes of education; they question "fundamental ideological issues pertaining to bureaucracy's meaning in a
democratic society" (Campbell, Fleming, Newell, & Bennion, 1987,
p. 73) and find that "it is inconsistent to endorse democracy in society
but to be skeptical of shared governance in our schools" (Glickman,
1990, p. 74; see also Fusarelli & Scribner, 1993). There are also scholars
who view bureaucracy as a form of operation that "deflect[s] attention from the central task of teaching and learning" (Elmore, 1990,
p. 5): "Since the student is the prime producer of learning and since
he is not part of the bureaucracy, and not subject to bureaucratic
accountability, bureaucracy and its whole value structure must be
seen as irrelevant at best, and obstructive at worst, to true learning
relationships" (Seeley, 1980, p. 8). Other reform proponents hold
that the existing organizational structure of schools is neither sufficiently flexible nor sufficiently robust to meet the needs of students
in a postindustrial society (Brown, 1992; Harvey & Crandall, 1988;
Sizer, 1984). Finally, some analysts who contend that the rigidities
of bureaucracy, by making schools "almost impenetrable by citizens
and unwieldy to professionals" (Candoli, 1991, p. 31), impede the
ability of parents and citizens to govern and reform schooling
(Campbell et al., 1987).

Not unexpected, given this tremendous attack on the basic organizational infrastructure of schooling, stakeholders at all levels are
arguing that "ambitious, if not radical, reforms are required to rectify
this situation" (Elmore, 1993, p. 34), that "the excessively centralized, bureaucratic control of . . . schools must end" (Carnegie Forum,
cited in E. M. Hanson, 1991, pp. 2-3): "Citizens increasingly are
demanding that the huge central bureaucracy be broken up into
smaller, more workable units that will give them the opportunity to
have input into the decisions and that will respond effectively,
efficiently, and quickly to demands and pleas being heard from the
clients" (Candoli, 1991, p. 31).

In its place, reformers are arguing for "a philosophy of devolved
decision-making and school self-determination" (Dellar, 1992, p. 5)
and "policies . . . that unleash productive local initiatives" (Guthrie,
1986, p. 306). The emerging alternative vision of administration for
tomorrow's schools includes methods of organizing and managing
schools that are generally consistent with the "quiet revolution [in]
organizational and administrative theory in Western societies" (Foster,
1988, p. 71). In the still-forming image of schools for the 21st century,

hierarchical bureaucratic organizational structures give way to systems that are more organic (Weick & McDaniel, 1989), more decentralized (Guthrie, 1986; Harvey & Crandall, 1988; Watkins & Lusi, 1989), and more professionally controlled (Houston, 1989; Weick & McDaniel, 1989), systems that "suggest a new paradigm for school organization and management" (Mulkeen, 1990, p. 105). The basic shift is from a *"power over* approach . . . to a *power to* approach" (Sergiovanni, 1991, p. 57). The focus is on local control and shared decision making. SBM moves to center stage.

Reinventing Learning and Teaching[11]

The advocates of adventurous instruction may be working near the beginning of a great, slow change in conceptions of knowledge, learning and teaching. (Cohen, 1988, p. 22)

From the onset of the industrial revolution, education in the United States has been largely defined by a behavioral psychological model of learning—a model that fits nicely with the bureaucratic system of school organization. This viewpoint in turn nurtured the development of the factory and medical models of instruction that have dominated schooling throughout the 20th century (Petrie, 1990; Schlechty, 1990). Under these two models, the belief that the role of schooling is to sort students into the able and less able—those who would work with their heads and those who would work with their hands (Goodlad, 1984)—became deeply embedded into the fabric of schooling (Oakes, 1985). Thus, up to the era of restructuring, "the actual operating goal of American society—whatever the ideal of rhetoric, or the commitment of individual schools or teachers—has been to provide educational services for all children, but to expect a 'bell curve' distribution of success, with large numbers of children falling in the 'mediocre' or 'failure' range" (Seeley, 1988, p. 34). Using analytic lenses inherent in these models, in the best case problems can be traced to deficiencies or dysfunctions in individuals that are subject to diagnosis, treatment, and remediation—problems and "solutions for human predicaments are to be found almost exclusively within the self, leaving the social order conveniently unaffected" (Prilleltensky, 1989, p. 796). In the worst case, as Seeley (1988) reminds us, failure is the inevitable consequence of the model of learning emphasized.

A shift in the operant model of learning is a fundamental dynamic of the struggle to redefine schools (Elmore, 1989; Marshall, 1992; Murphy, 1991). Of real significance, if rarely noted, is the fact that this new model reinforces the democratic tenets embedded in the postindustrial views of governance and administration discussed above. The behavioral psychological model that highlights the innate capacity of the learner is replaced by "cognitive or constructivist psychology" (Cohen, 1988, p. 19) and newer sociological perspectives on learning (Bransford, 1991). Under this approach to learning, which is at the heart of real restructuring efforts, schools that historically have been in the business of promoting student adaptation to the existing social order are being transformed to ensure equality of opportunity for all learners.

The emerging redefinition of teaching means that teachers, historically organized to carry out instructional designs and to implement curricular materials developed from afar, begin to exercise considerably more control over their profession and the routines of the workplace. Analysts see this reorganization playing out in a variety of ways at the school level. At the most fundamental level, teachers have a much more active voice in developing the goals and purposes of schooling (Conway & Jacobson, 1990)—goals that act to delimit or expand the conception of teaching itself. They also have a good deal more to say about the curricular structures and pedagogical approaches employed in their schools—"influences over the basic elements of instructional practice (time, material, student engagement, and so forth)" (Elmore, 1989, p. 20). Finally, teachers demonstrate more control over the supporting ingredients of schooling—such as budgets, personnel, and administration—that affect the way they carry out their responsibilities (Murphy, 1991).

Advocates of transformational change also see teaching becoming a more collegial activity. Isolation, so deeply ingrained in the structure and culture of the profession (Lortie, 1975), gives way to more collaborative efforts among teachers (McCarthey & Peterson, 1989; Wise, 1989). At the macro level, teachers are redefining their roles to include collaborative management of the profession, especially providing direction for professional standards. At a more micro level, new organizational structures are being created to allow teachers to plan and teach together and to make important decisions about the nature of their roles (Carnegie Forum on Education and the Economy, 1986; Holmes Group, 1986). A culture that recognizes the importance of collaborative efforts at professional development also characterizes teacher role redesign in restructuring schools (McCarthey & Peterson, 1989; Rallis, 1990).

New conceptions of teaching include other efforts to expand "teachers' roles and responsibilities beyond their regular classroom assignments" (Smylie & Denny, 1989, p. 4). The opening of decision-making forums historically closed to teachers is one example of this expansion. Thus, redefining teaching entails "acknowledging and institutionalizing the central managerial role of teachers" (Sykes & Elmore, 1989, p. 85)—a phenomenon that plays out in each individual teacher's expanded responsibility for the professionalization of colleagues and collectively in decision-making bodies such as school-site councils.

SUMMARY

In this chapter, the focus has been on the forces that are supporting—and in some cases driving—the SBM movement in education. We analyzed how powerful dynamics in the environment and in schools themselves are shaping education's efforts to redefine itself. In the next two chapters, we explore the history of SBM initiatives in the United States, beginning with the teacher councils movement in the early part of the 19th century and ending with the community control movement of the 1970s.

Notes

1. The framework for this analysis originally appeared in Murphy (1990). Many of the indices are taken from that source.

2. Somewhat paradoxically, this same set of external conditions has been employed to argue both for greater decentralization and for greater centralization. Those who maintain that centralized solutions are the most efficacious response to this complex environment held sway through much of the 1980s. More recently, those who maintain that decentralization-based responses will be more effective have taken center stage.

3. The fact that there is very little evidence to corroborate the assumption "of better schools as the engine for a leaner, stronger economy" (Cuban, 1994, p. 44) does not seem to bother most school reformers (for exceptions see Cuban, 1992, 1994; Kerr, 1991; and Tyack, 1993).

4. On the other hand, SBM in particular and decentralization initiatives in general may be viewed as attempts to pass downward problems that higher levels of government are unable or unwilling to address.

5. For a balanced analysis of the pros and cons of democracy, see Slater (1994).

6. Such conclusions about the failure of centralized reforms are not universally shared (see, for example, Murphy, 1989b).

7. Whether children of poverty were bypassed by Wave 1 reforms is open to debate (see Bartell & Noble, 1986; Grossman, Kirst, Negash, & Schmidt-Posnere, 1985; Murphy, 1989a, 1989c).

8. The beliefs that schools are overregulated and that this stranglehold on autonomy is hurting schools have been challenged by Hannaway (1992): "The claims of many analysts (e.g., Chubb and Moe, 1990) that excessive regulation is alienating public school teachers from their work and strangling their creativity are overstated. We argue that teachers in public systems are not overregulated; they are ignored!" (p. 8).

9. Ogawa (1992) does a good job of explaining this phenomenon. He notes that organizations

> such as public school systems, that do not possess clear technologies
> . . . and do not operate in competitive markets . . . are especially prone to
> adopting structures that mirror institutions. For, by doing so, they can
> gain legitimacy with stakeholders in their environments . . . without
> necessarily having to demonstrate the efficiency of their technical opera-
> tions. To the extent that legitimacy inclines stakeholders to invest resources
> in organizations, it contributes to organizations' survival, or effectiveness.
> (p. 2)

A second line of explanation centers on the ongoing infatuation that school administrators have had with the world of commerce and its prevailing theories of management (Beck & Murphy, 1993; Callahan, 1962; Murphy, 1992b). Although the benefits of this adaptive relationship are often glowingly explicated, potential costs should not be forgotten (Callahan, 1962; Murphy, 1991).

10. The bureaucratic story is more complex than its critics often acknowledge. On the nature of the intractability of bureaucracy, March and Olson (1983) remind us that "despite standard observations about bureaucratic rigidity, and the persist-ence of many forms of organizational routines and structures, any discussion of bureaucratic stability must be prefaced by a recognition of substantial bureaucratic change over time" (p. 281). On the search for bureaucratic villains, Sizer (1992) reports that

> there is, alas, no scapegoat here to ridicule and humiliate for the satisfac-
> tion of the rest of us. The system's power is deployed in the way it is because
> we wanted it that way. We trusted hierarchies and "systems" more than
> we trusted teachers' judgments. We believed that wisdom was more likely
> to be found at higher rather than lower levels of government. (p. 186)

And Cohen (1989) observes that one's perspective on bureaucracy is deeply influenced by where one resides in the organization:

> Top administrators in local school systems often turn out to be troubled
> by their agencies' unwieldy nature, much like teachers and parents. But
> when they explain the problem, ideas diverge. Administrators usually
> think they see unresponsiveness and resistance to change that are due to
> fragmented organization and dispersed authority; they regularly argue
> for more centralization and streamlining. Teachers and parents often
> think they see unresponsiveness and resistance to change due to central-
> ized bureaucratic hierarchy; they often argue for greater decentralization
> in order to disperse such agencies. (p. 6)

11. The material in this section is taken from Murphy (1992a, 1993a, 1993b).

4

SBM in Historical Perspective, 1900-1950

Richard Weise
Joseph Murphy

School-based management policies and research have long histories, way beyond the current generation of reforms, and . . . future policy and research agendas should advance along with the accumulated knowledge about school-based management (SBM). (Wohlstetter & Odden, 1992, p. 529)

To gain perspective on the current interest in school-based management, it is useful to examine the past history of the centralization-decentralization debate, not only in education but in society in general. (Lindelow, 1981, p. 95)

Because we believe that our understanding of school-based management should be informed by a historical analysis of decentralization efforts, we devote this chapter to the evolution of shared decision making in education. We begin by providing a snapshot of the forces that have promoted centralization in education, including developments within business that have reinforced centralization trends in schools. In the remainder of the chapter, we examine decentralization initiatives. We introduce Dewey as the first counterpoint to centralization. We then examine in greater detail two of the

AUTHORS' NOTE: Richard Weise is a doctoral student in the Department of Educational Administration at Peabody College, Vanderbilt University.

20th-century movements designed to diminish the impact of centralization—teacher councils and democratic administration. These movements are antecedents, if not progenitors, to the current school-based management reform initiatives.

Forces Promoting Centralization

School administration is responsive to social situations. It has, perhaps, an unusual sensitivity to public needs, though it may not interpret them or weigh them accurately. . . . The impact of new forces such as technology upon our society affects the needs and experiences of all persons and requires new services from the school. (Miller, 1942, p. 12)

The Industrial Revolution

Centralization began in the 1800s as an educational reform move-ment aimed at both responding to changing conditions resulting from the industrial revolution (Drost, 1971) and ending corruption within public education (Cronin, 1973). Broad changes in U.S. institutions were shifting the burden for the education of youth from traditional sources—home, trades, and church—to the schools (Cook, 1939; Counts, 1932/1978; Newlon, 1939). At the same time, child labor and compulsory attendance laws, as well as increased economic produc-tivity, diminished the child and youth labor force. This enabled young people to stay in school longer (Cremin, 1977; Tyack, 1974), but strained the schools' limited capacity.

In addition to shifting educational responsibilities and expand-ing the student population, the industrial revolution also created a demand for more prolonged socialization and specialized educations of consistent quality (Miller, 1942). For example, immigrants needed to be socialized to fit the culture of an industrialized workplace, and future office workers needed special training in bookkeeping. Throughout the late 1800s and early 1900s, schools were encouraged to expand efficiently both their curricula and their teachers' expertise beyond the teaching of the classics (Callahan, 1967).

Consolidation of Rural Schools

In the rural United States in 1916, there were over 200,000 public schools with a single teacher for all grades (U.S. Bureau of the Census,

1960), who often had no more than a grammar school education (Tyack, 1974). The curriculum "reflected a narrow range of texts and ideas whose purpose was to shore up the teachings of the home and church" (Mirel, 1990, p. 41). Educational demands of the industrial revolution strained rural education's meager resources. Reformers saw consolidation of many small districts into fewer, larger districts as a strategy for efficiently increasing educational quality in the U.S. heartland (Fuller, 1982).

Urbanization

The history of the 20th-century United States has been that of a continual migration from rural to urban areas. As Cremin (1988) points out, "urbanization was inextricably tied to the complex and interrelated phenomena that constituted the industrial, communications, and organizational revolutions of the late nineteenth and twentieth centuries" (p. 4). Not only did the population of the United States grow by 50%-60% each generation from 1890 to 1980, says Cremin (1988), but the percent of the population living in cities increased from 30% in 1890, to 50% in 1920, to almost 67% in 1950, to 75% in 1980. The growing population and the increased concentration of the population in cities taxed the resources of urban school systems.

Counterpoint to Corruption

In the urban United States, school districts at first were highly decentralized, being organized around neighborhoods and wards (Rogers, 1973). Each city contained many school districts, each with its own school board. Because selection of school personnel, vendors, even curricula and textbooks were many times tightly controlled by ward bosses, local control often led to abuse (Cronin, 1973; Mirel, 1990).[1]

Educational and political reformers saw school centralization as the best means to eliminate corruption (Callahan, 1962; Cronin, 1973; Tyack, 1974). They replaced ward-based school boards with small, city-wide boards "comprised predominantly of business and professional men" (Snauwaert, 1993, p. 2; see also Spring, 1986). They also moved away from the appointment of board members by ward bosses toward elected boards or boards appointed through nonpolitical offices (Cronin, 1973). Reformers also sought to increase the authority of

superintendents to decrease board influence in day-to-day operations of the schools (Snauwaert, 1993). However, in "depoliticizing"
school board appointments, reformers reduced board members' accountability to an identifiable constituency and thus community control of education (Tyack, 1974)—a consequence that was later to fuel
demands to decentralize schooling.

Scientific Management

Frederick Taylor (1916/1992) and Henri Fayol (1916/1992) revo-
lutionized business administration. They viewed top-down management, division of labor, specialization, and a regulated work
environment—for both workers and managers—as key strategies to
increase the efficiency and productivity of industry.

Educational administrators, eager to attain the status enjoyed
by the new "scientific" business managers (Callahan, 1962), quickly
adapted these centralizing management strategies to the public
schools. In 1908, David Snedden and William H. Allen "argued force-
fully . . . in favor of the schools' borrowing the methods of business
and applying them to social efficiency purposes" (Drost, 1971, p. 71).
In 1913, Frank E. Spaulding reported to a national meeting of school
superintendents that he had successfully introduced scientific management into the Newton, Massachusetts, school system (Campbell
& Newell, 1985). Spaulding and Franklin Bobbit "led the movement
to apply scientific management to education" (Callahan, 1962, p. 159),
in particular, the use of cost accounting to measure educational
value (Callahan, 1962). Simultaneous breakthroughs in educational
measurement further fueled scientific management by providing
educators the tools thought necessary to measure educational quality (Campbell & Newell, 1985). The sum total of these efforts led to a
dramatic centralization of the educational system in the United States.

In the Beginning Was John Dewey

During the era of centralization, a variety of forces were operating to prevent a more localized vision of schooling from being
completely overshadowed. Central to this movement is the work
of John Dewey who, in 1903—10 years prior to Spaulding's national report to superintendents—had already published the core

rationale for the future reform efforts that would rise in opposition to centralization.

In his often-excerpted 1903 article, "Democracy in Education," Dewey poses the following questions:

> What does democracy mean save that the individual is to have a share in determining the conditions and the aims of his own work and that on the whole, through the free and mutual harmonizing of different individuals, the work of the world is better done than when planned, arranged, and directed by a few, no matter how wise or of how good intent that few? How can we justify our belief in the democratic principle elsewhere, and then go back entirely upon it when we come to education? (p. 197)

Dewey (1903) points out that the educational and political re- formers who had attempted to eliminate corruption within munici- pal school boards had looked at only one solution: transferring author- ity to the school superintendent. However, in so doing, they had "tried to remedy one of the evils of democracy [corruption] by adopting the principle of autocracy" (p. 195). He argues that, "no matter how wise, expert, or benevolent the head of the school system, the one-man principle is autocracy," concluding that "the remedy is not to have one expert dictating educational methods and subject matter to a body of passive, recipient teachers but the adoption of intellectual initiative, discussion, and decision throughout the entire school corps" (pp. 195-196).

Regarding policy in the classroom, Dewey (1903) warns, "the dictation . . . of the subject-matter to be taught . . . and . . . the methods to be used in teaching, mean nothing more or less than the deliberate restriction of intelligence, the imprisoning of the spirit" (p. 196).

To those questioning the capacity of teachers to participate in policy making, Dewey (1903) first points out that if they are incapa- ble of participating in policy formation, how can one assume that they are capable of policy implementation? In fact, he claims that the opposite is true: "The more it is asserted that the existing corps of teachers is unfit to have voice in . . . important educational matters . . . to exercise intellectual initiative . . . , the more their unfitness to attempt the much more difficult and delicate task of guiding souls appears" (p. 197). He says "only by sharing in some responsible task does there come a fitness to share in it" (pp. 197-198).

For Dewey (1903), democracy is both the means and the end for the educational system. But, he contends:

> until the public-school system is organized in such a way that every teacher has some regular and representative way in which he or she can register judgement upon matters of educational importance, with the assurance that this judgement will somehow affect the school system, the assertion that the present system is not, from the internal standpoint, democratic seems to be justified. (p. 195)

However, despite the recognized need for such a democratic environment, Dewey (1903) points out that he is unaware of any school in which democratic administration existed.

In 1903, Dewey thus cast the seeds from which decentralization movements over the next century would take root: teacher councils (1909-1929), democratic administration (1930-1950), and community control (1965-1975).

Teacher Council Movement (1909-1929)

In 1923, Elmer Ortman reported,

> the years since 1910 have revealed many significant tendencies in school administration. Not least among these is the attempt made by school officials and teachers to secure a wider and more effective participation of teachers in formulating and directing the schools' educational policies. To secure this participation, school officials have in the past tried several different devices and organizations among which are the periodic general teachers' meetings, the various teachers' clubs and associations, the teacher committee appointed by the superintendent or the board of education and the individual teacher's report. (p. 1)

However, Ortman (1923) maintains that "no one nor all of [these decentralization strategies] have met all the hopes of school people"

(p. 1). He continues, "There has come into existence, therefore, within the past decade another organization which purports to secure a wider and more effective participation of teachers in formulating and directing the educational policies of the school. This organization is known as the teacher council" (p. 1).

The teacher council movement appears to be the first of several comprehensive attempts to reverse the trend toward centralization that gained a widespread following. It was able to do so in part because even though "school administration in the United States [had] changed vastly . . . , the classroom teacher['s] . . . influence on the shaping of policies and aims, as well as practical methods, [was] . . . almost nil" (School Administration and Teachers, 1918, p. 740). Teachers "chafed under . . . the factory plan of administration" and waged campaigns in several large cities to secure democratic participation in administration (p. 741).

Ironically, the teacher council movement emerged concurrently with education's infatuation with scientific management. As one set of reformers was attempting to democratize decision making, another group was working to centralize management control and to increase efficiency. Democracy versus efficiency would become one of the key sets of powerful oppositional forces in schooling throughout the 20th century.

Although teacher councils are mentioned in various writings of the time, Ortman's (1923) book *Teacher Councils* provides the most detailed description of their development between 1910 and 1923. We shall refer to it extensively in our discussion of this decentralization movement.

Purpose and Goals

According to Ortman (1923), the fundamental purpose of teacher councils is "the betterment of schools and education of children" (p. I). To this end, he identifies two primary goals of the movement: "the derivation of more workable policies" and "the improvement of educational workers in service through policy determining participation" (p. I). Like Dewey (1903), Ortman (1923) believes that people increase their democratic skills through practice, and also like Dewey, he urges schools not to make administrative skill a prerequisite for teacher participation in democratic administrative practice, for such a criterion "would have defeated every step in the democratic direction that has ever been taken" (Dewey, 1903, pp. 197-198).

Principles

From the above purpose and goals, Ortman (1923) culls three principles on which teacher councils were based—initiative, balancing authority and responsibility, and expert guidance.

Ortman (1923) states that "self-activity is one of the principles of learning" (p. I). Thus, teacher councils provide a policy classroom for not only teachers but "all educational workers" (p. I). However, declares Ortman (1923), a proper recognition of the policies of the teachers by the appropriate administrative officials is required if policy formation is to engender workers' genuine interest.

With authority, Ortman (1923) warns, comes responsibility. He exhorts teachers to develop "a willingness to do work acceptable to competent and impartial [though unspecified] judges" and awaken "a sense of responsibility for the results of the policies derived" (p. I).

Finally, Ortman (1923) prescribes guidance for the teacher council: "Expert opinion must have a place in the [teacher] council's deliberations" (p. I). He does not specify if the source of his proposed expertise would come from the principal, superintendent, teachers, or an external source. We shall see respect for expert opinion surface again in future decentralization movements.

Assumptions

Ortman's (1923) principles for teacher councils grow out of four assumptions. First, school policies must derive from the knowledge and experience of the workers in the school system. Second, workers in the school "at times offer valuable suggestions concerning the organization and operation of the schools" (p. II). Third, by participating in policy formation, school workers will better contextualize their problems within the larger administrative environment. Fourth, participation will increase workers' problem-solving skills.

Characteristics

The teacher council phenomenon was strongly influenced by the labor movement. This energizing movement provided a touchstone for educational reformers, who assumed that "a more equitable sharing of the rewards of labor and of the responsibilities for its highest productivity by all concerned are desirable" (Ortman, 1923, p. III). Teacher councils in fact shared a number of characteristics with industrial councils, including: being made up of elected representatives of the workers; aiming to increase worker participation in the "determination of the major policies that control industry in the shop, in the district, and in the nation" (Renolds, cited in Ortman, 1923, p. III); and raising workers up from the "cog in the machine status" (Renolds, cited in Ortman, 1923, p. III) by increasing both worker discretion and responsibility.

Additionally, Ortman (1923) specifies that teacher councils may be sanctioned by the school superintendent and the board of education and may be "guaranteed corporate existence by the city's charter, or the state legislature" (p. 3). In fact, he maintains that, for a

> completely organized teacher council to be effective [it] should probably be made legally possible by state legislative enactment; governed by a constitution and by-laws; its activities prescribed by a body of adopted rules and regulations; and its advisory relationship to the superintendent and the board of education accepted as desirable. (p. 3)

In assessing the extent of teacher council implementation, Ortman (1923) notes that "it is hardly necessary to say that very few councils today, are thus organized or established" (p. 3).

Implementation

Ortman (1923) documents that the first representative teacher council in the United States was formed in 1909 in Dallas, Texas. Between 1910 and 1917, only a half dozen other schools formed councils. However, by April 1922, Ortman (1923) determined that 86 cities in 29 states, including most major metropolitan areas, had active teacher councils.

Ortman (1923) claims that during their heyday, councils "attacked ten of the big problems in school administration" (p. 33). His Big 10 list includes the following:

1. Constructing or reorganizing courses of study

2. Adopting textbooks and materials for teaching
3. Establishing methods of instruction for subjects and classes
4. Building up teacher training requirements and courses
5. Constructing teacher rating systems
6. Modifying school building plans
7. Building up more comprehensive systems of reports
8. Helping increase salaries
9. Reorganizing the rules and regulations of the school
10. Cooperating in community work (p. 33)

Roles

Ortman (1923) explores various permutations of relationships between school boards, superintendents, and teacher councils. He demonstrates that in most districts, councils recommended policy for board approval. However, where superintendents declined to take council policy recommendations to the school board, the boards frequently listened to teacher councils directly. He concludes that the most "desirable relationship seems to be where the teacher council is responsible to the board of education through the superintendent of schools" (p. 14).

Ortman (1923) proposes in general "to make all the workers students of the problems of the schools and proficient helpers in solving those problems" (p. II; see also Follett, 1926/1992), and in particular, "to secure a wider and more effective participation of teachers in formulating and directing the educational policies of the school" (p. 1). He assumes that "every individual should be accustomed to cheerful submission to proper authority and to a ready acquiescence in meeting the requirements of the school insofar as these are necessary to the common welfare" (p. II; see also Fayol, 1916/1992). According to Ortman (1923), the role of the principal working with a teacher council is "to serve as a clearing house through which all business of the school must be transacted" (p. II).

For Ortman (1923), "the community is another group the teacher council may instruct" (p. 9). Teacher councils have instructed communities in the following ways: They have "helped board[s] mould public sentiment, planned programs for welfare work and carried them out, planned Americanization campaigns" (p. 9).

It is clear in retrospect that the teacher council movement focused on teacher participation in policy development to the exclusion of the community and parents. As we discuss later, some subsequent decentralization efforts have been much more sensitive to community participation.

Democratic Administration
Movement (1930-1950)

The democratic administration movement of the 1930s and 1940s is an antecedent to contemporary school-based management. World War II divided the movement into two distinct periods. The first period (1930-1944) was intellectual, antifascist, and driven by the idea of social change, which was "one of the most pervasive . . . ideas" (Krug, 1972, p. 225) of the Depression years. The second era (1945-1950) reflected the conservative, anti-Communist prosperity of the postwar years. Thus, the two periods are separated by an ideological shift precipitated by World War II.

The first wave was grounded in fields outside education, particularly philosophy and the social sciences. Following the war, however, purges of radicals in education and government appear to have discouraged later reformers from building on the movement's progressive prewar history. In the first wave, reformers were engaged in using the schools to form a more perfect, that is, more equal, union (Counts, 1932/1978). Democracy was the end toward which democratic school administration was the means (Morgan, 1939). When the Allies defeated fascism, democracy was viewed in the United States as a fait accompli. The U.S. perspective had changed. Compared to what had been seen during the war, the United States was all right. Thus, in the second wave of democratic administration, proponents sought to preserve the social contract for which the United States had fought—not to form a different one.

Definition and Characteristics

Though democratic administration was extensively written about well into the 1950s, a precise definition never emerged (Campbell & Newell, 1985). In particular, the actualization of the idea made the search for a definition problematic. As Morgan (1939) reminds us, "we do not disagree as to what democracy means in the abstract. It is when we strive to translate the spirit of democracy into working practice that we differ" (p. 30; see also Engelhardt, 1939). However, academics and practitioners did identify characteristics that they considered central to democratic administration. As we have seen previously, John Dewey spelled out in 1903 a principle that was repeatedly echoed by democratic administration reformers: "What does democracy mean save that the individual is to have a share in determining the conditions and the aims of his own work?" (p. 197).

Movement reformers extrapolated from Dewey's (1903) principle of individual determination. Newlon (1939), for example, argues that, "in a democracy all who are concerned with carrying out a policy or who are affected by it should participate in its formulation" (p. 143). Carr (1942) both specifies the means—"genuinely representative bodies must share in policy making"—(p. 83; see also Miller, 1942; Reeves, 1939) and includes students in the bodies to be represented. He believes that students

> should be allowed to participate in policy making to the limits of their abilities—not as a generous gesture to youth, but because young people contribute thoughtfully and capably to deliberations on matters within the range of their experience and understanding. Moreover, the experience of working with adults has great educational value for youth. Mature citizenship cannot be achieved through juvenile activities alone. (Carr, 1942, p. 83)

Carr's (1942) rationale for student participation in policy formation emerges from what Reeves (1939) reports as reformers' "universal respect for individual human worth and dignity, regardless of rank or class or race or sex or creed" (p. 16; see also Miller, 1942; Newlon, 1939). Reeves (1939) saw democratic administration's purpose as consisting "essentially in advancing the development of the personal potentialities of all who come within its orbit" (p. 28).

Assumptions

Advocates of democratic administration based their principles on certain assumptions about democracy, society, and education.

Democracy. Underlying the democratic administration literature of the 1930s was the belief that democracy would lead to a "good society" (Walter Lippman [1937], cited in Bellah, Madsen, Sullivan, Swidler, & Tipton, 1991, pp. 7-8). Miller (1942) unequivocally argues, "The goal of democracy is the realization of the abundant life for all" (p. 3). However, during the 1930s, democracy—and its promise —were assumed to be at risk (Kandel, 1939; Newlon, 1939). Fascism was on the rise in Europe and Asia, and its "virtues" were debated throughout the United States. Newlon (1939) documents that teachers and administrators of that era were "deeply concerned about [democracy's] future and the responsibility of education for its preservation" (p. 15).

Society. Educational reformers essentially describe a two-class society comprising elites and everyone else—which Counts (1927/ 1969) refers to as the "laboring classes" (p. 4). Many reformers believed that "American education . . . [was] too much under the influence of one social class" (Newlon, 1939, p. 127; see also Counts, 1927/1969). "If education is to serve its rightful [democratic] purpose," Newlon (1939) proposes, "control must be vested in the entire people" (p. 126). However, Newlon (1939) recognizes the complexity of his proposal:

> We have sought to remove the control of public schools as far as possible from the capriciousness of the moment and from the operation of selfish interests, keeping this control thoroughly democratic at the same time, but in the last analysis education will be controlled by the same forces that control the other political and social functions and that set the patterns of culture. Many of these influences are inherent in the long history of a community or a culture and are deep-seated and subtle in their operation. (pp. 133-134)

Education. Democratic administration reformers saw the school as having broad social responsibilities: "All that really enriches personal and social living must be the concern of the schools," said Newlon (1939, p. 124). At the top of educational reformers' list of concerns was democracy, its preservation, and its propagation in every social institution.

Though the best avenue for democracy's preservation was not agreed on, all assumed that a "school can be an effective teacher for democracy only to the extent that it recognizes for each member of the school community his right to share in determining school purposes" (Carr, 1942, p. 83). "Autocratic methods cannot be employed to achieve democratic purposes" (Newlon, 1939, p. 127; see also Miller, 1942). Nonetheless, autocratic methods were not uncommon during this era: "the administration of American schools and colleges has in many respects been undemocratic and in some instances autocratic and even authoritarian" (Newlon, 1939, p. 139).

With teacher enfranchisement through democratic administration came the belief that "a willingness to assume responsibility must accompany an acceptance of authority" (Miller, 1942, p. 46), for "to deny the essential relationship between authority and responsibility definitely endangers all our hopes for achievement of democracy in our schools" (Morgan, 1939, p. 32).

Environmental Forces That Spawned and Fueled Democratic Administration

As we report throughout this volume, schools do not exist in a vacuum, but are continually influenced by the external forces shaping the rest of society (Miller, 1942). In this section, we identify some of the societal forces to which democratic administration reformers responded.

Management Theory. During the 1920s, business theorists began to question scientific management's structural approach to efficiency. Mary Parker Follett (1926/1992) unveils her notion of participatory leadership: " 'power with' as opposed to 'power over' " (p. 150). She suggests letting the problem dictate leadership structure and staffing requirements for the particular situation, rather than constructing an all-purpose, hierarchical structure.

At that same time, in Western Electric's Hawthorne plant in Chicago, Elton Mayo was researching worker productivity and motivation (Shafritz & Ott, 1992). Conclusions of his study contain many implications for democratic administration. For example, he finds that morale increases under the following conditions: The work group participated in planning the conditions of their work, the atmosphere was friendly rather than autocratic, work varied, the group developed a team consciousness, groups enjoyed being together socially, and incentives were provided to the group rather than to individuals (cited in Koopman, Miel, & Misner, 1943).

Yauch (1949), discussing Lewin, Lippitt, and White's 1939 study comparing autocratic, democratic, and laissez-faire leadership in boys' clubs, finds that autocratic leadership produces frustration, peer aggression, and dependence. Work declines when the leader is not present. "It is better to let groups make their own choices," reports Yauch, "than it is to try to control [their] lives" (p. 40).

The Great Depression. The collapse of the stock market in 1929 undermined the decades-long assumption that business could provide the solutions to society's problems:

> With Hoover, the very symbol of efficiency, as President, greater and still greater triumphs were expected for and from our business civilization. Few realized at the time that the dominant culture in its very moment of victory was already doomed. Neither the boosters nor the critics of our business civilization foresaw the depression that would strip from business and industrial leaders their reputations as the guarantors of American social and economic welfare. (Krug, 1972, pp. 199-200)

Social Change. The Great Depression had a leveling effect on Americans' attitudes about their institutions: "In the 1930s, the number of casualties precipitated by the depression visibly demonstrated the inability of existing charities to deal with the [casualties of the social and economic system]" (Liebow, 1967, pp. 3-4). Every class of people came to see the United States—and much of the world—as troubled.

Enthusiasm for social change climbed the socioeconomic ladder all the way to the White House (Krug, 1972). In 1935, Roosevelt charged that "education must light the path for social change" (Educational Policies Commission, 1955, p. 5). Openness to social change may have been a means to control the change that appeared inevitable. As the number of people living in or near poverty grew, so did social unrest.

Spring (1986) detects a "general anxiety about the effect on youth of the Depression" (p. 274). Krug (1972) concurs: "the main problem of the 1930s was the problem of youth. . . . Youth served as both the victim and the alleged perpetrator of the chaos of the times" (p. 307). Spring (1986) argues that youths' reported "immorality" (p. 274) and "lack of idealism and rebelliousness" (p. 276) resulted from the impact on youth of forces such as the cynicism and sentimentality surrounding World War I and the prosperity of the 1920s followed by the hardship of the Great Depression.

Rise of Totalitarian Governments. Following World War I, the face of Europe changed as centuries-old monarchies disappeared overnight. The time for democracy should have arrived. However, the harsh conditions imposed by the Treaty of Versailles and the subsequent worldwide depression of the 1930s created the conditions for totalitarianism to emerge (Johnson, 1983/1991).

Active fascism started in Italy with Mussolini's rise to power in 1922. It soon was followed by fascist regimes in Germany and Spain. Even in the United States, fascism emerged in the form of Huey Long's populist movement in Louisiana.

In Russia, the intellectual and artistic spring that followed the Russian Revolution was suppressed by increasingly totalitarian elements. In the United States, increased Communist totalitarianism led to the expulsion of Communists in the 1930s and 1940s from the American Federation of Teachers (Urban, 1978, p. viii), as well as from other labor unions.

Prewar Radicalism/Postwar Conservatism and Repression. In the depth of the Depression and amid a worldwide military buildup, fascism and democracy competed for attention on both the world and the U.S. stage. The United States had not yet chosen sides in the 1930s, and there existed a questioning pessimism about the future of democracy (Cremin 1988; Yauch, 1949). At the same time that U.S. conservatives were toying with fascist ideology, many social reformers in the United States saw the Great Depression as an opportunity to democratize the country's social and economic life through a reconstruction of society (Krug, 1972; Spring, 1986; Urban, 1978). Some educational reformers, such as Newlon (1939), believed that "the public school is the most potent [agency of culture and communication] for molding the minds of people" (p. 126; see also Counts, 1932/1978). The sociopolitical debate continued until World War II, when political camps unified to fight common enemies abroad. However, "the Depression [had] set the stage for the next round of political battles, which were fought at the conclusion of World War II" (Spring, 1986, p. 279).

As the war came to an end, many elites became concerned that prewar political unrest would resume as soldiers returned to a less dynamic postwar economy. In June 1944, the *New York Times* predicted "a post-war period of great turmoil in labor relations" (Jezer, 1982, p. 78). Strategies such as the GI Bill were initiated to prolong the integration of men into the workforce. Following World War II, anti-Communist fervor replaced the intellectual freedom of the prewar years (Jezer, 1982).

Political Shifts in Education

Spring (1986) reports that "the economic depression of the 1930s caused several major political shifts in the educational world" (p. 269). Among these were growing criticism of elites and their control of school boards and splits between education and business, and education and the federal government.

Criticism of Elites and Their Control of School Boards. During the 1920s, sociologist George Counts conducted three studies of the public schools in which he "documented the failure of the public high school to reduce significantly the unequal distribution of wealth and privilege in American society; . . . demonstrated that school boards were controlled completely by the upper classes; and . . . chronicled the struggle of Chicago's teachers and citizens to free their schools from economic domination by elites" (Urban, 1978, p. vii). Counts's studies created empirical data and an ideological perspective that supported educational reformers' call to arms in the 1930s. In 1939, Reeves observes that though "the board of education is first of all intended to be a representative body . . . anyone intimately acquainted with the situation as it exists today knows that the picture drawn by Counts is still largely true" (p. 17; see also Newlon, 1939).

It was the economic crisis of the Depression that began splitting alliances that had formed among school administrators, school boards, and community elites: "Many school administrators and school boards wanted to maintain educational programs in the face of demands by other local leaders to reduce educational spending" (Spring, 1986, pp. 269-270).

Split With Business. Dissatisfaction with the society that business had created was emerging prior to the onset of the Depression. In 1929, John Dewey charged the public school system with turning out "efficient industrial fodder and citizenship in a state controlled by pecuniary industry, as other schools in other nations have turned out efficient cannon fodder" (p. 271).

As we have reported elsewhere (Beck & Murphy, 1993), the Great Depression led many educators to advocate use of the schools to restructure society. Newlon (1939) points out, "education is a social process that always has social consequences" (p. 211). Miller (1942) observes that "the school has moved into the front line of social conflict" (p. 16). Such statements "created the image that radicals were taking over the schools, which contributed to right-wing arguments in the 1940s and 1950s that public schools had come under the influence of communism" (Spring, 1986, p. 270).

Split With Federal Government. Mass concern about the problems of youth led the federal government to create new programs for youth (Krug, 1972; Spring, 1986). However, because Franklin D. Roosevelt "disliked and distrusted professional educators" (Spring, 1986, p. 274), his administration defined the youth problem as an unemployment problem and bypassed the schools (Cremin, 1988; Spring, 1986). Government initiatives "created tension between professional educators and the federal government as to each group's role in control of youth" (Spring, 1986, p. 270; see also Cremin, 1988; Krug, 1972). They also created a precedent for later intervention in the 1940s and 1950s (Spring, 1986).

Changing Roles

Democratic administration reformers distinguished between policy making and policy administration (Carr, 1942; Newlon, 1939). They sought to expand participation in policy formation to include teachers, students, and community members (Carr, 1942; Koopman et al., 1943) and to increase efficiency in policy administration (Newlon, 1939). Koopman et al. (1943) point out that "the designation of certain persons as administrators, consultants, or teachers should not suggest that these individuals pursue different goals" (p. 43), though they may perform different functions. Courtis (cited in Koopman et al., 1943) calls for teachers and administrators to engage in a "new cooperative effort" in which each acts as "highly specialized, individualistic, *creative* agents" (p. 44).

Boards of Education. Koopman et al. (1943) describe school boards as exercising positive leadership in "periods of conflict, breakdown, and transition" (p. 49). In other periods, say Koopman et al. (1943), they "usually exercise their leadership through delegation" (p. 49; see also Newlon, 1939). Newlon (1939) concurs; he also charges boards of education with representing "the interests and aspirations of the entire people and not merely of a group or class" (Newlon, 1939, p. 142; see also Counts, 1927/1969). Newlon (1939) elaborates:

> It is the responsibility of the board . . . to see to it that the schools are administered efficiently in accordance with the law and the best interests of the community. The board should be concerned primarily with policy, but if the interests of education are to be best served, it must share with the chief executive and his professional associates and with the community the determination of policies. It is essential that the board actively participate in this process and hold, with respect to certain matters at least, a veto power. (p. 143; see also Carr, 1942)

Reeves (1939) says that "the board of education should [not] be a rubber stamp. . . . The board is a policy-making body; it is responsible for the major planning of public education in its jurisdiction" (p. 2). However, Reeves (1939) also warns that the board should not go beyond its broad powers to approve and reject major policies.

Superintendents. According to Campbell and Newell (1985), administrators' primary function in an administrative democracy is to make participatory management work (p. 55). However, as late as 1943, Koopman et al. write, "the superintendent of schools is still, in most cases, both the channel of communication and the interpreter of the wishes of the board of education" (p. 49).

Morgan (1939) raises the issue of the "essential relationship between responsibility and authority" (p. 32): "To deny [it], . . . endangers all our hopes for achievement of democracy in the schools" (p. 32).

Principals. Yauch (1949) sees principals as executives of group policy, directors of interpersonal relations, as well as "expert handlers" of teachers. Koopman et al. (1943) identify four activities of a democratic principal: "(a) to create an environment in his school in which teachers attain maximum growth, (b) to offer technical resource service in some one or more specialized fields, (c) to serve as member of his building socialization committee,[2] (d) to execute specific administrative duties" (p. 47).

Teachers. Dewey (1903) stresses the necessity that "every teacher has some regular and representative way in which he or she can register judgement upon matters of educational importance" (p. 195; see also Carr, 1942; Koopman et al., 1943; Newlon, 1939). However, along with participatory leadership, reformers emphasize teacher responsibility. Koopman et al. (1943), for example, identify teachers' responsibility toward fellow teachers, administrators, learners, community adults, and the teaching profession.

Koopman et al. (1943) further identify seven "functional activities" of a teacher or group of teachers under democratic administration:

> (a) to take direct responsibility for child growth by providing adequate socializing experiences for children under his guidance, (b) to contribute some special service to faculty and school as a whole, (c) to work with room-groups of parents, (d) to execute administrative duties assigned by the faculty, (e) to operate as a creative unit in policy formation, (f) to operate as a primary agency in community relations, [and] (g) to carry on research and experimentation. (p. 47)

More broadly, Reeves (1939) states, "teachers should be really free to exercise without fear the rights of citizens . . . is a principle of modern democratic administration" (p. 26).

However, years of increasing centralization of school authority had marginalized teachers' influence on school conditions. In 1920, Blanton reports, "the iron of school-discipline has so deeply entered the souls of the great mass of teachers, that, . . . in regard to school affairs, they are as dumb [voiceless] as the bricks or stones of their own school buildings" (1920, pp. 156-157; see also School Administration and Teachers, 1918).

Students. Koopman et al. (1943) say that "students participating in . . . [a democratically administered school] will be dealing with problems which would not come under their jurisdiction in an authoritarian situation [e.g., participation in the] planning, execution, and evaluation of curriculum activities" (pp. 225-226). Many reformers agree with Miller (1942), who says that, "before any student leaves the school, not only must he be taught the values of the democratic way of life, but also must he be given opportunity to cultivate democratic behavior" (p. 22; see also Carr, 1942; Koopman et al., 1943). Caswell (cited in Koopman et al., 1943) cautions educators that student "operation of the school community must be given a significant part of school time. Democracy is more costly of time than the more autocratic types of government" (p. 232).

Community. In 1918, Hart (cited in Koopman et al., 1943) pointed out the importance of community in the education of children:

> The democratic problem in education is not primarily a problem of training children; it is the problem of making a community within which children cannot help growing up to be democratic, intelligent, disciplined to freedom, reverent of the goods of life, and eager to share in the tasks of the age. A school cannot produce this result; nothing but a community can do so. (p. 280)

Though many democratic administration reformers identify the importance of the community to education, the means by which the community participates varies from reformer to reformer.

Newlon (1939) sees the school as an integral part of the community and the community an integral part of the students' learning environment. The community is a learning laboratory to which children go for the "joy and educative experience of actual participation in work and community activities" (p. 122).

For Miller (1942), "the home, church, and community share responsibility in the educative process, and with the school mold the life of the individual" (p. 96). Miller (1942) proposes that the school link with other community organizations: "It is of vital importance today that the school administrator seek the advice and counsel of all who hold positions of leadership in these other social institutions" (p. 96). "To be effective," he continues, "community participation should operate in well-defined areas" (p. 97).

Koopman et al. (1943) identify school organizations as the means by which communities support their schools. They specify such organizations as parent-teacher associations, room-mother organizations, grade meetings, room groups, and parents' curriculum committees. However, they say, "one would be overly optimistic to conclude that adult participation in community education has reached significant proportions in this country at the present time" (p. 306).

Conclusions

In this chapter, we have shown that centralization, the successful—though not always effective—reform movement of the late 19th and early 20th centuries, stimulated counterreform in decentralization movements throughout the 20th century. Kingdon (1984) points out that in the public arena at any given time many potential policies compete for attention. It takes a precipitous event to enable one or another to come to the fore. We have shown that the industrial revolution and the Great Depression precipitated the centralization and decentralization movements of scientific management and democratic administration, respectively.

The legacy of scientific management—efficiency and expertise—exerted a strong influence on proponents of decentralization as well as those of centralization for decades after its introduction (Eaton, 1990) and arguably up to the present. The ongoing competition of simultaneous but oppositional influences in the policy process stems from, and results in, at least two tensions: democracy versus efficiency and lay versus professional influence. We see these tensions as creating ongoing dilemmas rather than being peculiar to an era.

We have thus far examined two decentralization movements: the teacher council movement and the democratic administration movement. The teacher council movement secured participation for teachers in policy formation but stopped short of community involvement. The democratic administration movement expanded the policy process to include all educational workers, students, parents, and the community. However, this inclusiveness gave rise to the aforementioned tensions.

We identified democracy and efficiency as powerful oppositional forces in schooling throughout the 20th century. Decentralization efforts have aimed at broadening professional and public participation in generating school policy. However, the more participative a system becomes, that is, the more people who are involved, the slower become its processes. Increased participation also means dispersed authority and responsibility. Reformers repeatedly emphasize the importance that new policy participants assume the responsibility that accompanies their increased authority.

In broadening public participation in the policy process, reformers increased the breadth of perspective and knowledge that would influence policy development; simultaneously the influence of professional expertise and experience decreased. Democratic administration reformers, well aware of this dilemma, often introduced provisions for expert opinion into their reform proposals (Ortman, 1923).

In Chapter 5, we will see how these tensions, as well as other ones, influenced reformers in the school-based budgeting and community control movements.

Notes

1. A similar pattern of abuse has been uncovered in the once-centralized urban districts that decentralized their educational systems during the late 1960s and early 1970s.

2. The essential functions of the Socialization Committee are the following:

(a) surveying and evaluating social life in order better to criticize the function of the school in society, (b) interpreting results of evaluation activities in terms of the unitary objective of education—democratic socialization, (c) determining steps, emphases, and sequences—the strategy of school administration, (d) reviewing, coordinating, and integrating activities of students, teachers, specialists, and community groups. (Koopman et al., 1943, p. 80)

5

SBM in Historical Perspective: The Community Control Movement, 1965-1975

Richard Weise

Joseph Murphy

In the previous chapter, we identified the teacher council movement and the democratic administration movement as the major decentralization movements of the first half of the 20th century. In Chapter 5, we assess the community control movement and other decentralization strategies that were initiated by or imposed on public school systems in the 1960s and 1970s. Our investigation reveals the community control movement to be a primary source of the participatory ethos that underlies public education in the 1990s.

We begin by presenting the definitions, goals and purposes, characteristics, and assumptions of the community control movement. We then examine the external forces that precipitated the community control movement. In the third section, we investigate how the responses of school actors shaped the movement's strategies. We then turn our attention to the circumstances surrounding implementation of community control, focusing on New York City. In the final two sections, we assess the results of the movement and discuss our conclusions.

The community control movement of the 1960s differs in several ways from the decentralization movements we previously examined —the teacher councils and democratic administration movements. First, the community control movement originated outside of education. Second, its implementation frequently led to confrontation. Third, it had a broad range of diverse participants, including leaders of community groups; minority parents; academics; foundations;

teacher unions; school administrators; and local, state, and federal levels of the executive, judicial, and legislative branches of government.

Structure of Community Control Movement

Definitions

As we discussed in Chapter 2, there are three pure forms of decentralization—administrative, professional, and community. Our concern here is with the third model, in which power is shifted not to teachers or administrators but to lay persons. In policy decentralization, that is, community control, control is shared with groups external to the school. In this formation, the community shares decision-making power with the school and central administration over the running of the schools. "Community" is not defined by the participants in a particular school, but by geographic area (Elmore, 1993; La Noue & Smith, 1973). Lewis (1993) aptly defines community in this paradigm as "the people who live near the school" (p. 91).

A range of perspectives helps to define community control. Boyd and O'Shea (1975) take a theoretical approach: "the devolution of significant policy-making power to citizens by subcommunity or neighborhood areas" (p. 357). La Noue and Smith (1973) specify a transfer of authority "in the areas of personnel (recruitment and discipline), curriculum, and budget from central boards and bureaucrats to local areas" (pp. 25-26). Ornstein (1983) specifies legislation of "an elected community school board functioning under specific guidelines and in conjunction with the central school board" (p. 3). Clark (1970) focuses on accountability. Community control, he says, is "a demand for school accountability by parents to whom the schools have never accounted, particularly those parents of low-status groups in Northern cities" (p. x). Lastly, Cronin (1973) cites the New Urban League in Boston, which called for "total control over the operation of the schools" (p. 186), including expenditures, banking, hiring and firing, building construction, and authority to contract with black construction companies.

Purposes and Goals

The dominant purpose of community control, according to La Noue and Smith (1973), is increased participation in the making of school policy, "especially by the poor and those not previously involved" (p. 229). In New York, where community control achieved the greatest implementation, Rogers (1981) writes that the "main goal was to decentralize the . . . school system into a series of smaller community school districts, with each governed by an elected community school board that would hold the educators of their district accountable for the quality of education there and would have significant power over budget, staffing, and program decisions" (p. 11). Boyd and O'Shea (1975) concisely identify the principal goal as "political accountability of educators to local area citizens" (p. 364). Underlying these calls for schools to decentralize authority and to be more accountable to the communities are the values of participation and equity (Cuban, 1990).

Characteristics

Decentralization may be characterized by examining the participants in the restructuring process (Wohlstetter & McCurdy, 1991). "The catalyst for the reform," say Wohlstetter and McCurdy (1991), "strongly influence the form of the decentralization adopted" (p. 394). When the decision to decentralize is internal—made by, for example, superintendents or teachers unions—the form taken is administrative or professional decentralization, and power is retained within the district structure. When impetus to decentralize comes from the external environment, for example, from state legislatures or civil rights groups, the form taken is often community control (Wohlstetter & McCurdy, 1991). Community control "shifts power from professionals and the central board to community groups not previously involved in school governance" (Ornstein, cited in Wohlstetter, 1990, p. 7).

Boyd and O'Shea (1975) identify a pattern of eight events leading to the emergence of community control as a school issue:

(1) changes in the demographic characteristics of the city's population; (2) emergence of low achievement outcomes from inner-city schools as an issue among parents; (3) demands for

desegregation as an approach to improving student achievement; (4) relatively little response to desegregation demands; (5) change from calls for desegregation to demands for some measure of local control to achieve accountability of schools to their clients; (6) protest activity and redirection of demands for restructuring the school system from the school board to partisan political leaders at the city and state levels; (7) informal alliances between minority leaders, on the one hand, and influential white liberals and/or conservatives, on the other; (8) adoption of a decentralization plan. (pp. 363-364)

Boyd and O'Shea (1975) do not identify the role played by teacher unions in this sequence of events; however, teacher unions are often a powerful force in shaping decentralization decisions. Struggles over community control frequently consisted of a three-way battle between central administration, teacher unions, and community organizers (Cronin, 1973).

Assumptions

In the 1960s, the belief that "public bureaucracies, especially school systems, were not responsive to the needs of the poor and that urban problems were caused by this unresponsiveness" was prevalent (Lewis, 1993, p. 87). It was argued that "poor children could be educated if the institutions were transformed" (p. 87). The assumption was that "if the institution could be controlled politically by external forces, schooling would improve" (Lewis, 1993, p. 89; see also Elmore, 1993; Epps, 1992). Embedded in this assumption was the belief that minority groups could "mobilize sufficient influence to obtain acceptance of part or all of their demands through political bargaining within the urban political system" (Boyd & O'Shea, 1975, p. 364). Fantini, Gittell, and Magat (cited in La Noue & Smith, 1973) declare: "We believe that the community-control movement, born of human deprivation, can direct the public school to a more humanistic purpose and performance" (p. 18).

Academic reformers and community groups alike anticipated that community control would provide the following benefits:

(1) more *accountability* of the educators to their school and district constituencies; (2) more parent and community

participation in educational decision making; (3) increasing educational *innovation*; (4) a more *organic relation of schools to communities* in curriculum and staffing and in program *linkages* to outside agencies; (5) more *jobs* within the school system for district residents; (6) *the development of more local-level leadership*; (7) improved *legitimacy* of the schools; and, ultimately, (8) *improved student performance*. (Rogers, 1981, p. 11)

External Forces That Spawned the Community Control Movement

The community control movement grew out of the coincident interests of three major actors: black community leaders who were disenchanted with the civil rights movement's lack of success at integrating Northern urban schools; private foundations; and the federal government. The effectiveness of the movement in ensuring community control of schools rested primarily on its ability to create and sustain broad-based coalitions comprised of black leaders, community organizers, academic activists, black and Spanish-speaking parents, state legislators, and sometimes, conservative ethnic or parent groups.

Black Leaders

Although civil rights activists desired to use public education as a tool to resolve contradictions between racism and democracy, "after from five to ten years of struggle to eliminate de facto segregation, [black leaders] grew cynical in the mid 1960s about the willingness of white leaders to move decisively" (Cronin, 1973, p. 182). For example, "between 1960 and 1965, the [New York] city schools underwent at least three separate attempts to desegregate, each less successful than the last, which left a legacy of frustration and demoralization among the city's civil rights leaders" (Elmore, 1993, p. 42). Boyd and O'Shea (1975) observe that

the frustration of years of demands for school desegregation intersected with the rise of the participatory movement . . . and the emergence in 1966 of the nationalistic black power ideology. These developments, then, combined with the distress and anger generated by the achievement problem to produce demands for community—or even racial—control of the schools. (p. 359; see also Epps, 1992)

Rogers (1981) concurs, "Blacks, in particular, resented the fact that the system had failed to improve the quality of education for them, either through compensatory programs or through desegregation" (p. 10).

In *Black Power: The Politics of Liberation in America*, Stokely Carmichael and Charles Hamilton identify the control of the schools as a core strategy in the new black politics (La Noue & Smith, 1973). They assert,

> We must begin to think of the black community as a base of organization to control institutions in the community. Control of the ghetto schools must be taken out of the hands of "professionals." . . . Black parents should seek as their goal the actual control of the public schools in their community. (cited in La Noue & Smith, 1973, p. 16)

"In this day and time," they continue, "it is crucial that race be taken into account in determining policy [for ghetto schools]" (p. 16).

Black leaders alienated traditional supporters of the civil rights movement, for example, Jewish liberals, when they changed focus from integration to community control. Former supporters charged the new leaders with racism. Carmichael and Hamilton (cited in La Noue & Smith, 1973) denied the assertions: "Some people will, again, view this as 'reverse segregation' or as 'racism.' It is not" (p. 16). Clark (1970) explains that the new community control leaders "have been consistent fighters for integration. Their support for decentralization is . . . a strategy of despair, a strategy determined by the broken promises of the white community" (p. x).

Foundations

In the late 1950s and early 1960s, foundations and federal government programs attempted to improve the operations of human services "by forcing [urban agencies] to turn outward to meet the challenges of poverty and race relations" (Marris & Rein, cited in Lewis, 1993, pp. 86-87). Private foundations, such as Danforth

(St. Louis), Russell Sage (San Francisco), and Ford (New York), promoted community control by providing seed money, technical advice, and legitimacy to local decentralization efforts "without which the movement might have collapsed" (La Noue & Smith, 1973, p. 228).

The Ford Foundation was the most influential in promoting community control (La Noue & Smith, 1973). Rogers (cited in Cronin, 1973) explains, "Ford was interested in urban development and public education and saw the reform of New York City schools as central to that interest" (p. 184). According to La Noue and Smith (1973), "much of the explicit thinking about the application of the community control concept to particular urban educational problems has come from Mario Fantini, the Ford Foundation's educational expert during the late 1960s, and Marilyn Gittell, Professor of Political Science and director of the Ford-funded Institute for Community Studies" (p. 18).

Elmore (1993) specifically charges that "the 'community control' project in Ocean Hill-Brownsville . . . had been the brainchild of officers at the Ford Foundation and was subsequently joined by education reformers in the city and by community activists in the neighborhood" (p. 41). Mayor Lindsey had asked the Ford Foundation president McGeorge Bundy to chair a committee to study decentralization in New York City schools. In summer 1967, the Ford Foundation granted financial support to the city for planning efforts to decentralize three districts, including Ocean Hill-Brownsville (Cronin, 1973; Elmore, 1993). "The Ford Foundation," continues Elmore (1993), "clearly believed that the city's schools had to become more closely connected to the emerging minority political activists in the city and that this connection would ultimately fuel an improvement in the quality of education for children" (p. 47).

Federal Government

In the mid-1960s, President Lyndon Johnson proposed a war on poverty. Underpinning this effort was the Economic Opportunity Act of 1964, which called for community action programs to mobilize resources that could be used in a direct attack on the roots of poverty (Krug, 1966). These programs would be "developed, conducted, and administered with the maximum feasible participation of residents of the areas and members of the groups served" (Public Law 88-452, cited in Krug, 1966, p. 151). Through the Economic Opportunity Act, Congress aided and augmented the community control movement (Boyd & O'Shea, 1975).

Congress also created substantial, new resources for education through the National Defense Education Act (NDEA) and the Elementary and Secondary Education Act of 1965 (ESEA) (Krug, 1966). ESEA and NDEA (amended in 1964) targeted funds for teaching disadvantaged youth (Krug, 1966); the Economic Opportunity Act funded community groups to mobilize new resources to be used in fighting the causes of poverty. Thus, Congress brought about "a significant shift in the sources of power affecting the control and support of schools" (Sizer, cited in Wayson, 1966, p. 333) and "opened a revolution in the politics of educational policy-making" (Wayson, 1966, p. 333). Through these three acts, Congress pitted schools and communities against each other.

These acts created new programs that were spread through many departments of the federal government. La Noue and Smith (1973) report that "by one count in 1971, some 180 new federal programs in the social services area had been initiated since 1965, many of which reflected the influence of the concepts of community participation" (p. 7). In some instances, community participation was "a prerequisite to achieving substantive goals" (p. 14). Federal money was used for financing everything from local elections to special governments for federal programs in inner-city neighborhoods. Because much of this money was controlled by a few federal officials, community leaders with access to these officials could leverage local school systems to either accept community participation on federal terms or forego funding (La Noue & Smith, 1973). Federal officials also directly urged schools to share power with community groups.

Harold Howe II (1966), U.S. Commissioner of Education, urged educators to engage citizens in school policy formation. Howe (1966) warned that, "The professional [educator] left unchecked becomes a dictator. . . . We should look for ways to put other kinds of professionalism to work for the schools" (pp. 449-450). He went on to call for local control of education in "densely populated urban areas" (p. 450) and to "encourage a responsible interest in the schools by laymen who hold no official position except that of citizen" (p. 450). "The concern many of us have today about the deficiencies of the schools and their lack of adequate service to poor and minority-group children," argues Howe (1966), "are concerns which will be answered best by efforts to enlist the lay governors of our schools in providing the answers" (p. 451).

The Schools' Response to Community Control

School Boards and Administration

Superintendents opposed community control everywhere (La Noue & Smith, 1973; Ornstein, 1983). They perceived it "rather like letting the passengers take over the ship" (Boyd & O'Shea, 1975, p. 362) and worried about opening education's door to politics. From their perspective, "there is—or ought to be—one broad public interest according to which educational policy should be shaped" (Boyd & O'Shea, 1975, p. 368). However, with social instability being such a serious problem as it was in the 1960s, "board members and administrators could not ignore any policy proposal that promised some relief. In this connection, demands for decentralization deserved careful consideration" (Peterson, 1975, p. 475).

As an alternative to community control, administrators chose administrative decentralization, which was "no less 'political' a choice than the proposals of community control advocates" (Boyd & O'Shea, 1975, pp. 364-365). Problems arose for school officials when they could not reach consensus on either desired levels of community involvement or which community to listen to (La Noue & Smith, 1973). Based on Crain's application of the community structure paradigm to study school desegregation in 15 cities, Wohlstetter (1990) hypothesizes that "conflict among the actors within the local school district will limit their policy making ability and provide an opportunity for outside actors to take control of the reform process" (p. 6). Crain (cited in Wohlstetter, 1990) observes, "the most important factor determining the behavior of the school boards we studied seems to be the amount of influence in the hands of the civic elite—the businessmen and others who participate in city decision making from outside the government and the political parties" (p. 5). If boards were in touch with civic elites, they certainly were not in touch with the minority members of their communities. It took student strikes, parent picket lines, and demonstrations at board meetings to convince board members that "the school system had lost touch with large segments of the minority communities" (O'Shea, 1975, p. 381).

Teacher Unions

Teacher unions were sympathetic to decentralization until the "racial implications . . . were highlighted" (La Noue & Smith, 1973, p. 226); from then on they strongly resisted community control (Epps, 1992). Educators argued that "the net result of such a politicized, racist, parochial, and inefficient system would be deteriorating schools and declining student performance" (Rogers, 1981, p. 12).

Teachers, through collective bargaining and political action, "achieved a large measure of autonomy and a great share in decision making" (Ornstein, 1983, p. 9). In New York, "the UFT [United Federation of Teachers] saw the attempt of the community organization to assert control of hiring, firing, and reassignment as a direct challenge to its hard-won efforts to ensure fair treatment and decent working conditions for its members across the whole city" (Elmore, 1993, p. 41). Minority leaders "judged that the 'so-called professionals' were more concerned about their own welfare than that of community children" (Cronin, 1973, p. 189). At the same time, academics at the university proclaimed that "the rights of the people are superior to the rights of professional educators" (Bortner, 1966, p. 62). Under attack on all sides, the teacher unions strengthened their resolve to fight community control.

Implementation

Community Control in New York City

In New York City, the UFT led teachers out on strike in 1960, in 1962, twice in 1964, and again in 1967. They won major concessions from the school district on salary and administrative processes. During the same period, civil rights leaders worked unsuccessfully to integrate city schools. In 1964, the school board finally made the concession of adopting a policy stipulating that any new school must be built on a site that would allow for integration. However, it would never be (Boyd & O'Shea, 1975). White parents mounted considerable opposition to integration plans.

Cronin (1973) recalls, "The most spectacular example of white resistance to racial integration was the planning of Intermediate School 201 in East Harlem" (p. 183). The board contradicted its own integration policy by building a new school in the heart of a ghetto (Boyd & O'Shea, 1975); however, it still promised to integrate I.S. 201. Early in 1966, the board announced its new integration plan: 50% black and 50% Puerto Rican. Angry community leaders blocked the opening of the school. The parents' council sought the political support of Mayor Lindsey, State Commissioner James Allen, and U.S. Commissioner of Education Harold Howe II (Cronin, 1973).

Frustrated by ongoing resistence to integration, parents changed their objective. If they could not have an integrated school, then they wanted I.S. 201 to be a quality segregated school run by a black principal. Superintendent Donovan agreed to community participation in selecting a black principal, but the Board of Education would not support his concessions. Instead, the board proposed administrative decentralization and a community advisory council to enable parental involvement (Cronin, 1973).

During 1966-1967, although several times announcing its intent to study decentralization, the board never did so. Then, on March 30, 1967, the New York State legislature agreed to grant additional school aid to the city on the condition that the mayor submit a plan to decentralize the school system the next year. In summer 1967, the Ford Foundation granted funds for decentralization planning efforts by the staffs and boards of three districts authorized by the central board: I.S. 201, Ocean Hill-Brownsville, and Two Bridges. (Cronin, 1973).

In spring and fall 1968, "things came to a head in the Ocean Hill-Brownsville district" (Porter, 1989, p. 83). At the heart of the conflict were the right of the community school board to dismiss teachers, the extent of disciplinary discretion allowed teachers, and the race and role of the principal. "The Ocean Hill-Brownsville board sent termination notices to six administrators and thirteen teachers and referred them to school board headquarters at 110 Livingston Street for reassignment. This move raised a storm of protest" (Cronin, 1973, p. 192). The UFT defined the issue as one of transfer rights and due process (Cronin, 1973). The union went on strike three times in 1968, exacerbating what the *New York Times* called "the worst of the city's racial fears and prejudices" (cited in Porter, 1989, p. 83).

The minority community perceived a black school principal as the guardian of students' rights and welfare. Because the UFT was predominantly white, minority parents and leaders "began to look upon the UFT demands for greater disciplinary authority as the racist domination of an anti-black, anti-Hispanic society. . . . Thus they were militantly opposed to circumventing the principal's authority in matters of discipline by giving teachers the power to expel students" (Porter, 1989, p. 82).

An advisory panel, assembled by Mayor Lindsey and chaired by McGeorge Bundy of the Ford Foundation, proposed that school governance be decentralized to community school district boards; however, the Bundy plan was rejected by the New York City school board and the state Board of Regents. After much conflict, the New York legislature passed the Decentralization Act of 1969. The act created 31 community school districts (eventually 32), ranging in size from 11,000 to 36,000 students, and provided for the election of district school boards with the power to appoint district superintendents and principals, determine curriculum priorities, and oversee schools—with many checks and balances from the central board and chancellor (Epps, 1992; Rogers, 1981).

Decentralization and Community Control in Other Cities

Beginning in New York City in 1966 with demands for community control of the schools, "the notion of community control and decentralization as a possible solution of the ills of urban education . . . spread rapidly to other large cities" (Boyd & O'Shea, 1975, p. 357). Several cities, including Detroit and Washington, D.C., implemented partial political decentralization, that is, community control, of schools. Most cities that decentralized school decision making chose to retain authority and implement administrative decentralization (Cronin, 1973; La Noue & Smith, 1973).

In 1980, Ornstein conducted a nationwide survey on decentralization of school systems with over 50,000 students. Forty-two (64%) reported that they were decentralized, and large systems reported being more decentralized than small systems (Ornstein, 1983). La Noue and Smith (1973) speculate that "the demand for decentralization has been strongest in the large cities because people are more likely to feel lost, alienated, and unable to participate in or to control their environment" (La Noue & Smith, 1973, p. 29).

Assessment of the Community Control Movement

Governance

Much of the criticism of community control has focused on governance. Schiff (cited in Epps, 1992), for example, found that "five years after the inception of decentralization in New York, its results were decidedly negative" (p. 145). First, many school district leaders were financially irresponsible, educationally incompetent, and patronage oriented. Second, districts were largely segregated. Third, "districts were often taken over by strident and militant elements who encouraged violence and chaos" (p. 145). By 1973, community boards had become more narrowly political, looking out for the interests of particular organizations, for example, teacher unions (Rogers & Chung, 1983). Mirel (1990) argues that community control efforts in New York City provide "evidence that if racial and ethnic strife will not severely damage the ability of schools to educate then corruption surely will. As of May 1989, 12 of the 32 regional boards in New York City were under investigation for some form of corruption" (p. 45). Ornstein (1983) asserts that "those elected to local boards in both cities (New York and Detroit) have not been well enough informed to function effectively" (p. 6).

Parent Participation

Participation was a dominant goal (La Noue & Smith, 1973) and underlying value (Cuban, 1990) of the community control movement, but voter turnout for even the first two community school board elections in New York City was low: 15% in one and 11% in another (Ornstein, 1983). Rogers and Chung (1983) report that "one of the disappointments of decentralization has been the limited participation of parents in school affairs" (p. 221). In part, they attribute limited participation to principal-initiated parent advisory councils. Principals undermined the interests of many parents by selecting certain parent leaders to serve on advisory councils where they became informants on activist parents still outside the system.

Student Performance

Rogers and Chung (1983) indicate that student performance, as assessed by reading scores, improved in New York City. Reading scores increased in all nine grades during a period in which the percentage of minority and low-income residents of the city increased. Thus, though the reason for improvement cannot with certainty be linked solely to decentralization, Rogers and Chung (1983) say that the results do disprove critics, such as teacher unions, who predicted that decentralization would cause student performance to decline. Elmore (1993) does note that "loosening central control, particularly in large urban systems . . . resulted in substantial variation among schools in curriculum and students' performance" (p. 37).

Transfer of Authority

Boyd and O'Shea (1975, August) observe that where community control was implemented it was only partially adopted. Rogers and Chung (1983) add that "the powers that were transferred from headquarters to the districts were limited, ambiguous, and hemmed in by many concurrent powers that remained with the chancellor" (p. xvi). Most cities' decentralization plans created the illusion of community control without significantly altering the power structure (Tyack, 1993).

Resources

The federal government poured money into cities to initiate community control movements; however, following Nixon's election in 1968, funding for cities dried up. Thus, as community control and decentralization were entering implementation phases, cities were plunged into acute financial crisis (Rogers & Chung, 1983). At the same time, school districts were adding costly layers of bureaucracy to implement decentralization.

Conclusions

We have shown that the community control movement emerged from the common interests of black leaders with community bases of power, the federal government, and private foundations. The federal government and private foundations ignited the movement by pouring funds into poor urban communities in which parents were disgruntled with the school system's rejection of racial integration, its inability to educate their children, and its unresponsiveness to their complaints and recommendations. In directing financial and other assistance toward effecting community control of schools, the federal government and foundations empowered local leaders and organizations. Once funding was withdrawn, however, the community control movement died as a catalyst for educational change. An irony of the community control movement was that minority groups' principal allies in pressing for local control of schools were the federal government and the elite of private foundations (La Noue & Smith, 1973).

The poor schooling provided to minority students was a compelling rationale and rallying point for the community control movement. However, there was never evidence that community control would lead to improved student performance, and such an outcome was rarely measured. When schools had to make choices between being accountable to community adults and being accountable to schoolchildren, they always chose the adults (Elmore, 1993).

Schools had no basis for choosing between various decentralization proposals, because no criteria existed (Boyd & O'Shea, 1975). Cronin (1973) points out that "there is little research evidence that [either community control or administrative decentralization], alone or combined, have positive effects" (p. 9).

School districts decentralized in compliance with state legislation or in compromises with community leaders; however, the decentralized administrative structures they created frequently required additional personnel and procedures. Consequently, the large bureaucracy against which community control advocates protested often expanded. Additionally, the new bureaucracy was less coherent, less orderly (Tyack, 1993), and more factional (Elmore, 1993); moreover, the distribution of power remained intact (Tyack, 1993). What the movement did accomplish was to embed in the public mind the "participatory ethos" (La Noue & Smith, 1973, p. 230).

6

Examining Evidence From the Current Reform Era

Rhetoric about centralization and decentralization has promised much, for reformers have not been shy in their claims. (Tyack, 1993, p. 1)

It has almost become an article of faith that greater freedom from the effects of centralized bureaucracy, hierarchy, and administrative rules will serve the interest of improving U.S. schools. (Bimber, 1993, p. IX)

Though widely discussed as a reform measure, the experience with and knowledge base for understanding site-based management remain relatively limited. (Wagstaff & Reyes, 1993, p. ii)

In this chapter, we investigate the evidence assembled to date on SBM, paying particular attention to studies undertaken during the current round of SBM that coincides with the restructuring movement. We begin with a discussion that grounds the analysis, pointing out some of the limitations of our examination. In the second part of the chapter, we study the extent to which participatory decision making meets the assumptions embedded in the SBM model presented in Chapter 1 (see Figure 1.2). We conclude that the effectiveness of SBM is greater in theory than in practice.

Grounding the Discussion

The Need for Exploration

School based management remains an empirically-elusive notion. (Malen et al., 1989, p. 7)

For all the attention given to SBM in its various incarnations over the past century, we have enjoyed only limited success in constructing an explanatory framework that allows us to understand effects of shared decision making in schools. Prior to the current "restructuring" version of SBM, the most thoughtful reviews of shared governance and management in education reached three conclusions. First, despite the popularity of this educational reform, analysts consistently pointed out that there was "surprisingly little empirical research on the topic" (David, 1989, p. 45). Most of what was available was conceptual, or more often, testimonial in nature. There were "more slogans than carefully worked-out concepts with consequences understood and accounted for" (Ornstein, 1983, p. 9). It was argued that the "body of research on the subject, though growing, still [did] not constitute a sizeable enough collection to permit generalizations to be made" (Imber, 1983, p. 38). As we discuss more fully later, this finding is "consistent with a theory of democratic accountability" (Clune & White, 1988, p. v) and as noted earlier, with the history of institutional reorganizations (see March & Olson, 1983; Tyack, 1993).

Second, existing evidence suggested that the path to school improvement via decentralization should be approached with caution. Jenni (1990), for example, reported that "the outcomes derived from this movement to decentralize schools have eluded what the framers intended" (p. 3). In his influential review, Conway (1984) concluded that findings about the effectiveness of participatory decision making "have been mostly negative" (p. 22). In their review, Chapman and Boyd (1986), in turn, noted that scholars "who have studied administrative reorganization in government agree that such efforts rarely achieve success in terms of the usual goals of increased efficiency, effectiveness, or responsiveness" (p. 50). Finally, in the most comprehensive review of the pre-restructuring SBM literature, Malen and her colleagues (1989) affirmed that "evidence gleaned from related literature question rather than confirm the central premises of school based management proposals" (p. 26).

Third, the data that were collected were not used as well as they might be: "In those rare cases where information is available, it is not attended to reliably" (March & Olson, 1983, p. 289). School reformers at all levels displayed a remarkable ability to ignore what they did not wish to see.

None of these constraints seemed to influence the onslaught in the late 1980s of the most comprehensive era of decentralization in the history of educational reform. Fueled by the forces described in Chapter 3, advocates began touting SBM as the much-needed balm for a very distressed educational system. Unencumbered by historical insights from previous efforts at decentralization, thinly tethered to the available research base, and armed with an unassailable belief that this time—for a variety of reasons—shared decision making would produce dramatic results, SBM began to take root throughout the nation, and indeed, around the world. The results of these recent efforts occupy our attention in this chapter.

A Word About Alternative Investigations

School-based management appears to have brought many changes to the roles of personnel. (Brown, 1990, p. 238)

Before moving into our analysis of the effects of SBM, it is important to note that results can be explored in a variety of ways. As outlined earlier, in this volume we investigate how shared decision making does or does not alter important organizational processes and outcomes. An alternative strategy, which space precludes us from exploring in depth,[1] would be to study how the roles of various stakeholders evolve under more democratic models of governance and management. It is widely held that "implementing shared decision making in school-based management requires changes in traditional attitudes and behaviors on the part of people throughout the school community" (Duttweiler & Mutchler, 1990, p. 48)—that "SBM requires the restructuring of most roles in the school district: superintendent, school board, students, teachers, parents and the community" (Clune & White, 1988, p. 7). In short, reformers argue that "relationships will be altered and many people will be forced to play new roles" (Chapman, 1990, p. 226).[2]

Initial studies appear to provide some support for the role change hypothesis: "Roles and responsibilities are now in the process of being redefined," reports the Pacific Regional Educational Laboratory (1992, p. 16). Once SBM appeared in Kentucky, "the roles of everyone involved began to change" (Steffy, 1993, p. 83).

At the central office, there are "profound changes in the roles of school board members, superintendents, and district staff" (David, 1993, p. 42). "Boards behave differently in significant ways. Central office functions are affected" (Brown, 1990, p. 162). In particular, "site-based management changes the role of the superintendent and board of education in relation to schools" (Wagstaff & Reyes, 1993, p. 1).

At the site level, "school improvement through democratic, school-based management, with extensive community and staff involvement necessitates a revised management role for principals" (Chapman & Boyd, 1986, p. 29). Indeed, "empowerment . . . has meant a drastic change in the way principals view their work" (Epps, 1992, p. 153). In fact, initial studies on SBM suggest that the principalship may be being redefined more dramatically than any other role (Duttweiler & Mutchler, 1990; Murphy, 1994b).

Although early efforts at decentralization did "not require major changes in the roles and responsibilities of teachers" (Clune & White, 1988, p. 21),[3] new roles and new leadership responsibilities for teachers now appear to be emerging. Brown's (1990) assessment on teachers' roles seems representative of the larger body of scholarship: "The effects of school-based management on teachers are quite evident but far less pronounced than those on principals."

In terms of support staff, "not much evidence is available about how [their] roles . . . are affected by decentralization (Brown, 1991, p. 82). "The role of parents under school-based management will vary greatly depending on whether the district is decentralized organizationally or politically" (p. 83). To date, the evidence suggests that parents' roles are being altered considerably less than SBM advocates had hoped (David, 1993; Wagstaff & Reyes, 1993).

Revisiting Guiding Concerns

> The decentralization implied by SBM contains ambiguities that depend on context. (Goldman et al., 1991, p. 2)

Before proceeding, it may be helpful to reinforce some of the concerns about conducting our investigation raised in earlier chapters. In particular, it is instructive to recall that in testing the inherent logic of SBM, we are providing a general picture of effects. We have assembled considerable evidence and aggregated it to provide a macro-level analysis of SBM. Consistent with the purpose of the volume, we are primarily interested in searching for general patterns in the larger landscape. Our goal is to provide guidance to those who are or will be touched by the current decentralization movement, especially site-level, district, and state policymakers. As noted repeatedly, whether any large-scale pattern fits a particular experiment with shared decision making depends a good deal on the context in question[4]—or as Miles (1969) puts it, "any particular planned change effort is deeply conditioned by the state of the system in which it takes place" (p. 375). It is also important to remember that SBM has a "developmental nature" (Rutherford, 1991, p. 10)—self-managed schools are likely to evolve over time (Etheridge et al., 1992). Aggregating evidence in the manner we do here has the potential to mask this fact.

A Caveat About Our Model

> By using a broad perspective to look for indicators that point to outcomes, one runs the risk of missing the target altogether. (Jenni, 1990, p. 2)

Inherent in the model we employ in this volume is the belief that the "purpose of these new patterns of management must be expressed unmistakably in terms of their contribution to an end, that is quality of schooling" (Caldwell, 1990, p. 20). The key question is: "Have substantial improvements in student learning occurred?" (Bryk, 1993, p. 3). Such an instrumental approach to SBM "implies the use of the input, process, output model broadly conceived" (Brown, 1990, p. 180), explicated in Chapter 1 and tested here. This framework permits us to track intermediate measures of progress (Zuckerman, 1992) and "ongoing organizational rearrangements" (Bryk, 1993, p. 3) in addition to variations in student learning. At the same time, as with all models, it blinds as well as enlightens. A strong case can be developed for the desirability of infusing democratic principles into education regardless of their effects on cognitive outcomes, but the model itself tends to minimize this intrinsic "value position" (Burke, 1992, p. 36) of the intervention—especially the importance of SBM serving "as a moral doctrine by which students can regulate their behavior" (Fusarelli & Scribner, 1993, p. 8). The framework also provides insufficient attention to the symbolic and political dimensions of SBM, particularly the goal of legitimizing schooling in its larger environment. Finally, on the other side of the ledger, the model fails to acknowledge adequately the dark side of SBM: "Managerial reforms can thus be seen as an instrumental response introduced for other, political, reasons rather than for their own merits" (S. B. Lawton, 1991, p. 11). In this case, the model fails to reveal that SBM may have more to do with any of the following four goals than with improving education: (a) the desire "by politicians to wrest control over education away from educators and to place it under their own control" (S. B. Lawton, 1991, p. 11); (b) the desire "on the part of some to transfer tens of billions of dollars from the public to the private sector" (Murphy, 1993a, p. 9)—"to undermine public authority and responsibility for education while enhancing the control of private agencies and interests" (Lewis, 1993, p. 86); (c) the desire by many to push intractable problems downward while ensuring that "central agencies will no longer carry the political burden of confronting those who accuse them of ineffectiveness and inefficiency" (S. B. Lawton, 1991, p. 18); and (d) the desire of some "to satisfy demands for change without having to invest enormous resources in schools" (Ornstein, 1983, p. 6). We return to all of these issues in the concluding chapter, but it is important to introduce them before reviewing the recent evidence on SBM.

Sifting the Evidence

As the empowerment movement has coalesced and spread during the past few years, researchers have begun to assess outcomes. . . . Research to date generally has reported conclusions that appear more neutral and disappointing than positive and encouraging. (Levine & Eubanks, 1992, p. 66)

Although several of these schools were drawn from districts with highly publicized reform programs, the changes that SDM brought about were clearly limited. Perhaps changes in other institutional rules would have more potency; this one, without supplementation by other organizational arrangements, shows meager promise. (Weiss, 1993, p. 17)

Empowerment

> *For the reasons identified, we conclude that it is extraordinarily difficult to determine what authority has been delegated to site participants, how that authority is distributed, and how discretion is affected by the web of rules embedded in the broader system. (Malen et al., 1989, p. 8)*

At the very core of SBM—the beginning link in the chain of logic we formulated in Figure 1.2—is the assumption that revisions in "formal decisionmaking arrangements . . . will alter influence relationships in several ways" (Malen et al., 1989, p. 10). As discussed earlier, the hope is that empowerment will overcome the general state of decisional deprivation among teachers (Conway, 1976; Riley, 1984) and parents, and in so doing, promote more effective education and better student performance. The question here is: Are reasoned generalizations from the recent round of SBM experiments available?

Some Hopeful Signs. Evidence on whether SBM actually empowers local stakeholders is mixed, although there is a decidedly pessimistic flavor to the data. On the positive side of the ledger, empowerment is generally portrayed as accruing to a wider assortment of stakeholders—teachers, principals, parents, students, and general members of the community—than has been the case in the past. There is also considerably more attention to the state agenda for local empowerment than we have seen previously (Murphy, 1994a).

Respondents under existing models of participatory governance often report that they feel more empowered—"that engagement in site-based management is positively affecting teachers' perceptions of their involvement in the decision-making process" (Rice & Schneider, 1992, p. 12) in terms of (a) the influence they can exert in schools and on decision councils (Gips & Wilkes, 1993; Jenni & Mauriel, 1990); (b) the general authority they have in important decision areas (Davidson, 1992; Goldman et al., 1991; Hess, 1992); (c) a diminution in autocratic control exercised by school administrators (Collins & Hanson, 1991); (d) the management of site-level improvement programs, including planning and goal setting (Bredeson, 1992; Goldman et al., 1991); and (e) control over the general operation of the school (Pacific Region Educational Laboratory, 1992).

In addition, the recent round of SBM does appear to be successful in devolving decision-making influence to the school level in areas of real importance—budget, personnel, and curriculum: "Districts with school-based management have achieved a considerable amount of vertical decentralization. Authority once resident in the board and central office has been passed to schools" (Brown, 1990, p. 226). More important, at least in some locales, stakeholders in SBM environments are exercising this influence. David (1993), in her review of recent activity in Kentucky, for example, concludes that "councils are meeting and making important decisions" (p. 35). In a study of Oregon's 2020 schools, Goldman and his associates (1991) reach a similar conclusion:

> Committees had real authority over managing the 2020 projects, and almost all of them reported concrete powers and concrete accomplishments. In most schools, the teachers are fiscal managers of the grant. This is a new role for teachers. They reported making decisions about supplies budgets, distribution of special education funding, implementation of computer labs, and so on, that would have traditionally been handled by the principal. (p. 7)

This pattern of substantive decision making has also been uncovered by Brown and Wohlstetter in their influential studies of recent SBM initiatives:

> The findings from this study propose new patterns of decision making that effectively empower building-level educators with substantial discretion over, at least, some resources. (Wohlstetter & Buffett, 1991, p. 12)

> The evidence, on a case-by-case basis, seems to indicate that school personnel are able to make and carry out decisions which may not have been possible under more centralized management. Schools appear to be taking more control of their personnel, equipment, maintenance, utilities and supplies. (Brown, 1990, p. 157)

Cause for Concern. As exciting as these findings are, it is important to note that they are shrouded by a larger body of work that provides a more pessimistic backdrop, raising doubts about the vigor of the connections between altered patterns of decision making and influence transfer.

The most thoughtful theoretical and empirical reviews on this issue are uniformly gloomy in their assessments:

> Reviews of the literature on school-site management find that the authority of schools and of school-site councils—which typically represent some combination of parents, administrators, and staff—is either very vaguely specified or highly circumscribed; seldom if ever does school-site management actually mean real control over the core elements of the organization (budgeting, staffing, curriculum, organizational structure, and governance). In most instances, school-site management means some incremental shift of responsibility from central administration to the school site on some limited set of dimensions. . . . The idea that school-site management involves decentralization of authority and responsibility to "the school," then, is a convenient fiction. (Elmore, 1993, pp. 44, 45)

> School-based management generates involvement in decisionmaking, but it does not appear to substantially alter the policymaking influence of site participants generally, the relative influence of principals and teachers or the relative influence of professionals and patrons. While there is little evidence that school-based management alters influence relationships typically and traditionally found in schools, there is some evidence that it maintains those relationships. A variety of factors converge to restrict the ability of school based management to fundamentally change influence relationships. (Malen et al., 1989, p. 11)

The more fine-grained studies of recent decentralization efforts often reinforce these judgments. There is some concern "that the extent of decision-making responsibility transferred to site teachers and administrators is [more] limited" (Wohlstetter & Mohrman, 1993, p. 2) than advocates for SBM suggest. More troubling is that fact that, even when there is documented evidence of "formal policy making authority that gave teachers and parents substantial control over decision making, influence relationships traditionally found in schools were maintained and principals retained control" (Wohlstetter & Odden, 1992, p. 4). "The outcome reported in most studies was a low degree of teacher and parent influence on school policy decisions" (Duttweiler & Mutchler, 1990, p. 40). The "overall distribution of power" (Tyack, 1993, p. 19) was rarely altered. There "is little evidence that teachers exert meaningful influence" or that "professional-patron influence relationships are substantially altered" (Malen et al., 1989, pp. 12-13). Involvement does not appear to translate into influence (Duttweiler & Mutchler, 1990; Fusarelli & Scribner, 1993).

Four recent studies in particular lend credence to the belief that changing decision-making structures—implementing SBM—may not lead to empowerment of local stakeholders.[5] Malen and Ogawa's (1988) exemplary research on site councils in Salt Lake City leads them to conclude, "The research casts doubt on the efficacy of site-based governance as a reform strategy or, more precisely, it underscores the difficulty of establishing arrangements that will fundamentally alter principal, teacher, and parent influence relationships" (p. 266). Lindquist and Mauriel (1989) also report that "it is not clear that substantive decisions are made by the site Council" (p. 413)— that is, even when authority is devolved, local stakeholders may not exercise it effectively. In fact, says Jenni (1990), "the activities of the site council tend to be observational and discussional," and it "appeared that the site council meetings were a place where information was shared, discussion ensued, but serious decisionmaking was generally avoided" (pp. 19, 21). In his inside look at local school advisory councils in Cincinnati (as a member), Daresh (1992) contends that council members "had little control over matters of importance" (p. 115), "degrees of freedom were greatly limited" (p. 119), and "traditional patterns of influence in school decision making remained clear and unchanged" (p. 115). The results, according to many who have investigated shared decision making, are that SBM often leads to involvement but not to empowerment, and the role of local stakeholders becomes one of "ratify[ing] decisions made at another level" (Daresh, 1992, p. 113). According to Malen and her colleagues (1989), "the dominant pattern illustrates that school councils operate more as ancillary advisors or pro forma endorsers than as major policy makers or primary policy actors at both the school and the district level" (p. 12).

Overall, the evidence from the recent restructuring era of SBM suggests that changes in patterns of decision making have been more successful than in the past in decentralizing influence within school districts. There are data to support the assumption that influence is pushed down to the school level. At the same time, it appears that most schools have generally been unwilling or unable to take advantage of this newly devolved authority. Perhaps the most that can be said is "that some alteration [is taking place] in the influence relations between principals and teachers" (M. Hanson, 1991, p. 11).

Ownership/Participation

> *Shared decision making conceivably contributes to an individual's feeling of being part of a collective enterprise. The notion that one has a stake in the future of an enterprise sometimes is referred to as a feeling of shared owner-ship. (Duke et al., 1980, p. 99)*

> *The existence of such decision-making structures is not an automatic guar-antee of participatory decision-making. (Conley, 1991, p. 37)*

Earlier—in Chapter 1 in our analysis of the SBM framework and in Chapter 2 in our discussion of "models" and "domains" of shared decision making—we grappled conceptually with the meaning of participation. Here, as a guiding caveat, we simply reintroduce the conclusion "that despite consensus regarding the importance of participation . . . [it] remain[s] an elusive construct that means[s] different things to different actors in the process" (Mills, 1992, p. 28). As we demonstrated, "there are varying shades of participation" (Alutto & Belasco, 1972, p. 118); "participation can be thought of in terms of a continuum reflecting several levels of actual involvement and influence of organizational members in a decision-making en-terprise" (Wood, 1984, p. 60). Using this as a contextual jumping-off point, the relevant question is: What can we learn from the recent literature about the empirical relationship between empowerment and ownership/participation?

Entering the recent round of SBM studies, we knew that teachers desired to participate in decision making more than they usually did (Conway, 1976, 1984). Likewise, the involvement of parents (and community members) in decision making at the site level has been limited. "Despite a long tradition of community participation in North America, considerable research suggests that a hierarchical model of decision-making based on professional values and technical authority prevails" (Chapman, 1990, p. 237). We were also aware that as with empowerment, there is a dark side to participation that has received little attention. There is reason to believe that participation may have as much to do with "increased administrative control" (Alutto & Belasco, 1972, p. 117) as it does with the promotion of democratic values (High et al., 1989). In addition, "there is no strong empirical confirmation for theoretical claims that high levels of teacher participation in school decision making would improve schools" (Imber & Duke, 1984, p. 24; see also Conway, 1984).

In Chapter 1, we allowed that one of the key objectives of SBM is "to increase involvement of school staff, parents and community (to create a sense of school ownership)" (Clune & White, 1988, p. 14). Evidence to date on the extent to which students participate in self-managing schools is quite limited. What we can discern, both from what is and from what is not discussed in the research, is that few SBM sites are giving much thought "to involving students in any significant way" (Fusarelli & Scribner, 1993, p. 18) in school decisions.[6]

In terms of enhancing the participation and ownership of parents—the effectiveness of SBM as "a policy tool for opening up school systems to involve 'outsiders' . . . in school governance" (Wohlstetter, 1990, p. 2)—the studies completed over the past decade are fairly pessimistic (Bradley, 1993), reinforcing conclusions from the last round of political decentralization in the 1960s and 1970s (see Chapter 5; see also Epps, 1992; Ornstein, 1983).[7] Although some analysts discern a silver lining in the data on voter turnout for school councils, and "enhanced [parental] participation has emerged in many schools" (Bryk, 1993, p. 37), in the aggregate, David's (1993) findings on SBM in Kentucky are representative of the picture elsewhere: "Across the state, parent participation in running for the council and voting in elections is dismally small. Reflecting historical patterns of involvement, overall participation is low and that of poor and minority parents virtually non-existent" (p. 33). Even in the highly touted Chicago experiment, voter turnout for the second round of elections was only half of what it was for the first round in 1989 (Hess, 1992).[8]

What about the participation of teachers in self-managing schools? Here the studies allow us to draw a more positive picture.

In his comprehensive assessment of SBM, Brown (1990) has discovered considerable evidence of staff involvement in decision making. Similar conclusions have been reached in investigations by Gips and Wilkes (1993); Carnoy and MacDonnell (1990); Taylor and Bogotch (1992)—"Clearly the district's program had the effect of increasing teachers' rates of participation for schools in this study" (p. 10); Bryk (1993)—"Combining these figures, slightly more than one-half of the schools are reporting moderate to extensive activity in the faculty as a site of power" (p. 71); and Goldman and his colleagues (1991)— "Typically, existing faculty groups (like faculty or curriculum councils) at these sites became more actively involved in budget and curricular decisions previously made by the principal and were consulted more often by the principal in areas where the principal still made the final decision" (p. 8). Perhaps the most thorough analysis of teacher participation under participatory management can be found in the investigation of Dade County's decentralization reform effort. According to the study's authors, Collins and Hanson (1991), the focus of the Dade County SBM project was "the involvement of teachers in critical decision-making processes at the individual school level" (p. ii). At the end of 3 years of study, they found "substantial evidence that the involvement ha[d] taken place" (p. ii).

These studies also reinforce findings reported in Chapter 2— that participation ranges across a wide array of domains and subareas and along a continuum from information input to decision making. They also convey the importance of collaborative or collegial types of participation (Goldman et al., 1991; Rutherford, 1991; Smith, 1993).

There is a downside to teacher participation in shared decision making, however. Four issues receive special attention in the literature: (a) the high costs of participation in terms of time (Collins & Hanson, 1991; Duke et al., 1980)—especially time away from teaching and other interactions with students (Bredeson, 1992; Chapman, 1990; Hannaway, 1992); (b) a drop-off in the amount and intensity of participation as decentralization projects mature (Collins & Hanson, 1991);[9] (c) the possibility that participation may become disconnected from influence (Duke et al., 1980; Malen & Ogawa, 1988; Rice & Schneider, 1992); and (d) the potential for participation to become the venue of a small cadre of teachers with the majority of the staff increasingly removed from the center of action (M. Hanson, 1991; Smith, 1993).

Professionalism

> *During the implementation of SDM at Silver Hill, teachers reported personal changes because of their involvement in the process. They believed they gained understandings through their involvement in SDM and changed the way they perceived themselves. (Smith, 1993, p. 16)*

> *The teachers expressed renewed sense of professionalism resulting from the opportunity to express their opinions and to have those opinions respected and/or implemented. (Davidson, 1992, p. 19)*

As defined in Chapter 1, professionalism comprises a bundle of components such as commitment, morale, satisfaction, efficacy. At the outset of the current wave of shared decision making, there was some support for the belief that participatory modes of management could enhance employees' assessments of these conditions (Imber, 1983; Lindelow, 1981; Rice & Schneider, 1992; Wood, 1984). However, the picture was far from clear (Alutto & Belasco, 1972) and the evidence specifically in the area of education was spotty and "extremely thin" (Malen et al., 1989, p. 16).

Commitment. What empirical insights have been mined over the past decade on the connections between SBM and teacher professionalism? On the topic of commitment, we know little more now than we did when restructuring began. There does appear, however, to be a linkage between SBM and collegiality (Fusarelli & Scribner, 1993), although it is much stronger for teachers who are most active in local governance (Goldman et al., 1991; Smith, 1993). Of particular importance in the area of collegiality is the power of SBM to help break down "traditional norms of isolation and noninterference" (Smith, 1993, p. 34).

Satisfaction/Morale. The evidence on the relationship between SBM and satisfaction/morale is mixed.[10] The current era of SBM began with appeals to the larger body of literature that demonstrated the connection between "teachers' perceived levels of influence . . . and job satisfaction" (Rice & Schneider, 1992, p. 11) as well as skepticism about the long-term effects of SBM on teacher morale and motivation (Malen et al., 1989). There was an undercurrent of concern that "teacher morale and motivation may increase in the initial stage of implementation but soon return to depressed levels" (Duttweiler & Mutchler, 1990, p. 34).

Holding aside the issue of context for the moment, the bulk of recent evidence suggests that (a) SBM, when implemented in a meaningful fashion, has a positive effect on teacher satisfaction[11] (Brown, 1990; Clune & White, 1988; Rungeling & Glover, 1991); (b) "teacher involvement in decision making must be perceived as influential in order to increase teachers' levels of job satisfaction" (Rice & Schneider, 1992, p. 6); (c) the sense of teacher satisfaction in the same school is variable (Chapman & Boyd, 1986; Collins & Hanson, 1991; Smith, 1993); (d) satisfaction lies behind other indicators of professionalism such as collaboration (Rutherford, 1991) and status (Collins & Hanson, 1991); (e) satisfaction is enhanced when one looks at the more successful SBM initiatives (Bryk, 1993; Rice & Schneider, 1992) and those in which "the administration took a positive, supportive role" (Steffy, 1993, p. 83); and (f) consistent with the hypothesis noted above, satisfaction and morale rise in the short run only to decline as SBM initiatives unfold (Carnoy & MacDonnell, 1990; Collins & Hanson, 1991).

Efficacy. Following the work of Brookover and his colleagues (1978, 1982), we define efficacy as a combination of two beliefs: (a) that one is capable, and (b) that one's efforts can make a difference (Murphy, Weil, Hallinger, & Mitman, 1982)—that is, that the system will not block one's sense of personal efficacy. Chapman (1990) refers to this as a "sense of mastery over the destiny of the school and of [oneself] in that school" (p. 231). Although it is premature to draw generalizations in this area, many of the more carefully crafted studies reveal that SBM can and does positively affect teachers' sense of efficacy. In their work on the 2020 project in Oregon, Conley and his colleagues (Conley, 1991) find that SBM "grants are creating a greater sense of efficacy based on . . . [teachers'] ability to influence the conditions of their work environment" (p. 44). In his thoughtful study of SBM, Smith (1993) reaches a similar conclusion: "A second change attributed to SDM was an enhanced sense of efficacy associated with their belief that SDM enabled them to enact fundamental school reform" (p. 20). There is also a hint in the recent set of studies on SBM that efficacy may be the fulcrum to translate empowerment and ownership into commitment, satisfaction, and collegiality. This is a clue worthy of further exploration.

Organizational Health:
General Organizational Processes

One might rather wish to study assumptions of the current school-based management movement regarding increased efficiency through reorganization and increased innovation through autonomy. (M. Hanson, 1991, p. 15)

Flexibility and Responsiveness. A central premise of SBM is that flexibility and responsiveness will be enhanced. Specifically, advocates hold that SBM will (a) "make schools more responsive to their constituencies" (Malen et al., 1989, p. 10), especially "more open and responsive to parents" (Chapman & Boyd, 1986, p. 46); (b) provide schools with "the ability to adapt resources and procedures to student needs" (Brown, 1990, p. 259); (c) improve "the fit between the schools and the community" (Epps, 1992, p. 146); and as a consequence, (d) enhance accountability. Available studies suggest that SBM does indeed enhance the responsiveness of the school site. In his 7-year study of decentralization, Brown (1991) reported that enhanced "flexibility was the most widely agreed-on outcome" (p. 25). There were both objective indicators of increased flexibility and widespread recognition of these new degrees of freedom by site-level personnel. There is also some evidence that educators believe that such flexibility "is critically important to address school specific problems" (Hannaway, 1992, p. 11).

Flexibility seems to play out in a variety of ways in self-managed schools. At the most basic level, there is a sense of liberation from the tight constraints imposed by central authorities. There is a feeling that activities can be accomplished more quickly than they were in the past. Educators are able to discern new opportunities in all the domains detailed in Chapter 2, especially in the areas of curriculum and budget.

The story on responsiveness as the development of more client-centered forms of accountability is a good deal sketchier, however. Although "advocates claim that the aims of accountability are better served through SBM" (Clune & White, 1988, p. 6), there are little data on the matter—a silence, we believe, that should be of concern to reformers who draw linkages between participatory governance and customer-oriented accountability.[12]

Change. Although there is widespread agreement that SBM does encourage a loosening of centralized controls and the augmentation of flexibility at the local level, conclusions about the ability of schools to translate newfound freedoms into new ways of doing business—in short, to change—are considerably less sanguine. Moving into the current restructuring era of SBM, "preliminary information and logic . . . suggest[ed] that school site management and budgeting would produce a much greater variety of educational services" (Garms et al., 1978, p. 288). And in her baseline review, David (1989) reported that "there is evidence that there are greater differences among schools under a system of school-based management than under one of centralized management" (p. 51). Optimism that the current movement toward "decentralized governance would enable school communities to shape distinctive forms of school life particularly sensitive to needs of their students and families" (Bryk, 1993, p. 14) was also fueled by Lindelow's (1981) assertion that "in general a district's implementation of school-based management has led to an increase in the diversity of educational approaches in that district" (p. 122).

Studies document fairly conclusively, however, that SBM has fallen far short of expectations. Although self-governing schools do implement some innovations (Brown, 1991; M. Hanson, 1991; Strusinski, 1991), very few of them are of the variety envisioned by reformers. There seems to be a strong strain of conservatism in the ways school personnel plan to take advantage of the new opportunities they have been afforded (Anderson & Dixon, 1993; Johnson, 1993)—"in the majority of schools, the plans call for more of the same in educational programming" (Hess, 1992, p. 18). Not surprising, "decentralization has not impacted schools in ways that trigger diversity" (Collins, 1994, p. 94). "Differences among schools in allocation patterns are relatively minor" (Hannaway, 1992, p. 11) and "variation in the configuration of personnel across schools is again small" (pp. 11-12). By and large, decentralization has not led to the implementation of dramatic changes (Rothstein, 1990). Adaptations tend to be "conservative" (Collins & Hanson, 1991, p. v) and "at the margin" (Sackney & Dibski, 1992, p. 17)—and to "show remarkably similar patterns of conformity to mainstream 'norms' " (Anderson & Dixon, 1993, p. 56). They are not "particularly innovative" (Etheridge et al., 1992, p. 18). Most improvements under way in self-governing schools are of the first-order variety (M. Hanson, 1991;

Hess, 1992).[13] Research conducted over the past decade also reveals that the supposition that "staff acting independently will be more innovative than under the direction of the school bureaucracy [has] not [been] strongly borne out" (M. Hanson, 1991, p. 15). SBM and non-SBM schools show "very similar profiles" (Weiss, 1993, p. 11; see also Collins & Hanson, 1991).

If there is a generalization about the relationship between the earlier links of the SBM model (empowerment → ownership → professionalism) and change, it is this: SBM appears to offer the opportunity for change, but schools have largely failed to translate that flexibility into (a) significant educational innovations, (b) more innovations than are found in schools without participatory management, and (c) and innovations that look different from the popular improvement strategies of the day. "The findings call into question the assumption . . . of increased innovation through autonomy" (M. Hanson, 1991, p. i). "School-based management does not appear to be a key stimulus for innovation" (Brown, 1990, p. 259).[14] There is also little support for the claim that the quality of decision making is improved (Ovando, 1993).

Efficiency. Although past studies reveal that in general, reorganizations, whether of the centralized or decentralized variety, "cannot result in major savings" (March & Olson, 1983, p. 283), woven throughout the literature on SBM is the claim that participatory governance will promote economic efficiency in schools. Although the evidence on this assumption from the recent round of SBM is hardly conclusive, it is suggestive on a number of issues. To begin with, consistent with the findings on responsiveness, it does appear that SBM reallocates funds and responsibilities from the district office to the school level, thereby reducing central office costs (Carnoy & MacDonell, 1990; Hess, 1992).

On the other hand, the early hope that SBM "may actually save money" (Clune & White, 1988, p. 29) in the aggregate appears unfounded. Although more work is needed on the issue of "efficiency as overall cost savings," the major studies completed to date find that: "SCBM [school/community-based management] does not necessarily streamline operations" (Pacific Region Educational Laboratory, 1992, p. 31), "efficiency ratings do not change systematically" (Collins & Hanson, 1991, p. 21), and the "assertion that decentralization would reduce costs [is] not supported" (Brown, 1990, p. 248). In summary,

> Two assumptions of school-based management must be questioned: first, that there are more resources in a school that can be tapped merely by changing the structure of the organization and not increasing the resources flowing to it; second, that a school staff will necessarily be more resourceful when acting independently than when administered by a larger bureaucracy. (M. Hanson, 1991, p. 14)

The relationship between SBM and "technical efficiency" (Brown, 1990, p. 247), what we refer to in Chapter 1 as the welfare gain from securing a better match between expenditures and local interests and needs, is less clear. Part of the confusion arises because of the complexity of the issue: "There is no simple formula for establishing a relationship between decentralized authority and efficient use of resources, there is only a series of complex, interrelated puzzles" (Elmore, 1993, p. 50). Notwithstanding measurement concerns, it is proposed by many that SBM will produce "greater efficiency in the allocation of resources" (Clune & White, 1988, p. 4) and "a more efficient use of resources" (Duttweiller & Mutchler, 1990, p. 45). Advocates of shared decision making maintain that technical efficiency is improved because, under decentralization (a) "cost awareness is raised" (Brown, 1990, p. 187)—what Hannaway (1992) refers to as "the increased efficiency that results from the decisions of more knowledgeable agents" (p. 3); (b) "resources are [better] matched to school tasks" (Brown, 1990, p. 260) or "to accomplish tasks seen as important by school personnel" (p. 191)—thus money is not wasted on unneeded and unwanted programs (Clune & White, 1988) and goods and services "previously underfunded from a school perspective" (Brown, 1990, p. 188) will be increased; and (c) spending may be shifted "away from activities that are distinct from learning to activities that are closely related to learning" (Carnoy & MacDonnell, 1990, p. 59).[15] Recent studies of decentralization efforts have produced little evidence to support the viability of the assumption of technical efficiency under SBM. It appears that such claims may be significantly overstated. On the other side of the ledger, there is considerable evidence of additional workload costs associated with participatory models of governance (Murphy, 1991, 1994b), an issue to which we return in Chapter 7.

Equity. The effects of SBM on equity have been the subject of much conceptual and theoretical conjecture, but little empirical investigation (see Murphy, 1993b). Particularly thoughtful analyses of the potentially disequalizing effects of decentralization have been produced by Watt (1989), S. B. Lawton (1991), and Mirel (1990). Watt (1989) maintains that the threads of inequity are an inherent part of the restructuring tapestry. He asserts that self-managing schools "must disadvantage poor children" (p. 23). In analyzing localized curriculum planning, Watt (1989) sees "a tendency which seems almost inevitable: to design for schools in affluent areas curricula which will be culturally rich and cognitively demanding, and for schools in poor areas curricula which impose much lower expectations on the students' capacity for intellectual development and hard work" (p. 23). He reports that since the implementation of SBM in schools in South Australia, there has been an increasing inequality of provision of favorable conditions of learning between rich and poor schools. He concludes that "this increasing inequality of provision is not an accidental and avoidable by-product of sweeping devolution of power, but a central and virtually inevitable outcome" (p. 22).

S. B. Lawton (1991) echoes many of Watt's (1989) concerns, suggesting that because deregulation "will ultimately favor those with greater personal and financial resources (p. 18) . . . radical decentralization can be a major threat to the welfare of many of those who benefit from government services" (p. 16). He also warns that "the allocation of political responsibility to local communities or collectivities absolves the central authority of much of the responsibility for the welfare of minorities" (p. 16). "It is a way of the state arrogantly shirking its social responsibility for providing an equitable quality education for all" (Smyth, 1993b, p. 8). S. B. Lawton (1991) adds a new equity concern when he introduces the possibility that SBM may allow teachers "to capture the process of school governance" (p. 19).

Addressing the issue of equity from a historical perspective, Mirel (1990) assembles a different set of concerns, offering warnings in terms of the potential equity costs of decentralization. The first cost, he contends, is the potential rise of "provincialism—the narrow viewpoint that the norms and values of your region, town, or neighborhood represent the essence of human achievement" (p. 41). Based on lessons from previous attempts to deregulate schools, Mirel (1990) cautions that recent efforts at school-site management "may provide access to power for groups that see the schools as a forum for enacting narrow, ethnic or racial agendas, agendas that will separate our children from one another in a new form of self-imposed segregation" (pp. 41-42). He also reveals how "even modern decentralized control of schools can breed corruption and malfeasance" (p. 44), conditions that foster inequities. Indeed, newly completed investigations have concluded that "New York City's most recent community-based elections were . . . plagued by fraud and corruption" (Schmidt, 1994, p. 11).

Overall, available data on the relationship between recent SBM initiatives and equity are quite tentative, yet more positive in nature than might be expected. Both Brown (1990) and Hess (1992) conclude that "decentralization provides a measure of equal access to educational resources for students" (Brown, 1990, p. 260)—"that resources appear to be distributed more equitably with decentralized districts" (p. 246).[16] Bryk (1993) also concludes that the opportunities provided by reform initiatives "for school improvement have been equitably accessed by schools across the system" (p. 19). At least in Chicago, indications are that SBM has also dramatically augmented minority representation in school governance. In fact, the Chicago school reform "nearly doubled the number of African Americans and Hispanics making educational policy decisions in the United States" (Designs for Change, 1991, p. 1). Clearly more work is needed to assess the effects of SBM on a variety of dimensions of educational equity, especially to test the concerns raised by Watt (1989), S. B. Lawton (1991), and Mirel (1990).

Organizational Health: Learning and Teaching

> *But nearly all of the contending parties seem to agree that decentralization and choice would affect instruction. Though advocates and analysts disagree about how these reforms would affect practice, most of them seem to assume that there would be direct effects. (Cohen, 1989, pp. 7-8)*

From past efforts at participatory management, we know that "reform rhetoric about governance has often obscured more than it

revealed about actual practice in classrooms" (Tyack, 1993, p. 7)—
that reform "policy and administrative structure are uncoupled
from the central task of the enterprise—teaching and learning"
(Elmore, 1993, p. 50). However, there is a pervasive feeling in the
current literature that "decentralization *should* direct teachers' attention to their central functions" (Hannaway, 1992, p. i, emphasis added)
and that instructional improvement and "improved school program
practices" (Stevenson, 1990, p. 1) will result. Not surprising, then,
considerable effort is being devoted to trying to uncover "to what
extent and how SBDM contributes to the ultimate goal of transforming curriculum and instruction in ways that increase student performance" (David, 1993, p. 31). Four areas, in particular, are being
explored to develop an answer to this question: (a) how the governance structure, especially the site council, attends to matters of
learning and teaching; (b) how school planning and improvement
projects spotlight the core technology; (c) how actual change occurs
in learning and teaching; and (d) how, in terms of time allocations,
operating a decentralized school system pulls teachers toward or
pushes them away from their central function.

Site-Council Activities. Studies of school-site councils, with a few
exceptions (Ovando, 1993; Wohlstetter & Buffett, 1991), conclude
that these formal governance mechanisms are largely inattentive
to learning and teaching matters. In one study, for example, Malen
and Ogawa (1988) find that "program issues received scant, episodic,
superficial attention" (p. 256). School councils rarely involve
themselves in curricular or instructional matters (Collins & Hanson,
1991; David, 1993; Jenni, 1990). "Neither do leadership councils
. . . spend a lot of time planning staff development" (Rothstein,
1990, p. 12). Their scope of operations is much more likely to be
confined to "issues of discipline and sports" (David, 1993, p. 30),
"business matters" (Sackney & Dibski, 1992, p. 12), and "scheduling school events" (Rothstein, 1990, p. 9)—issues that are "peripheral
to fundamental instructional content or methodology" (Duttweiler
& Mutchler, 1990, p. 36). In summary, "In many schools, the first
years of site-based management are dominated by contention
about adult working conditions—labor management relations
and fair allocation of parking spaces, telephones, and hall and
playground duty—rather than by serious efforts to improve services to students" (Hill & Bonan, 1991, p. 27). School-based coun-

cils, by and large, "do not get at the problem of meaning for the everyday teacher" (Fullan, 1991, p. 201).[17] Even when one finds a focus on technical core issues in self-governing schools, it often has much more to do with the leadership of the school principal (Bryk, 1993; Weiss, 1993) or with outside consultants "who work with individual schools, or other activities that teachers choose to participate in rather than council decisions" (Malen et al., 1989, p. 21).

School Improvement Plans. Analyses of school improvement plans and projects tend to reinforce conclusions drawn from investigations of site-council activities. According to Wohlstetter and Odden (1992): "School-based management initiatives rarely become centrally involved in technical core issues of curriculum and instruction. . . . Instead, SBM projects tend to focus on peripheral issues, such as school climate, campus beautification, career education, remedial education, parent involvement, scheduling, safety and use of the copying machine" (p. 5). The actual effects of such projects are often "limited to changes in the lives of adults at the school" (Marsh, 1992, p. 33). When planning and innovations address the core technology, the focus is on "add-on" programs rather than a reconfiguration of the base program. In Chicago, for example, Hess (1992) reports that "in only about a quarter [of the schools] are they [school improvement plans] likely to significantly alter the way students encounter schools" (p. 50)—roughly the result one would expect by chance, given the resources Chicago has devoted to reform. Similarly, Brown (1990) notes that most of the respondents in his study "did not associate school-based management with either an increase or decrease in the educational opportunities afforded students" (p. 186).

Instructional Practice. Not surprising given what we just reported about council activities and school improvement plans, analysts are able to muster little support for the premise that SBM improves curriculum and instruction. We have already examined in some depth the issue of curricular change. Here we just reintroduce two findings: (a) that the linkage between SBM and curricular change is weak (Collins & Hanson, 1991; Diegmueller, 1991)—that schools, in general, do not "seize the opportunity to develop their own curricula" (Brown, 1991, p. 36); and (b) that most studies do not establish "school-based management as providing an avenue for innovation or the exercise of creative behaviour" (Brown, 1990, p. 236). In fact, there are few differences in curriculum between SBM and non-SBM schools (Taylor & Bogotch, 1992; Weiss, 1993).

There also seems to be no direct and positive linkage between teacher involvement in decision making and improved teacher practice. Although a few studies report either more effective teaching in SBM schools, or that SBM "fosters instructional change" (Bryk, 1993, p. 23; Crosby, 1991; Goldman et al., 1991), the bulk of the evidence suggests otherwise. SBM tends to wash over classrooms, leaving the instructional program largely unaffected (Griffin, in press; Hess, 1992; Taylor & Bogotch, 1992). "There are few if any indications, that early movement toward site-based management has been associated with substantial change in instructional delivery" (Levine & Eubanks, 1992, p. 74). Not unexpected, therefore, investigators uncover few signs of "qualitative differences in the instructional techniques chosen by teachers" (Taylor & Bogotch, 1992, p. 17) in SBM and non-SBM schools.

Time Allocations of Teachers. Throughout the early years of the current era of SBM, warnings were being made that participatory decision making could negatively affect the core technology of schooling by drawing the energy and time of school professionals away from learning, students, and the classroom. Based on her earlier research, Chapman (1990) cautioned that the "impact of increased teacher participation in decision-making on face-to-face teaching may be more negative than positive as teachers report that involvement in committee work distracts teachers' energy away from teaching, correction and classroom practice" (p. 237). A similar note of concern was raised by Caldwell (1990), who reported: "There has been concern that the shifting of management responsibilities to the school level is in some way a distraction from the central processes of schooling, namely, learning and teaching, and that principals and teachers will become accountants" (p. 20).

Studies completed over the past decade provide ample evidence that these warnings should be heeded. Shared models of leadership do have the potential to reduce the time teachers have available for instructional planning as well as, in some instances, the amount of time they can devote to working with students (Hannaway, 1992;

Rutherford, 1991; Wallace & Wildy, 1993). Thus, "under current patterns of time allocation in schools, participation in shared decision making often is a cost rather than a benefit to teachers" (Mutchler, 1990a, p. 1). "Collective decision making can be a burden" (Sackney & Dibski, 1992, p. 7) when committee assignments "take teachers out of classrooms, affect the time they [have] for preparation and marking, and disrupt the education of students" (Dellar, 1992, p. 14) and when it "divert[s] human resources from the main purpose of the school—the teaching/learning process—to administration" (Chapman & Boyd, 1986, p. 44). Similarly, shared governance can become dysfunctional when it redefines the role of the school principal away from that of educator to that of manager. Again, early studies reveal that just such a change is precipitated by SBM (Murphy, 1994b).

Despite some optimism that "enhanced democratic participation can be an effective lever for systemic educational change" (Bryk, 1993, p. 21) and that "over time, schools can use a process of shared governance to control their own destinies and to reorganize themselves in creative ways to help students and teachers become more successful" (Glickman, 1990, p. 70), in general, "devolution of authority and responsibility for the core technology has not impacted teaching-learning" (Collins, 1994, p. 91), has "generally failed to alter basic patterns of instruction" (Tyack, 1993, p. 25), and "does not seem to be affecting the major substance of curriculum" (Ovando, 1993, p. 2).

Performance

> The real challenge and test for SBM is to see if it does produce the types of changes in educational inputs and processes that result in enhanced and improved learning outcomes. (Sackney & Dibski, 1992, p. 9)

> Output defined as learning outcomes may be the most valid indicator of productivity for schools, but the satisfaction with that output is another way in which productivity may be conceived. (Brown, 1990, p. 193)

School Improvement and Student Outcomes. As E. M. Hanson (1991) correctly asserts, "the principal outstanding question is, will school-based management in any of its forms improve the quality of education in local public schools?" (p. 26). More specifically, the "question that must eventually be answered is whether administrative decentralization accompanied by community participation or control improves the educational progress of students" (Ornstein, 1983, p. 8). However, because "the notion of productivity in education is difficult to work with" (Conway, 1984, p. 27), educators have tended to avoid defining their successes in terms of outcomes, especially measures of student performance (Cohen, March, & Olsen, 1972; Meyer & Rowan, 1975). Consequently, "criteria of success for SBM programs [have tended to] pertain to process rather than outcomes (increased autonomy, flexibility, communication). Systematic monitoring is rare, whether of student achievement or other outcomes" (Clune & White, 1988, p. 23). "The impact on student learning is usually ignored. . . . As a result, SBM has not been accountable for improving student learning" (Wohlstetter & Odden, 1992, pp. 6, 5).

Given this aversion to the inspection of outcomes, the current round of SBM initiatives has taken root with "precious little research to suggest any close connection between management and leadership *structures* and improved student *performance*" (Sokoloff & Fagan, 1991, p. 2), in particular with "very little empirical data . . . available on the effects of decentralization or community control" (Ornstein, 1983, p. 8). This "lack of evidence linking school-based budgeting to increased school productivity" (Wohlstetter & Buffett, 1991, p. 6)—or the lack of a "clear linear . . . link from teacher participation in school decision making to better achievement by students" (Weiss et al., 1991, p. 23)—makes "arguments supporting school-based budgeting and decision-making as means of improving student learning . . . at best speculative" (Sackney & Dibski, 1992, p. 9).

Speculative or not, as we documented in Chapter 1, a fundamental premise of current SBM reforms "is that when schools have the power, resources, and freedom from constraint to resolve their own problems, the payoff will be increased levels of learning" (E. M. Hanson, 1991, p. 3). "The expectation is that school level actors, freed from state and district prescriptions, [will] focus their efforts in ways that lead to greater student achievement" (Hannaway, 1992, p. 3). The data assembled over the past decade cast a pall over this basic premise of self-managing schools. A few investigators conclude "that school-based management is an effective vehicle for school improvement" (Crosby, 1991, p. 10) or "that shared decision making teams can be an effective engine of school restructuring"

(Zuckerman, 1992, p. 19), but the weight of the evidence suggests that the development of characteristics of more effective schools does not occur (Duttweiler & Mutchler, 1990; Malen et al., 1989) and that there are "no concrete or measurable indicators of . . . improvement in most schools" (Rutherford, 1991, p. 12; see also Wagstaff & Reyes, 1993).

SBM studies focusing on student outcomes arrive at a similar conclusion. Results on the connections between local autonomy and student achievement are particularly disheartening. Taylor and Bogotch (1992), for example, recently found that "participation did not improve outcomes for . . . students" (p. 17)—"the anticipated link between participation in the core technology dimensions and student achievement did not emerge" (p. 13). In a comprehensive assessment of the Dade County Public Schools (DCPS) SBM experiment, Collins and Hanson (1991) discovered that, "as was the case with the previous Stanford comparison, it is fair to say that students in SBM schools performed no differently, on the average [on the state Student Assessment Test] than students in other DCPS schools" (p. 27). In Kentucky, recent test scores "evinced no clear difference between schools that have been deeply involved in reform efforts and others that have made no changes" (Harp, 1993b, p. 15). In Chicago, as the "reform implementation effort reached its mid-point, it would be fair to say that it has not yet had a significant impact upon student learning" (Hess, 1992, p. 49). Confirming evidence has also been assembled in reviews by Marsh (1992) and Malen and her colleagues (1989) and in studies by Duttweiler and Mutchler (1990) and Rumbaut (1992). The likelihood that recent reforms aimed at creating self-managing schools will lead to improved schooling outcomes is extremely problematic. We see almost no evidence from research conducted over the past decade that the current round of SBM measures is any more effective in enhancing student achievement than were previous decentralization initiatives.

Recently, some analysts have proposed that examining "the link between school-based management and student achievement focused on achievement test data as the sole measure of outcome" (Duttweiler & Mutchler, 1990, p. 42) is "inadequate" and "inappropriate" (p. 42). They call for "a much broader array of student assessment and program evaluation measures" (pp. 42-43). Data on these additional measures of student performance are in short supply, however. Nonetheless, there are indications that improvements on such measures as student dropout rates, suspensions, and attendance are possible (Collins & Hanson, 1991), although the evidence is far from clear (Hess, 1992).

Broader Measures. On the topic of the macro-level performance of SBM, four indicators seem most relevant: (a) "the broader public interest" (Sackney & Dibski, 1992, p. 17), (b) community well-being, (c) environmental legitimacy, and (d) parental satisfaction. Unfortunately, our understanding of how decentralized systems of governance and management influence these outcome variables is extremely limited. On the first two measures, there is some conceptual speculation that SBM will have a positive influence (Bryk, 1993; Burke, 1992). Others, however, are much more cautious in their assessments (Sackney & Dibski, 1992).

Malen and her colleagues (1989) have proposed that the real impact of SBM is more symbolic than substantive—that the fundamental purpose of self-managing schools is (a) to help educators "survive the stress" (p. 27) of the environmental pressures we described in Chapter 3, (b) to realign schooling "with the dominant values of its environment" (p. 27), and (c) to restore the mantle of legitimacy to schools. There is considerable support for this viewpoint in the larger body of work on the reorganization of institutions (March & Olson, 1983; Meyer & Rowan, 1975; Tyack, 1993). However, whether SBM has been successful in restoring legitimacy to the educational enterprise remains an open question at this time. Certainly a case can be made that in selected communities some of the luster of the educational system has been restored. On the other hand, the continued barrage of criticism being leveled at schools and the increasing tendency of reformers to search for more radical improvement strategies such as choice and charter schools imply that rejuvenated models of shared governance may be inadequate to restore legitimacy to education.

A number of analysts believe "that decentralization and community control are programs designed to produce parental and community *satisfaction*" (Epps, 1992, p. 154). Data on the level of client satisfaction with SBM, however, are insufficient to form any firm conclusions. In those few places where information has been systematically collected, the landscape is far from clear. Although parents in some studies feel that schools are improving under decentralized approaches to management governance (Designs for

Change, 1991; Epps, 1992), other "parents do not seem to perceive advantages to SBM schools" (Collins & Hanson, 1991, p. 34). Given that "the assessment people make of SBM is closely related to how well they feel it is achieving its objects" (Jenni & Mauriel, 1990, p. 14), it is not surprising to discover that the preliminary reports on parental satisfaction are also mixed. Even the positive evidence must be tempered, however. Positive effects may peak early in the life of the intervention (Duttweiler & Mutchler, 1990) and may be largely confined to parents who work closely with the school, especially those serving on the site council.[18]

Looking Ahead

In this chapter, we reviewed the recent evidence on SBM. The major focus was on testing the assumptions, or embedded logic, in the SBM model. We examined effects from empowerment to performance, mediated along the way by ownership, professionalism, and organizational health. In Chapter 7, we turn our attention to explaining these findings.

Notes

1. For analyses of role changes under SBM, see the following: for teachers (Murphy, 1991, in press d), for principals (Louis & Murphy, 1994; Murphy, 1994b), and for superintendents and other central office staff (Murphy, in press b, in press c).

2. Although it is beyond the scope of this volume to treat changes in roles of stakeholders at the state level under SBM, it is argued that important changes at this level are critical to the successful adoption of decentralized systems of management and governance (Armstrong, 1990; David, Cohen, Honetschlager, & Traiman, 1990; Murphy, 1994b).

3. For a particularly thoughtful analysis of this conclusion, see Smith (1993).

4. The research on the issue of the context for SBM is instructive. To date, it has been demonstrated that a variety of factors influence the implementation of shared management (Chapman, 1990). For example, at the district level, the political context (Wohlstetter, 1990), district size (Clune & White, 1988; Riley, 1984), and urbanism (Jacobson & Woodworth, 1991) all appear to color how participants view SBM and "both complicate and enrich" (Hannaway, 1992, p. 8) the investigation of effects.

At the school level, the history of reform is an important context variable (Cohen, 1989). For example, Gips and Wilkes (1993) have shown that site-level personnel "react to new situations related to site-based decision making based on their past relationships and experiences" (p. 8). Also important are the level of harmony or conflict (Wohlstetter, 1990), amount of administrative support (Chapman, 1990; Weiss

& Cambone, 1993), and the "manner in which site-based decision making was introduced and considered" (Gips & Wilkes, 1993, p. 9). Timing appears important— "different times, different meaning" (Malen & Ogawa, 1988, p. 288), as does school size (Gips & Wilkes, 1993; Robertson & Buffett (1991), level of instruction (Gips & Wilkes, 1993; Jenni & Mauriel, 1990), and student and faculty diversity.

Personal factors such as the type of working environment in which one feels most comfortable (Reed, 1992), the "level of involvement with the innovation" (Gips & Wilkes, 1993, p. 8), closeness to the decision making body in the school (Smith, 1993), and gender (Gips & Wilkes, 1993) appear to be relevant context variables as well.

5. All four studies focus on empowerment via site-council operations. This, however, is only one mechanism, among many, by which empowerment can be actualized. This limitation should not be overlooked.

6. It is our belief that although it is instructive to examine the role of students in the governance of decentralized schools, the key participation issues for students reside closer to the classroom (Evertson & Murphy, 1992).

7. Like Mirel (1990), we are not overly impressed by the voter turnout in Chicago. Based on our historical analysis of SBM, we also agree that this "low voter turnout for the LSC elections is a sure fire path to political manipulation" (p. 46).

8. Although we return to this issue in the last chapter, it is worth noting here that one reason for the anemic level of participation of parents in SBM is that neither teachers (Murphy, Evertson, & Radnofsky, 1991) nor principals (Hallinger et al., 1992) are particularly supportive of the idea.

9. The most common explanation for the phenomenon focuses on the issues of teacher burnout and overload—teachers doing too much and needing to pull back. As we discuss later in this chapter and in Chapter 7, concerns about neglecting the classroom are paramount in this line of analysis (Bredeson, 1992; Carnoy & Mac-Donell, 1990). On the other hand, alternative explanations are worthy of consideration. For example, it may be that teachers feel less need to participate directly in making decisions after they secure the right to participate. According to this line of analysis, "the right to participate in curriculum decision making is, perhaps, more important to teachers than actually making decisions. Teachers know they have easy access to the decision process through a representative if they want it" (Hannaway, 1992, p. 22). Likewise, participation may facilitate the development of trust, especially in the principal or the elected council, which in turn, may reduce the need for direct involvement in decision making (Hallinger et al., 1992). Such a possibility was surfaced by Conway (1984) when he noted, "there is some indication that *trust* is a better predictor of satisfaction than is participation" (p. 32).

10. It is important to emphasize that "no empirically strong or theoretically compelling relationship between satisfaction and performance is apparent" (Mitchell, cited in Conway, 1984, p. 16)—"employee satisfaction by no means automatically translates into improvements in productivity or other performance outputs" (Levine & Eubanks, 1992, p. 74). More important for our purposes here, based on the work of Brookover and Lezotte who found that "teachers in low-achieving schools tended to have higher job satisfaction scores than teachers in improving schools" (Epps, 1992, p. 157), Levine and Eubanks (1992) argue that "unless site-based management is clearly part of a much more comprehensive and serious reform effort in the future, indications of increase in faculty satisfaction should not necessarily be interpreted as a positive development" (pp. 74-75).

11. Satisfaction for teachers under SBM does not necessarily translate into satisfaction for principals (see Murphy, 1994b; Louis & Murphy, 1994). Trestrail

(1992) captures the issue well when he reports that in a revolutionary context like SBM, administrators often "see themselves as in the centre of a conflagration" (p. 1).

12. A thoughtful analysis of the issue of accountability under SBM has been provided by Elmore (1993),

> To say that decentralization increases "accountability" in educational systems is to say very little in the absence of some set of beliefs about who is to be accountable to whom for what. On the surface, most decentralizing efforts express a common theme on the subject of accountability: schools are to be held accountable to the public for the results that they produce with students. Below the surface of this simple (some would say simplistic) formula lie roiling ambiguity and outright contradiction. (p. 45)

Equally thoughtful is Mirel (1990), who suggests that SBM is likely "to replace one form of non-accountability with another form of non-accountability" (p. 43). Both scholars urge reformers to avoid the trap of "substitut[ing] democratic sentiment for analysis" (Elmore, 1993, p. 46).

13. Even if SBM did result in significant changes, some analysts discern a downside to this diversity. In particular, Sackney and Dibski (1992) question

> whether individual schools in making goal and program decisions that serve the interests of their own clientele are also making decisions that serve the broader public interest in education. . . . Particular concern is voiced about school-based curriculum that might result in schools that are committed to ethno-cultural ideals outside the mainstream. A vision of social fragmentation in which centrifugal forces tear apart the body politic dominates this perspective. (pp. 16, 19)

14. Brown (1990) hypothesizes that this may be due to a lack of incentives for schools to improve. For a helpful analysis of the introduction of incentives into the dialogue on SBM, see Wohlstetter and Mohrman (1993).

15. Elmore (1993), for one, is skeptical of this assumption. He contends that one "cannot assume that just because resources are being used at the school level, they are being efficiently allocated for maximum impact on students' learning" (p. 50).

16. It is important to note here—as Brown (1990) does—that equity as access to aggregated resources tells us little about how equitably those resources are distributed within schools, or the more fine-grained issue of equity as access to knowledge (Murphy, 1993b; Murphy & Hallinger, 1989).

17. There are some hints that as councils mature they "appear to be moving into areas of staffing, curriculum, and instruction" (David, 1993, p. 36; also Hess, 1992).

18. A similar pattern may hold for teachers as well (Smith, 1993).

7

Explaining Effects

> In any specific case, decentralizing reforms seem, at least on the surface, to provide very plausible answers to the ills of public education. (Elmore, 1993, p. 34)

> The focus on site-based management is not justified because of its brilliant track record in education. (Marsh, 1992, p. 3)

If, as we argued in Chapter 6, the recent round of SBM initiatives has largely failed to fulfill its promise,[1] our remaining task is to attempt to explain why. We undertake to fulfill that charge in two ways. In the first half of this chapter, we examine implementation issues that reveal why shared decision making is working much less effectively in education than supporters had hoped it would. In the second, we describe a more significant problem—a misdirected focus that would probably doom SBM to the backwaters of educational reform even if it were well implemented.

Before proceeding, we should acknowledge the possibility that participatory models of governance are not working well because they are not supposed to work—at least in the terms we employed in Chapter 6. SBM might have much less to do with outcomes such as organizational health and student achievement than it does with the divestiture of responsibility for intractable problems from central authorities to local communities (Brown, 1991; Sackney & Dibski, 1992):

District thrusts toward site-based management may divert attention from central decision makers' responsibility for initiating and supporting comprehensive and fundamental reforms in the design and delivery of educational services. If power and resources can be shifted to the school level, central authorities also may be able to shift most or all of the responsibility for failure to improve student performance to teachers and administrators in the schools. (Levine & Eubanks, 1992, p. 75)

It is also possible that the movement may have less to do with school change than with efforts to use decentralization and deregulation as foils to shift massive amounts of money from the public to the private sector (Murphy, 1993a).

Implementation Issues

It is idle to judge the strategy effective if it has not been fully implemented. (Wood, 1984, p. 63)

Of the variety of implementation problems that appear to be undermining the potential of SBM, four seem most significant: weak implementation, resistance, lack of support, and a confining task environment.

Weak Implementation

The first conclusion is that site-based management (SBM) in educational settings has not been successful to date and that weak implementation processes were part of the problem. (Marsh, 1992, p. 33)

Unquestionably, one of the key difficulties with the SBM movement is that many initiatives have been only partially implemented (Rutherford, 1991).[2] A number of important reviews of shared decision making (David, 1989; Malen et al., 1989; Wohlstetter & Odden, 1992) have concluded that "school decentralization is often marginalized and incomplete" (Bimber, 1993, p. 35). Various investigators have discovered the "greatly limited degrees of freedom" (Daresh, 1992, p. 119) of SBM, "the limited scope of Shared Decision Making authority," and the fact that SBM in practice often does not align well with the definition of SBM promulgated by advocates (Lindquist & Mauriel, 1989). As Wood (1984) reminds us, "it may be that participatory decision making does not work in these instances because it was never actually attempted" (p. 60). One tangible measure of weak implementation is the extent to which school communities must rely on requests and waivers of various state, district, and union policies to implement changes, as opposed to being granted the requisite authority outright (Murphy, 1991).[3]

Resistance

> It is apparent that power is perceived as an important consideration in determining and implementing devolution policy. There is the strong suggestion that powerful vested interests are apt to subvert the policy and planning at all levels because of the threat such moves pose to existing power relations which currently favor such interest groups. (Burke, 1992, p. 47)

> If more authority is to be given to the schools to chart their own courses, those agencies previously assigned to direct these schools must be eliminated. Keeping them around—"revising their mission"—is an evasion. If new missions derive from new powers, let them do so de novo. But asking previous "power centers" to give up power, and the habits that accrue with it, and to figure out something else to do is futile. They will not give up power. (Sizer, 1992, pp. 186-187)

Gips and Wilkes (1993) maintain that "decentralizing schools to a site-based model will not happen without resistance" (p. 1). Brown (1990) concurs,

> The range of courses of opposition spans board members, central office personnel who may encounter loss of control of some functions, principals who do not all welcome decentralization sometimes because of small school size, teacher associations who may lose control of some functions, staff unions who may be concerned about job security and due process, and individual parents who may not accept the change. (p. 215)

Garms et al. (1978) assert that "those people who benefit from the existing order will naturally oppose the reform" (p. 289). In addition, a more "passive resistance" (Duttweiler & Mutchler, 1990, p. 5) to change will characterize those who are comfortable with the status quo (Glickman, 1990).

School Boards. A number of analysts have asserted that school boards often consider SBM and school-site councils "as threats to their own political power" (Guthrie, 1986, p. 307) "and the resources they control" (Brown, 1991, p. 39). Thus, it "is not at all clear that a school board will want to delegate its decision-making authority to the extent required by SBM theory" (Lindquist & Mauriel, 1989, p. 405). Indeed, the literature is dotted with cases where school boards have actively or passively resisted the implementation of SBM (Brown, 1990; Lindquist & Mauriel, 1989).

District Office Staff. At the core of SBM is a "restructuring of the relationship between central office administrators and school-level professionals" (Taylor & Bogotch, 1992, p. 19). Yet because "central office employees have much to lose under decentralized management" (Brown, 1990, p. 226), they tend to be "the most prominent among the groups that work against the implementation of decentralization" (p. 293).[4] Therefore, "the effectiveness of SBM is limited by superintendents and central administrators who are reluctant to share authority" (Clune & White, 1988, p. 20).

For these employees, there is a palpable sense of loss associated with shared governance (Brown, 1990; Murphy, 1993a, in press c, in press d)—a sense of loss rooted in a diminished sense of authority (Thompson, 1988), efficacy (Brown, 1991), prerogatives (Levine & Eubanks, 1992), influence (Wissler & Ortiz, 1988), power (Brown, 1990; Heller et al., 1989; Mutchler, 1990a), control (Clear, 1990), role status (Garms et al., 1978; Stoll & Fink, 1992), and position security (Brown, 1990, 1992; Wagstaff & Reyes, 1993), as well as in a perceived distancing in the relationship between central office personnel and school staff (Murphy, 1993a, in press c, in press d). Not unexpected, because these new conditions are often "scary for a central office" (Sommerfeld, 1992a, p. 10) and because district staff often feel left "on the fringes" (Stoll & Fink, 1992, p. 34) and "off-balance" (McPherson & Crowson, 1992, p. 3), many district employees have "a particular difficulty accommodating decentralization" (Brown, 1991, p. 78), especially in the absence of training (Harrison et al., 1989).

Central office administrators have been shown in a number of studies to have "actively blocked the practice of school-based decision making" (Harrison et al., 1989, p. 56; see also Brown, 1990; Smith, 1993) and to have reshaped reform "to maintain the equilibrium from which they . . . profit" (Finn, 1991, p. 182). Some reform analysts question whether central office staff can and will make the types of changes needed to permit SBM to work (Chubb, 1988; Sizer, 1992): "it cannot be taken for granted that these same people can readily convert and adapt to the values, and become proficient in the management style, which are nearly the antitheses of those inherent in the system which rewarded them over a long period of time" (Burke, 1992, p. 40).

Principals. Objections to the implementation of SBM can also stem from school site administrators, who like their central office colleagues, may be reluctant to give up power (Duttweiler & Mutchler, 1990) and "fearful of losing their authority" (Smith, 1993, p. 26), autonomy (Chapman, 1990), privileges (Brown, 1990), and "personal influence" (Brown, 1991, p. 24). In addition, as we have documented elsewhere (Murphy, 1994b), changing authority relations entails a "process of abandonment" (p. 43) that has the potential to undermine principals' sense of self as well as the accountability foundations on which they construct their understanding of their roles. Finally, some principals oppose SBM because they are comfortable with "the traditional top-down management system and are resistant to the adoption of a new system of management" (Clune & White, 1988, p. 27). Principal antipathy to SBM is not the norm (Weiss, 1993), but there are sufficient examples of both active and passive resistance by site leaders to attribute to them some of the blame for the difficulty in implementing shared models of governance in schools (Carnoy & MacDonell, 1990; Chapman, 1990; Epps, 1992; Etheridge et al., 1990; Hill & Bonan, 1991; Jewell & Rosen, 1993; Levine & Eubanks, 1992; Rothstein, 1990).

Teacher Unions. Although at first blush it may seem surprising, some reviewers have suggested that teachers may be less than enamored with SBM and may act as a brake on the implementation of participatory forms of management. A few analysts contend that "the concerns of teachers unions do not significantly conflict with the concerns of school-based management" (Lindelow, 1981, p. 123), but others see the situation quite differently. These reformers discern two types of union antipathy to SBM. First, there is hostility from union leaders, who like principals and district office administrators, are likely to lose influence—"to see their power to make rules for schools shift to their membership" (Brown, 1991, p. 88). Second, there is opposition from the union members when they discover how SBM "complicates their organizational task" (Garms et al., 1978, p. 290) by limiting their power "to impose a uniformity of conditions on schools via precise contract clauses" (Brown, 1992, p. 294) and by undermining "the interests they had developed in centralized bargaining power" (Chapman, 1990, p. 240). Specifically, there is "concern that they might lose hard won contract agreements" (Gips & Wilkes, 1993, p. 8) and "jeopardize the collective bargaining position of teachers at the district level" (Duke et al., 1980, p. 97).

Teachers. Through their actions or inactions at the school site, teachers, both individually and collectively, may hinder the implementation of shared decision making. Some teachers express considerable skepticism over the purported benefits of SBM. Many believe "SBM is like other educational reforms, a passing fad" (Reed et al., 1990, p. 12) that "in due time [will] fade away" (Gips & Wilkes, 1993, p. 9). Other teachers have "a certain comfort level with the status quo" (p. 9) and tend "to view site-based decision making unfavorably" (p. 91). In other schools, "resistance in the form of apathy toward shared decision making" (Mutchler & Duttweiler, 1990, p. 5) prevails, especially where teachers enjoy a good relationship with their principal. For example, in their in-depth investigation of SBM, Weiss and Cambone (1993) concluded (a) the norms of the profession are not supportive of collaborative models of management—"most teachers tended to be conservative, wanting to maintain things much as they had been, with minor changes to take care of problems" (p. 14); (b) because of this "pervasive complacency" (p. 14) and "climate of inertia" (pp. 15-16), "relatively few teachers saw a need for basic change" (p. 14); and (c) on a recurring basis, "teachers articulated a sense that the principal should make decisions" (p. 16). Not surprising, analysts of SBM often record "an unwillingness among teachers to assume responsibilities different from those they traditionally have held" (Mutchler & Duttweiler, 1990, p. 5).

Although we engage this issue in more detail below, it is important to note here that teachers may exhibit antipathy toward SBM because the costs of involvement in participatory management of the school may be too high and may be "counterproductive . . . [to] teachers' perceived self-interest" (Levine & Eubanks, 1992, p. 64). In addition to the extra time commitment necessitated by participatory management, two classroom-related costs of SBM are often experienced by teachers. There is the cost associated with spending additional time outside the classroom, time away from students and teaching (Bredeson, 1992; Hannaway, 1992). There are also the costs linked with opening up one's personal domain—the classroom—to the scrutiny of others (Weiss, 1993):

> In a decentralized arrangement, when teachers are involved in decisions about their work, their professional life is more observable and therefore more open to monitoring and influence by others.[5] At least their views of their work, the way they go about planning for it, and their reports about what goes on in their classrooms are more public than in a traditionally organized school where individual teachers function isolated in their classrooms. (Hannaway, 1992, p. 6)

As Reed (1992) reveals, teachers are sometimes reluctant to give up the autonomy[6] that working in isolation provides:[7]

> Though it took me a long time to see it, I finally understood that some teachers did not want to lose their traditional authority, no matter how "aware" they might become and, indeed, they resisted activity that could bring greater "awareness." As a good friend explained, "Carol, when I'm inside my classroom, I'm on top. I get to make the decisions. I get to decide what happens. When I step across the threshold into the hallway, I lose that position. Why would I want to step across that threshold?" For my friend, as for so many of the teachers in the four schools in which this study was implemented, an increase in group capacity meant a loss of individual authority. (p. 18)

Teachers are committed to the integrity of their own turf. Their classroom is their kingdom, and they do not welcome anyone—even another teacher—into their space. What they do in the classroom is private; it is a matter between them and their students. Although they submit to the necessity, and even the reasonableness, of the periodic supervisory visit, they value their autonomy within the walls of the classroom. (Weiss, 1993, pp. 5-6)

SBM is, therefore, not being embraced by teachers as warmly as many analysts believed it would.

Professional Hostility to Lay Control. Studies document fairly conclusively that "it is in the arena of professional versus lay that the egalitarian principle underlying SBM/SDM [is] most severely threatened" (Jewell & Rosen, 1993, p. 8). Investigators conclude that both teachers (Gips & Wilkes, 1993; Murphy et al., 1991) and principals (Fusarelli & Scribner, 1993; Hallinger et al., 1992) express "deep-felt concern about the participation of parents and community members in school decision-making" (Dellar, 1992, p. 7), especially when "parents [are allowed] to have any say in curriculum or other areas of student learning" (Jewell & Rosen, 1993, p. 10) or when participation takes on traces of control (Epps, 1992; Malen & Ogawa, 1988; Ornstein, 1983). Fusarelli and Scribner (1993) report, "It is clear from our study that both principals and teachers are interested in controlling the shared decision making component of site-based management such that it excludes parents and community members from significant participation in the decision making process" (p. 16). Citing concerns about "self-interestedness of parental involvement" (p. 14), "parents' ability and motivation" (Brown, 1990, p. 240), and "level of interest and competence" (Dellar, 1992, p. 7) and clinging to the mantles of professional expertise (Gips & Wilkes, 1993) and professional autonomy (Malen & Ogawa, 1988), school professionals have vigorously resisted the ideal of "critical democratic pluralism" (Fusarelli & Scribner, 1993, p. 16) that is at the core of SBM.[8] Reinforcing this active resistance by professionals to inclusive models of shared management is a natural inclination on the part of many parents to defer to teachers and principals, to avoid trespassing on the professional turf of educators, and to sustain norms of civility even when doing so limits their ability to participate in decision making (Malen & Ogawa, 1988; Malen et al., 1989).

Lack of Support

> *Site management offers teachers the opportunity to take initiative and solve problems. But it imposes corresponding burdens. (Hill & Bonan, 1991, p. 19)*

> *While many people want greater control over their destiny, the price for many of them may be too high. (Wagstaff & Reyes, 1993, p. 8)*

There is a nearly endless list of reasons why the considerable costs of SBM might strangle the implementation of even the most energized and enthusiastic reform efforts. Yet in terms of potential to choke off or support participatory management, four issues seem most critical: additional workload demands, opportunity costs of participation, disruption to the existing social fabric, and a shortage of needed support.

Additional Workload Demands. A recurring theme in studies reviewed in this volume is that "school-based management places new demands on teachers' and administrators' time" (Bachus, 1991, p. 1): "The evidence is conclusive, . . . one of the most immediate costs of increased teacher involvement in school management is 'time'" (Chapman, 1990, p. 223; see also Carnoy & MacDonell, 1990; Duke et al., 1980; Hill & Bonan, 1991). In fact, time is generally cited by stakeholders as the major reason for their lack of participation in SBM (Brown, 1990; Collins & Hanson, 1991). Two issues exacerbate the time problem. First, because "pre-existing responsibilities [generally] continue, staff who participate in shared decisionmaking experience a major increase in workload" (Hill & Bonan, 1991, p. 21). Second, the fact that involvement in SBM is placed "on top of the regular workload" (Wagstaff & Reyes, 1993, p. 3) is aggravated by the fact that "concomitant compensation" (p. 3) is generally conspicuous by its absence. It is not surprising, therefore, that some administrators and teachers find "the additional responsibilities associated with decentralization a heavy burden" (Chapman & Boyd, 1986, p. 43). Neither is it difficult to understand why some school personnel elect not to participate in SBM (Collins & Hanson, 1991), others end up returning decision authority to principals, and still others become "disillusioned and embittered with the Shared Decision Making Process" (Rothstein, 1990, p. 19); "even more dangerous to the long-term success of devolution, however, was the cynicism that excessive work demands created" (Chapman & Boyd, 1986, p. 44).

Opportunity Costs of Participation. Time spent in participatory decision making is time that cannot be devoted to other activities. Under SBM, these opportunity costs can be quite heavy for both teachers and administrators. For principals, studies portray a picture of men and women who are "involved in a massive increase" (Earley et al., 1990, p. 7) in work with governing boards and teacher councils (Ford, 1991; McConnell & Jeffries, 1991). School leaders also find themselves devoting considerably more time to the managerial aspects of the job (McConnell & Jeffries, 1991; McPherson & Crowson, 1992; Murphy, 1994b). Unfortunately, the opportunity cost of this heightened managerial responsibility is often diminished attention to the principals' educational/instructional role (Bennett et al., 1992; Ford, 1992; McConnell & Jeffries, 1992; Murphy, 1994b).

For teachers, similar opportunity costs are evident.[9] Despite thoughtful pleas that SBM "arrangements must ensure that participation in decision making does not detract from teaching" (Chapman, 1990, p. 233; Hannaway, 1992), there is considerable evidence that for many teachers shared decision making is leading to the augmentation of "non-instructional duties" (Bredeson, 1992, p. 18) and is requiring "them to leave their classrooms and their students" (p. 12). "Specifically, for teachers, time devoted to participating in decision making processes is time not devoted to 'teaching' activities—preparing and leading classes, grading papers, counseling students, advising extra-curricular activities" (Duke et al., 1980, p. 95). "The dissonance created as committee demands compete with teaching responsibilities" (Malen et al., 1989, p. 17) and "committee work distracts teachers' energy away from teaching, correction and classroom practice" (Chapman, 1990, p. 237) has led some researchers to view "participation in shared decision making . . . as a cost rather than as a benefit to teachers" (Mutchler & Duttweiler, 1990, p. 10) and conclude that the additional responsibilities of SBM are a "disruption to what they [see] as their major task" (Chapman & Boyd, 1986, p. 44). The dampened enthusiasm and retrenchment that often follow undermine the successful implementation of SBM (Bredeson, 1992; Rothstein, 1990).

Disruption to the Social Fabric. Harrison and her colleagues (1989) remind us that "change on a large scale threatens the established order and comfortable way of doing things" (p. 58). "Where the proposed change involves a fundamental alteration to existing decision-making structures and procedure, conflict would seem inevitable" (Dellar, 1992, p. 17). And sure enough, "adoption of decentralization appears to have generated some controversy in most of the districts" (Brown, 1992, p. 248) where it has been attempted. At the most basic level, by altering role conceptions and daily routines SBM has the potential to create considerable "personal uncertainty" (Gips & Wilkes, 1993, p. 9) among teachers and administrators. Looking specifically at school principals, Conley (1993) maintains that this "new way of doing business can be fraught with difficulty. . . . Essentially, these people are being asked to modify their personalities" (p. 83; see also Alexander, 1992; Prestine, 1991). A similar redefinition is required of teachers (Glickman, 1990). Organizationally, SBM has the potential to introduce considerable "confusion, anxiety, . . . contention" (Malen et al., 1989, p. 17) and "ambiguity" (Malen & Ogawa, 1988, p. 263) and to enhance tensions (Glickman, 1990). "Role conflict . . . and role strain" (Bredeson, 1992, p. 18) often follow. Particularly vexing for the successful implementation of SBM is the not-infrequent occurrence of "tensions between teachers and administrators" (Wagstaff & Reyes, 1993, p. 10) and conflicts between "teachers with traditional status" (Weiss et al., 1991, p. 5) and their newly empowered colleagues.

A Shortage of Needed Support. Elsewhere we have sketched out in detail the support structures required to make restructuring-anchored reforms work (Murphy, 1991; Murphy & Hallinger, 1993). We have also described more specifically the imperatives needed to reshape SBM in the service of educational improvement (Murphy & Beck, in press). Here we underscore two points: (a) For shared governance to be successful, a variety of support mechanisms must be in place; and (b) such supports are often absent or only dimly discernible in many current SBM-based reforms. We have already outlined some of the time barriers to the implementation of shared decision making. Investigators also frequently describe SBM initiatives with "resource liabilities" (Malen & Ogawa, 1988, p. 263) and without "the *resources* necessary to create new norms, 'learn' new behaviors, and make the personal and interpersonal changes required by school-based management" (Duttweiler & Mutchler, 1990, p. 41). M. Hanson (1991) characterizes the operative fiscal policy in SBM schools as that of "robbing Peter to pay Paul" (p. 15), hardly a viable strategy to ensure the health of participatory management. Duttweiler and Mutchler (1990) also document that "school-based management is frequently implemented without accompanying supportive changes in the professional life of teachers" (p. 38). Given the fact that there is often "a critical lack of knowledge and skills needed for shared decision making at [school] sites" (Mutchler & Duttweiler, 1990, p. 7), this inattention to professional development is particularly troublesome (Daresh, 1992).

Confining Task Environment

> More significant in the longer term may be the constraints which are imposed by forces external to the school, especially those associated with the demands of a centralized system in a time of economic constraint. (Chapman, 1990, p. 232)

> As the focus strengthens on the development of innovative organizational systems aimed at increasing participant involvement in decision making at the school level, traditional methods of policy making will need to be reassessed. Current policies as they now exist at the state, district, and building levels may greatly impede the empowerment effort. (Short & Greer, 1989, p. 23)

Duttweiler and Mutchler (1990) observe that "increased authority at the school site is not always accompanied by release from highly restrictive district or state regulatory requirements" (p. 38). Worse, "despite the lip-service paid to individual school initiative, education policies at all levels of government mandate uniformity in standards and programs" (M. Hanson, 1991, p. 8).

Wohlstetter and Odden (1992) report that "many SBM programs have suffered from inconsistent signals from their local and state policy makers on subjects that ranged from budgeting, curriculum and teaching to student learning" (p. 6).[10] These "inherent hierarchial constraints" (Short & Greer, 1989, p. 11) characterizing the "larger external realities" (Bryk, 1993, p. 39) that surround self-managing schools limit the flexibility of participatory models of governance and management (Brown, 1990; Duttweiler & Mutchler, 1990; Malen et al., 1989).

Constraints in the task environment of self-managing schools emanate from four sectors.[11] To begin, community norms exert considerably more pressure on efforts to use participatory governance in the service of fundamental change than the literature on SBM acknowledges (for an exception, see Malen & Ogawa, 1988). In addition, states continue to maintain existing regulations as well as to promulgate new legislation and procedures that "hinder the school-based management movement" (Stevenson & Pellicer, 1992, p. 135; Brown, 1990, 1992; Carnoy & MacDonell, 1990; Collins, 1994). Indeed, "many states have passed reform legislation that may preclude teacher initiated programmatic decisions" (Short & Greer, 1989, p. 19). Site governance has also been held in check by district policies and hierarchical structures (Daresh, 1992; M. Hanson, 1991; Heller et al., 1989). In fact, based on their work with empowering teachers, Short and Greer (1989) contend that "district level policy will, most likely, present the greatest need for change" (p. 20) to make SBM work. Finally, there is the hard "reality of union contracts" (Mirel, 1990, p. 46), which with their specific rules and regulations, often undermine the vitality of participatory governance at the site level (Brown, 1990; Daresh, 1992; Epps, 1992; Garms et al., 1978).

Misdirected Focus

The politics of structural reform in education has increasingly become a politics about the authority and legitimacy of various institutional arrangements, disconnected from any serious treatment of whether these arrangements can be expected to have any impact on what students learn in school. The stakes of structural reform are largely reckoned in terms of who gains and who loses influence within the governance structure, not in terms of whether structural change leads to changes in the conditions of teaching and learning. (Elmore, 1993, p. 39)

The relations between policy and organization on the one hand, and instructional practice on the other have been a frustrating problem for US policymakers, educators, and researchers. While connections are regularly assumed and asserted, they are much less often confirmed by research or experience. (Cohen, 1989, p. 2)

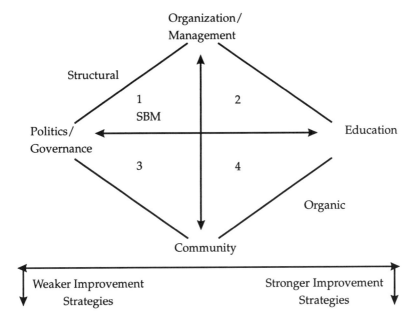

Figure 7.1. Foci of School Reform

After reviewing the literature on SBM and laying the school improvement template over that information, one arrives at the conclusion that even if well implemented, SBM-anchored reforms are not likely to bring about much significant school improvement. This is the case primarily because the four central foci of SBM—politics, governance, management, and organization—are distally and weakly connected to the central issues of student performance and democratic community.[12] In this section, we expand on this premise, examining how these four foci underscore structural as opposed to more powerful frames for improvement such as education and community (see Figure 7.1). We close the volume with a few thoughts about how SBM can be redirected in the service of enhanced student learning.

At its core, SBM-based reform "conceives of politics as a constructive force for school improvement" (Bryk, 1993, p. 5). It is primarily a political intervention designed to shift power to teachers and community members, especially parents.[13] Many analysts have concluded, therefore, that it "seems appropriate to examine site-based management as a political response to conflict and a strategy to stabilize school systems" (Ogawa & Malen, cited in Levine & Eubanks, 1992, p. 69). Unfortunately, "policy . . . is uncoupled from the central task of the enterprise—teaching and learning" (Elmore, 1993, p. 50). Its ability to promote school improvement is thus severely compromised (Sackney & Dibski, 1992).

Concomitantly, SBM represents an attempt to reform education "by radically altering its governance structure" (Hess, 1992, p. 1); it is viewed as a "reformation in the way that schools [are] governed" (Bryk, 1993, p. 2). Both in theory (Clune & White, 1988) and in practice (Smith, 1993), SBM is generally described as a "significant innovation in educational governance" (Clune & White, 1988, p. 11). The SBM model is concerned with "who has authority in the school— who gets to tell whom what to do. It had little to say about other aspects of the situation that may affect low achievement" (Lewis, 1993, p. 91).[14] The troubling conclusion that "governance reforms have been mostly disconnected from what students learn" (Tyack, 1993, p. 1) is often conveniently overlooked by SBM reformers.

If politics and governance are the soul of SBM, then management and organization are its heart. Under SBM, schools are depicted much more "as bases for management" than "as centers of renewal" (Sirotnik & Clark, 1988, p. 660, emphasis deleted). Bradley (1992) maintains that "empowerment is a management strategy, not a tool for improving education" (p. 10):

> For the most part the discourse suggests an acceptance of devolution as an *administrative* exercise. There is evidence of critical comment about devolution among senior officials, but little in the way of deeper critical reflection, or substantive social critique. For this reason the discourse may be characterized in mainly instrumentalist (i.e., administrative/ operational) rather than socially critical terms. (Burke, 1992, p. 50)

By providing SBM with a management and administration overcoat, shared decision making often (a) becomes viewed as an additional program, as opposed to something central to the life of the organization; (b) throws the spotlight on "the 'technology' of school-site management" (Mojkowski & Fleming, 1988, p. 14); and (c) is seen as "a way for a group of teachers to make better decisions than administration could make" (Smith, 1993, p. 10) rather than as a vehicle for school improvement. Issues of learning and teaching rarely reach center stage (Murphy, 1991, 1994b; Sackney & Dibski, 1992), or as Sirotnik and Clark (1988) state, "choosing to talk about *management* focuses attention on a broad spectrum of activities, many of which are only indirectly related to instructional programs" (p. 660).

Finally, "decentralization [is] conceived as a change in the organizational structure" (Brown, 1990, pp. 120-121) of the educational system. One form of organization gives way to another: "What may happen under SBM is that one level of bureaucracy may be juxtaposed for another" (Sackney & Dibski, 1992, p. 4). Again, the evidence suggests that "educators have learned to play the game of structural reform in ways that are consistent with the prevailing form of interest-group politics" (Elmore, 1993, p. 40). Organizational revisions may function to maintain rather than to alter influence relationships (Malen et al., 1989). By focusing on organizational issues, "school districts and principals put form before function" (Weiss & Cambone, 1993, p. 20). Finally, as with the other foci of SBM—politics, governance, and management—concentration on organizational structure directs attention away from the central issue of schooling, that is, learning and teaching. As Sokoloff and Fagan (1991) remind us, "what is important in restructuring is not that we change the organizational structure, but that those changes focus more sharply on the core tasks of teaching and learning" (p. 2).

Collectively, its four central foci demarcate SBM as a structurally grounded reform (see Figure 7.1), one characterized by two systemic flaws. First, its energy is marshaled in the service of replacing one type of bureaucracy with another (Sackney & Dibski, 1992). In so doing, it does not "anchor site-based management in a context that stimulates or even forces participants to address important issues" (Levine & Eubanks, 1992, p. 77). Second, it leads to a situation in which "teachers [think] of SDM and teaching as two separate activities" (Smith, 1993, p. 27), and "support for SDM and support for change in curriculum and instruction . . . vie for primacy" (Weiss & Cambone, 1993, p. 18). In short, SBM—at least in its most recent incarnation—generally reinforces rather than helps overcome widespread inattention to the central issues of learning and teaching in schools.

Refocusing SBM

In essence what is being argued here is that the traditional rational bureau-cratic organization may still be well and alive even though structural changes have taken place. (Sackney & Dibski, 1992, p. 5)

The more we study SBM the more we are convinced that it is a fairly weak intervention in our arsenal of school reform measures. As we discuss above and show in Figure 7.1, its structural focus tends to pull stakeholders at local school sites in certain directions—toward issues of governance and organization—that reinforce traditional aspects of schooling, specifically the centrality of hierarchy and the neglect of learning and teaching. Given the intensity of these forces, it is clear that although attention to the implementation issues discussed earlier will be necessary, more significant efforts will be required to harness shared decision making to the service of organizational health and student performance.

Without such work, three powerful tendencies will probably overwhelm the marginal benefits currently available from SBM and make the likelihood of important changes exceedingly problematic. First, the existing array of "traditional norms and behaviors" (Duttweiler & Mutchler, 1990, p. 41) will remain largely unaltered. "Values, beliefs, norms and assumptions" will remain anchored "in the old paradigm" (Sackney & Dibski, 1992, p. 5). Change will become increasingly difficult to foster. Second, the improvements that do unfold will tend to map onto current frameworks and blueprints, adapting themselves to existing ways of doing business (Hill & Bonan, 1991; Smith, 1993). Over time, changes will become modified to fit what is rather than what was, or might be, envisioned. Third, by focusing on organization and governance—the structural dimension of school improvement shown in Figure 7.1—SBM will fail to redefine the deeper cultural dimensions of education. In so doing, it will leave open the possibility, some would say the likelihood (Brown, 1992), that the system will recentralize (M. Hanson, 1991; Hill & Bonan, 1991, S. B. Lawton, 1991)—most damagingly, that there will be "regression toward the classroom," or teachers increasingly gravitating back toward their classroom kingdoms (Collins & Hanson, 1991; Smith, 1993; Taylor & Bogotch, 1992; Weiss, 1993).

It is not our intention here to suggest that stakeholders in the educational community should abandon efforts at shared decision making at the school level. At the same time, it is clear to us that unless SBM is refocused, it will never approximate the expectations of its advocates. Specifically, we maintain that SBM must be shifted from Quadrant 1 to Quadrant 4 of our model in Figure 7.1. This will entail two fundamental changes. First, politics will need to be directed to the task of creating an educational community. Second, organization and management will need to be formed in response to the needs of the learning environment, rather than vice versa.

Four conditions appear critical for the refocusing of SBM to occur. To begin with, support on a broad array of fronts is necessary—time, money, technical assistance, professional development, and so forth. Second, shared decision making must become at its core a strategy for improving the education of children and youth. Currently, in terms of substance, SBM is fairly empty. To redirect SBM, shared decision-making processes will need to wrap around powerful conceptions of learning and teaching. Third, SBM must begin the transformation from a set of organizational operations to an environmental fabric that nurtures the deep involvement of teachers and parents in the life of the school community. Finally, strong yet facilitative leadership is needed to reorient shared decision making from the organizational-governance axis to an educational-community one.

Notes

1. We acknowledge that the perception of failure can at least to some extent be attributed to the use of the linear, structural framework employed in this volume (see Figure 1.2) and the corresponding rational evaluation strategy (Murphy, 1989b). Adding symbolic criteria to the assessment may reveal that SBM has had a larger impact than we claim. However, again, at least on the issue of legitimization as a nonrational outcome (March & Olson, 1983; Ogawa, 1992), SBM does not appear to be very successful.

2. Originally it was argued that a key problem was "the relative newness of the change effort" (Fusarelli & Scribner, 1993, p. 12; Taylor & Bogotch, 1992)—what Wohlstetter and Buffett (1991) refer to as the "learning curve" (p. 4) phenomenon. Reformers suggested that with time implementation efforts would become more focused and more robust. The preponderance of evidence does not support this hypothesis. If anything, there appears to be a slight tendency for these efforts to deteriorate over time (Carnoy & MacDonell, 1990; Collins & Hanson, 1991; Duttweiler & Mutchler, 1990; Jenni, 1990; Rothstein, 1990; Weiss & Cambone, 1993).

3. Elsewhere (Murphy, 1991), we have argued that by legitimizing the status quo, reliance on waivers inhibits change efforts.

4. On the other hand, Candoli (1991) suggests that, "although historically, central office administrators have resisted attempts to decentralize authority, many have

been attracted by the opportunity to be further insulated from the field as a result of the decentralization and have changed their minds about the realities and difficulties of decentralization because it provides still another scapegoat to blunt the thrust of community groups who are asking penetrating and difficult questions" (p. 33).

5. Whether the monitoring and influencing of teachers by teachers is more acceptable than similar work by school administrators is an open question. What is not in doubt is the fact that "the boundaries between individual teacher's autonomy and collective decisionmaking can lead to time consuming and painful conflicts" (Hill & Bonan, 1991, p. 21).

6. In at least one important study, "loss of autonomy" was not perceived by teachers to be an "important reason for avoiding shared decision making" (Duke et al., 1980, p. 100).

7. Sizer (1984) does a particularly nice job of revealing how isolation is a perversion of real professionalism.

8. Fusarelli and Scribner (1993) contend that "restructuring based upon the premise of democracy is preferable to arguments based upon the premise of teacher professionalism" (p. 6). It is, however, important to note that there is little empirical support for this claim in terms of the outcomes examined in Chapter 6.

9. In addition, there are real opportunity costs in terms of time devoted to personal and family matters (David, 1993; Riley, 1984).

10. Although Guthrie (1986) has argued conceptually that "school-based management strategies appropriately tailored to the circumstances of each state and local school district, hold the potential for resolving the tensions that currently exist between state-level policy makers and local school personnel" (p. 306), in most places the conflict has not been dealt with constructively. Actually, states have often exacerbated the tension by developing contradictory sets of educational policies.

11. It is important to remember that some of these constraints are by-products of the way that schools have been run for the past century. Even when given additional degrees of freedom, local school personnel are often unable to envision new ways of conducting business (Hallinger et al., 1992; Murphy et al., 1991) and/or are "reluctant to question established instructional 'techniques' " (Duttweiler & Mutchler, 1990, p. 38). The work of Malen and Ogawa (1988) on how deeply ingrained norms operate to constrain participatory governance at the site level is particularly instructive.

12. Given the model employed in this volume, our concern is primarily with student performance and its antecedents. For a fuller account of the shortcomings of SBM in promoting community, see Fusarelli and Scribner (1993) and Smyth (1993a).

13. Note again that there is only a marginal empowerment of students in the political processes at the heart of SBM.

14. Perhaps no aspect of the governance issue is more difficult to reconcile than the vigorous attacks on the viability of local school boards on the one hand and the mushrooming belief that replicating the board model at the individual school level (via local governing councils) represents a decided improvement to the educational system.

References

Alexander, G. C. (1992, April). *The transformation of an urban principal: Uncertain times, uncertain roles.* Paper presented at the annual meeting of the American Educational Research Association, San Francisco.

Alutto, J. A., & Belasco, J. A. (1972, March). A typology for participation in organizational decision making. *Administrative Science Quarterly, 17,* 117-125.

Anderson, G. L., & Dixon, A. (1993). Paradigm shifts and site-based management in the United States: Toward a paradigm of social empowerment. In J. Smyth (Ed.), *A socially critical view of the self-managing school* (pp. 49-61). London: Taylor & Francis.

Armstrong, J. (1990, March). A road map for restructuring schools. *Education Week, 9*(27), 24.

Association for Supervision and Curriculum Development. (1986, September). *School reform policy: A call for reason.* Alexandria, VA: Author.

Astuto, T. A. (1990, September). *Reinventing school leadership* [Working memo prepared for the Reinventing School Leadership Conference]. Cambridge, MA: National Center for Educational Leadership.

Bachus, G. S. (1991, October). *The shifting format of administration in small schools: Participatory school decision making.* Paper presented at the annual conference of the National Rural Education Association, Jackson, MS.

Banathy, B. H. (1988). An outside-in approach to design inquiry in education. In Far West Laboratory for Educational Research and Development (Ed.), *The redesign of education: A collection of papers concerned with comprehensive educational reform* (Vol. 1, pp. 51-71). San Francisco: Far West Laboratory.

Barber, B. R. (1994). *An aristocracy of everyone.* New York: Oxford University Press.

Bartell, T., & Noble, J. (1986, April). *Changes in course selection by high school students: The impact of national educational reform.* Paper presented at the annual meeting of the American Educational Research Association, San Francisco.

Barth, R. S. (1986). On sheep and goats and school reform. *Phi Delta Kappan, 68*(4), 293-296.

Barth, R. S. (1991, October). Restructuring schools: Some questions for teachers and principals. *Phi Delta Kappan, 73*(2), 123-128.

Beare, H. (1989, September). *Educational administration in the 1990s.* Paper presented at the national conference of the Australian Council for Educational Administration, Armidale, New South Wales, Australia.

Beck, L., & Murphy, J. (1993). *Understanding the principalship: Metaphorical themes, 1920 to 1990s.* New York: Teachers College Press.

Beck, L. G., & Murphy, J. (in press). *Reinventing school-based management for school improvement.* Thousand Oaks, CA: Corwin.

Bellah, R. N., Madsen, R., Sullivan, W. M., Swidler, A., & Tipton, S. M. (1991). *The good society.* New York: Vintage Books.

Bennett, A. L., Bryk, A. S., Easton, J. Y., Kerbow, D., Luppescu, S., & Sebring, P. A. (1992, December). *Charting reform: The principals' perspective.* Chicago: Consortium on Chicago School Research.

Bernas, T. G. (1992, April). *Documenting the implementation of school based management/shared decision making in a non-Chapter 1 elementary school.* Paper presented at the annual meeting of the American Educational Research Association, San Francisco.

Bimber, B. (1993). *School decentralization: Lessons from the study of bureaucracy.* Santa Monica, CA: Rand.

Blanton, A. W. (1920, April). Democracy in school administration. *High School Quarterly, 8,* 155-159.

Blumberg, A. (1985). *The school superintendent: Living with conflict.* New York: Teachers College Press.

Bolin, F. S. (1989, Fall). Empowering leadership. *Teachers College Record, 19*(1), 81-96.

Bortner, D. M. (1966, February). Educational policy is public policy. *American School Board Journal, 152*(2), 62.

Boyd, W. L. (1987, Summer). Public education's last hurrah? Schizophrenia, amnesia, and ignorance in school politics. *Educational Evaluation and Policy Analysis, 9*(2), 85-100.

Boyd, W. L., & Hartman, W. T. (1987). The politics of educational productivity. In D. Monk & J. Underwood (Eds.), *Distributing educational resources within nations, states, school districts, and schools* (pp. 271-308). Cambridge, MA: Ballinger.

Boyd, W. L., & O'Shea, D. W. (1975, August). Theoretical perspectives on school district decentralization. *Education and Urban Society, 7*(4), 464-479.

Bradley, A. (1989). North Carolina schools draft reform plan to gain flexibility. *Education Week, 9*(14), 16.

Bradley, A. (1992, October). Crusaders in Detroit fight to keep board seats. *Education Week, 12*(7), 1, 10.

Bradley, A. (1993). Shortcomings of decentralized decisionmaking in NYC detailed. *Education Week, 13*(6), 14.

Bransford, J. D. (1991). *Reflections on a decade of research on thinking.* Paper presented at the Conference on Cognition and School Leadership, Vanderbilt University, National Center for Educational Leadership, Nashville, TN.

Bredeson, P. V. (1992, April). *Responses to restructuring and empowerment initiatives: A study of teachers' and principals' perceptions of organizational leadership, decisionmaking and climate.* Paper presented at the annual meeting of the American Educational Research Association, San Francisco.

Brookover, W., Beamer, L., Efthim, H., Hathaway, D., Lezotte, L., Miller, S., Passalacqua, J., & Tornatzhy, L. (1982). *Creating effective schools: An in-service program for enhancing school learning climate and achievement.* Holmes Beach, FL: Learning Publications.

Brookover, W. B., Schweitzer, J. H., Schneider, J. M., Beady, C. H., Flood, P. K., & Wisenbaker, J. M. (1978, Spring). Elementary school social climate and school achievement. *American Educational Research Journal, 15*(2), 301-318.

Brown, D. J. (1990). *Decentralization and school-based management.* London: Falmer.

Brown, D. J. (1991). *Decentralization: The administrator's guidebook to school district change.* Newbury Park, CA: Corwin.

Brown, D. J. (1992, September). The recentralization of school districts. *Educational Policy, 6*(3), 289-297.

Bryk, A. S. (1993, July). *A view from the elementary schools: The state of reform in Chicago.* Chicago: Consortium on Chicago School Research.

Burke, C. (1992). Devolution of responsibility to Queensland schools: Clarifying the rhetoric critiquing the reality. *Journal of Educational Administration, 30*(4), 33-52.

Caldwell, B. (1990). School-based decision-making and management: International developments. In J. Chapman (Ed.), *School-based decision-making and management* (pp. 3-26). London: Falmer.

Callahan, R. E. (1962). *Education and the cult of efficiency: A study of the social forces that have shaped the administration of the public schools.* Chicago: University of Chicago Press.

Callahan, R. E. (1967). *An introduction to education in American society: A text with readings.* New York: Knopf.

Campbell, R. F., Fleming, T., Newell, L., & Bennion, J. W. (1987). *A history of thought and practice in educational administration.* New York: Teachers College Press.

Campbell, R. F., & Newell, L. J. (1985). History of administration. In T. Husen & T. N. Postlethwaite (Eds.), *The international encyclopedia of education: Research and studies* (Vol. 1: A-B; pp. 51-59). Elmsford, NY: Pergamon.

Candoli, I. C. (1991). *School system administration: A strategic plan for site-based management.* Lancaster, PA: Technomic.

Carlson, R. (1989). *Restructuring schools* [Internal memorandum]. Washington, DC: Public Schools.

Carnegie Council on Adolescent Development. (1989). *Turning points.* Washington, DC: Author.

Carnegie Forum on Education and the Economy. (1986, May). *A nation prepared: Teachers for the 21st century.* Washington, DC: Author.

Carnoy, M., & MacDonnell, J. (1990). School district restructuring in Santa Fe, New Mexico. *Educational Policy, 4*(1), 49-64.

Carr, W. G. (1942). Efficiency through democratic administration. *Journal of the National Education Association, 31*(3), 83-84.

Chapman, J. (1990). School-based decision-making and management: Implications for school personnel. In C. Chapman (Ed.),

School-based decision-making and management (pp. 221-244). London: Falmer.

Chapman, J., & Boyd, W. L. (1986, Fall). Decentralization, devolution, and the school principal: Australian lessons on statewide educational reform. *Educational Administration Quarterly, 22*(4), 28-58.

Chubb, J. E. (1988, Winter). Why the current wave of school reform will fail. *Public Interest,* (90), 28-49.

Clark, D. L. (1990, September). *Reinventing school leadership* [Working memo prepared for the Reinventing School Leadership Conference]. Cambridge, MA: National Center for Educational Leadership.

Clark, D. L., Lotto, L. S., & Astuto, T. A. (1984, Summer). Effective schools and school improvement: A comparative analysis of two lines of inquiry. *Educational Administration Quarterly, 20*(3), 41-68.

Clark, D. L., & Meloy, J. M. (1989). Renouncing bureaucracy: A democratic structure for leadership in schools. In T. J. Sergiovanni & J. A. Moore (Eds.), *Schooling for tomorrow: Directing reform to issues that count* (pp. 272-294). Boston: Allyn & Bacon.

Clark, K. B. (1970). Introduction. In M. Fantini, M. Gittell, & R. Magat, *Community control and the urban school* (pp. ix-xi). New York: Praeger.

Clear, D. K. (1990, October). *Changes in roles and responsibilities of central office supervisors: Organizational and functional outcomes.* Paper presented at the annual convention of the University Council for Educational Administration, Pittsburgh, PA.

Clinchy, E. (1989, December). Public school choice: Absolutely necessary but not wholly sufficient. *Phi Delta Kappan, 70*(4), 289-294.

Clune, W. H., & White, P. A. (1988, September). *School-based management: Institutional variation, implementation, and issues for further research.* New Brunswick, NJ: Rutgers University, Eagleton Institute of Politics, Center for Policy Research in Education.

Cohen, D. K. (1988, September). *Teaching practice: Plus ça change . . .* (Issue Paper 88-3). East Lansing: Michigan State University, National Center for Research on Teacher Education.

Cohen, D. K. (1989, May). *Can decentralization or choice improve public education?* Paper presented at the Conference on Choice and Control in American Education. Madison: University of Wisconsin-Madison.

Cohen, D. L. (1991). Inordinate share of poverty said to rest on children. *Education Week, 11*(6), 4.

Cohen, D. L. (1992a). Children without "traditional family" support seen posing complex challenge for schools. *Education Week, 12*(8), 5.

Cohen, D. L. (1992b). Nation found losing ground on measures of child well-being. *Education Week, 12*(28), 14.

Cohen D. L. (1993). Half of Black, Hispanic children may be poor by 2010. *Education Week, 8*(9), 11.

Cohen, D. L. (1994). "Distressed" communities jeopardize children's well-being, report says. *Education Week, 13*(31), 5.

Cohen, M. D., March, J. G., & Olsen, J. P. (1972, March). A garbage can model of organizational choice. *Administrative Science Quarterly, 17*(1), 1-26.

Collins, O. T. (1994). *Emerging central office roles in a decentralizing school district.* Unpublished doctoral dissertation, Vanderbilt University, Nashville, TN.

Collins, R. A., & Hanson, M. K. (1991, January). *School-based management/shared decision-making project 1987-88 through 1989-90: Summative evaluation report.* Miami, FL: Dade County Public Schools, Office of Educational Accountability.

Combs, A. W. (1988, February). New assumptions for educational reform. *Educational Leadership, 45*(5), 38-40.

Conley, D. (1993). *Roadmap to restructuring.* Eugene: University of Oregon, ERIC Clearinghouse on Education Management.

Conley, D. T. (1991, March). Lessons from laboratories in school restructuring and site-based decision making. *Oregon School Study Council Bulletin, 34*(7), 1-61.

Conley, S. C. (1989, March). *Who's on first? School reform, teacher participation, and the decision-making process.* Paper presented at the annual meeting of the American Educational Research Association, San Francisco.

Conley, S. C., & Bacharach, S. B. (1990, March). From school-based management to participatory school-site management. *Phi Delta Kappan, 71*(7), 539-544.

Conway, J. A. (1976, March). Test of linearity between teachers' participation in decision making and their perceptions of their schools as organizations. *Administrative Science Quarterly, 21,* 130-139.

Conway, J. A. (1984, Summer). The myth, mystery, and mastery of participative decision making in education. *Educational Administration Quarterly, 20*(3), 11-40.

Conway, J. A., & Jacobson, S. L. (1990). An epilogue: Where is educational leadership going? In S. L. Jacobson & J. A. Conway (Eds.), *Educational leadership in an age of reform* (pp. 181-195). New York: Longman.

Cook, F. A. (1939). Democracy as an agency of social control. In W. C. Reavis (Ed.), *Democratic practices in school administration: Proceedings of the eighth annual conference for administrative officers of public and private schools: 1939* (pp. 3-15). Chicago: University of Chicago Press.

Counts, G. S. (1969). *The social composition of boards of education.* New York: Arno & *New York Times.* (Original work published in 1927)

Counts, G. S. (1978). *Dare the schools build a new social order?* Carbondale and Edwardsville: Southern Illinois University Press. (Original work published 1932)

Cremin, L. A. (1977). *Traditions of American education.* New York: Basic Books.

Cremin, L. A. (1988). *American education: The metropolitan experience: 1876-1980.* New York: Harper & Row.

Cronin, J. M. (1973). *The control of urban schools: Perspective on the power of educational reformers.* New York: Free Press.

Crosby, S. (1991, December). *Teachers' opinions of school-based management.* (ERIC Document Reproduction Service No. ED 343 241 EA 023 785)

Cuban, L. (1984, November). School reform by remote control: SB813 in California. *Phi Delta Kappan, 66*(3), 213-215.

Cuban, L. (1989). The "at-risk" label and the problem of urban school reform. *Phi Delta Kappan, 70*(10), 780-784, 799.

Cuban, L. (1990, January). Reforming again, again, and again. *Educational Researcher, 19*(1), 3-13.

Cuban, L. (1992, October). The corporate myth of reforming public schools. *Phi Delta Kappan, 74*(2), 157-159.

Cuban, L. (1994). The great school scam. *Education Week, 13*(38), 44.

Dade County Public Schools. (1989). *Renaissance in education.* Miami, FL: Author.

Daresh, J. C. (1992). Impressions of school-based management: The Cincinnati story. In J. J. Lane & E. G. Epps (Eds.), *Restruc-*

turing the schools: Problems and prospects (pp. 109-121). Berkeley, CA: McCutchan.

David, J. L. (1989, May). Synthesis of research on school-based management. *Educational Leadership, 46*(8), 45-53.

David, J. L. (1993, August). *School-based decision making: Progress and promise* (Report prepared for the Prichard Committee [KY] for Academic Excellence).

David, J. L., Cohen, M., Honetschlager, D., & Traiman, S. (1990). *State actions to restructure schools: First steps.* Washington, DC: National Governors' Association.

Davidson, B. M. (1992, April). *Transforming schools: Foundations for school restructuring focusing on the role of the teacher in four elementary schools.* Paper presented at the annual meeting of the Association for Supervision and Curriculum Development, New Orleans, LA.

Dellar, G. B. (1992, April). *Connections between macro and micro implementation of educational policy: A study of school restructuring in Western Australia.* Paper presented at the annual meeting of the American Educational Research Association, San Francisco.

Designs for Change. (1991, February). *Chicago School Reform, 1*, 1-5.

Dewey, J. (1903, December). Democracy in education. *Elementary School Teacher, 4*(4), 193-204.

Dewey, J. (1929, April 24). The house divided against itself. *New Republic, 58*, 271.

Diegmueller, K. (1991, February). Backed by N.E.A., Memphis schools serve as "laboratories" for reforms. *Education Week, 10*(20), 1, 12-13.

Diegmueller, K. (1994). Inequities lead to dual system in N.Y., panel finds. *Education Week, 13*(16), 14.

Downs, A. (1967). *Inside bureaucracy.* Boston: Little, Brown.

Dreyfuss, G. O., Cistone, P. J., & Divita, C. (1992). Restructuring in a large district: Dade County, Florida. In C. Glickman (Ed.), *Supervision in transition* (pp. 77-96). Alexandria, VA: Association for Supervision and Curriculum Development.

Drost, W. H. (1971). Educational administration: History. In L. C. Deighton (Ed.), *The encyclopedia of education* (Vol. 1, pp. 68-77). New York: Macmillan & Free Press.

Duke, D. L., Showers, B. K., & Imber, M. (1980, Winter). Teachers and shared decision making: The costs and benefits of involvement. *Educational Administration Quarterly, 16*(1), 93-106.

Duttweiler, P. C. (1990, July). Recommendations for implementing school-based management/shared decision making. *Insights on Educational Policy and Practice*, (21), 1-4.

Duttweiler, P. C., & Mutchler, S. E. (1990). *Organizing the educational system for excellence: Harnessing the energy of people.* Austin, TX: Southwest Educational Development Laboratory.

Earley, P., Baker, L., & Weindling, D. (1990). *"Keeping the raft afloat": Secondary headship five years on.* National Foundation for Educational Research in England and Wales.

Eaton, W. E. (1990). *Shaping the superintendency: A reexamination of Callahan and the cult of efficiency.* New York: Teachers College Press, Columbia University.

Education Commission of the States. (1983). *Action for excellence.* Denver: Author.

Education Week. (1991). Drinking among teenagers widespread, C.D.C. says. *Education Week, 11*(6), 12.

Education Week. (1992a). Community-foundation official touts new coalition on children. *Education Week, 11*(19), 6-7.

Education Week. (1992b). Dimensions: Social well-being. *Education Week, 12*(7), 3.

Education Week. (1992c). Study charts decline in children's economic, social welfare. *Education Week, 11*(17), 11.

Education Week. (1993). Dimensions: Children in poverty. *Education Week, 13*(4), 3.

Educational Policies Commission. (1955). *Public education and the future of America.* Washington, DC: National Education Association of the United States and the American Association of School Administrators.

Educational Testing Service. (1994). NAEP writing report card released. *Access, 4*(39), 1.

Elmore, R. F. (1988a). Choice in public education. In W. L. Boyd & C. T. Kerchner (Eds.), *The politics of excellence and choice in education* (pp. 79-98). New York: Falmer.

Elmore, R. F. (1988b). *Early experience in restructuring schools: Voices from the field.* Washington, DC: National Governors' Association.

Elmore, R. F. (1989, March). *Models of restructured schools.* Paper presented at the annual meeting of the American Educational Research Association, San Francisco.

Elmore, R. (1990). Introduction: On changing the structure of public schools. In R. Elmore & Associates (Eds.), *Restructuring* schools: *The next generation of educational reforms* (pp. 1-29). San Francisco: Jossey-Bass.

Elmore, R. F. (1991, April). *Teaching, learning and organization: School restructuring and the recurring dilemmas of reform.* Paper presented at the annual meeting of the American Educational Research Association, Chicago.

Elmore, R. F. (1993). School decentralization: Who gains? Who loses? In J. Hannaway & M. Carnoy (Eds.), *Decentralization and school improvement* (pp. 33-54). San Francisco: Jossey-Bass.

Engelhardt, N. L. (1939). The practice of democracy in educational administration. *Phi Delta Kappan, 21,* 412-413.

Epps, E. G. (1992). School-based management: Implications for minority parents. In J. J. Lande & E. G. Epps (Eds.), *Restructuring the schools: Problems and prospects* (pp. 143-163). Berkeley, CA: McCutchan.

Etheridge, C. P., Hall, M. L., & Brown, N. (1990). *Leadership, control, communication and comprehension: Key factors in successful implementation of SBDM.* Paper presented at the annual meeting of the Mid-South Educational Research Association, New Orleans, LA.

Etheridge, C. P., Valesky, T. C., Horgan, D. D., Nunnery, J., & Smith, D. (1992, April). *School based decision making: An investigation into effective and ineffective decision making processes and the impact on school climate variables.* Paper presented at the annual meeting of the American Educational Research Association, San Francisco.

Evertson, C., & Murphy, J. (1992). Beginning with classrooms: Implications for restructuring schools. In H. H. Marshall (Ed.), *Redefining student learning* (pp. 293-320). Norwood, NJ: Ablex.

Fayol, F. (1992). Principles of management. In J. M. Shafritz & J. S. Ott (Eds.), *Classics of organization theory* (3rd ed., pp. 56-68). Pacific Grove, CA: Brooks/Cole. (Original work published in 1916)

Fernandez, J. A. (1989, May). *Dade County Public Schools' blueprint for restructured schools.* Paper presented at the conference on choice and control in American education, University of Wisconsin-Madison.

Finn, C. E. (1991). *We must take charge: Our schools and our future.* New York: Free Press.

Finn, C. E., & Clements, S. K. (1989, July). *Reconnoitering Chicago's school reform efforts: Some early impressions* (A report to the Joyce Foundation). Washington, DC: Educational Excellence Network.

Flax, E. (1989a). South Carolina board adopts regulatory relief for top-scoring schools. *Education Week, 9*(12), 1, 16.

Flax, E. (1989b). South Carolina considering "flexibility" for high-scoring schools. *Education Week, 8*(21), 1, 14.

Flax, E. (1991). Teenage-drinking study spurs questions on efficacy of drug-prevention efforts. *Education Week, 10*(39), 13.

Follett, M. P. (1992). The giving of orders. In J. M. Shafritz & J. S. Ott (Eds.), *Classics of organization theory* (3rd ed., pp. 150-158). Pacific Grove, CA: Brooks/Cole. (Original work published in 1926)

Ford, D. J. (1991, March). *The school principal and Chicago school reform: Principals' early perceptions of reform initiatives.* Chicago: Chicago Panel on Public School Policy and Finance. (ERIC Document Reproduction Service No. ED 330 109)

Ford, D. J. (1992, April). *Chicago principals under school based management: New roles and realities of the job.* Paper presented at the annual meeting of the American Educational Research Association, San Francisco.

Foster, W. (1988). Educational administration: A critical appraisal. In D. E. Griffiths, R. T. Stout, & R. B. Forsyth (Eds.), *Leaders for America's schools* (pp. 68-81). Berkeley, CA: McCutchan.

Frymier, J. (1987). Bureaucracy and the neutering of teachers. *Phi Delta Kappan, 69*(1), 9-14.

Fullan, M. (1991). *The new meaning of educational change.* New York: Teachers College Press.

Fuller, W. E. (1982). *The old country school: The story of rural education in the Middle West.* Chicago: University of Chicago Press.

Fusarelli, L. D., & Scribner, J. D. (1993, October). *Site-based management and critical democratic pluralism: An analysis of promises, problems, and possibilities.* Paper presented at the annual conference of the University Council for Educational Administration, Houston, TX.

Garms, W. I., Guthrie, J. W., & Pierce, L. C. (1978). *School finance: The economics and politics of public education.* Englewood Cliffs, NJ: Prentice Hall.

Gerstner, L. V. (1994). *Reinventing education: Entrepreneurship in America's public schools.* New York: Dutton.

Gips, C. J., & Wilkes, M. (1993, April). *Teacher concerns as they consider an organizational change to site-based decision making.* Paper presented at the annual meeting of the American Educational Research Association, Atlanta, GA.

Glickman, C. D. (1990, September). Pushing school reform to a new edge: The seven ironies of school empowerment. *Phi Delta Kappan, 71*(1), 68-75.

Goldman, P., Dunlap, D. M., & Conley, D. T. (1991, April). *Administrative facilitation and site-based school reform projects.* Paper presented at the annual meeting of the American Educational Research Association, Chicago.

Goldring, E. B. (1992). System-wide diversity in Israel: Principals as transformational and environmental leaders. *Journal of Educational Administration, 30*(3), 49-62.

Goodlad, J. I. (1984). *A place called school: Prospects for the future.* New York: McGraw-Hill.

Griffin, G. A. (in press). Matters of consequence: School restructuring and classroom activity. *Elementary School Journal.*

Grossman, P., Kirst, M. W., Negash, W., & Schmidt-Posnere, J. (1985, July). *Curricular change in California comprehensive high schools 1982-83 to 1984-85.* Stanford, CA: Policy Analysis for California Education.

Gursky, D. (1992). Cincinnati cuts more than half of central office. *Education Week, 11*(35), 1, 13.

Guskey, T. R. (1986, May). Staff development and the process of teacher change. *Educational Researcher, 15*(5), 5-12.

Guthrie, J. W. (1986, December). School-based management: The next needed education reform. *Phi Delta Kappan, 68*(4), 305-309.

Hallinger, P., Murphy, J., & Hausman, C. (1992, August). Restructuring schools: Principals' perceptions of fundamental educational reform. *Educational Administration Quarterly, 28*(3), 330-349.

Hannaway, J. (1992, March). *Decentralization in education: Technical demands as a critical ingredient.* (ERIC Document Reproduction Service No. ED 345 362)

Hanson, E. M. (1991). *School-based management and educational reform: Cases in the USA and Spain.* (ERIC Document Reproduction Service No. ED 336 832)

Hanson, M. (1991, April). *Alteration of influence relations in school-based management innovations.* Paper presented at the annual meeting of the American Educational Research Association, Chicago.

Harp, L. (1993a). Engler's choice plan includes student grants. *Education Week, 13*(6), 1, 18.

Harp, L. (1993b). Widely mixed test results leave some in Kentucky puzzled. *Education Week, 13*(6), 15.

Harrison, C. R., Killion, J. P., & Mitchell, J. E. (1989, May). Site-based management: The realities of implementation. *Educational Leadership, 46*(8), 55-58.

Harvey, G., & Crandall, D. P. (1988). A beginning look at the what and how of restructuring. In C. Jenks (Ed.), *The redesign of education: A collection of papers concerned with comprehensive educational reform* (pp. 1-37). San Francisco: Far West Laboratory.

Heller, R. W., Woodworth, B. E., Jacobson, S. L., & Conway, J. A. (1989, November). You like school-based power, but you wonder if others do. *Executive Educator, 11*(11), 15-18.

Hess, G. A. (1991). *Restructuring schools: Chicago style.* Newbury Park, CA: Corwin.

Hess, G. A. (1992, February). *School restructuring, Chicago style: A midway report.* Chicago: Chicago Panel on Public School Policy and Finance.

Hess, G. A., & Easton, J. O. (1991, April). *Who's making what decisions: Monitoring authority shifts in Chicago school reform.* Paper presented at the annual meeting of the American Educational Research Association, Chicago.

High, R. M., Achilles, C. M., & High, K. (1989, March). *Involvement in what? Teacher actual and preferred involvement in selected school activities.* (ERIC Document Reproduction Service No. ED 336 856)

Hill, P. T., & Bonan, J. (1991). *Decentralization and accountability in public education.* Santa Monica, CA: Rand.

Hirsh, S., & Sparks, D. (1991, September). A look at the new central-office administrators. *School Administrator, 48*(7), 16-17, 19.

Holmes Group. (1986, April). *Tomorrow's teachers.* East Lansing, MI: Author.

Houston, H. M. (1989, March). *Professional development for restructuring: Analyses and recommendations.* Paper presented at the annual meeting of the American Educational Research Association, San Francisco.

Howe, H. II. (1966, December). A nation of amateurs in education. *School and Society, 94*(2283), 448-451.

Hoy, W. K., & Ferguson, J. (1985, Spring). A theoretical framework and exploration of organizational effectiveness of schools. *Educational Administration Quarterly, 21*(2), 117-134.

Hutchins, C. L. (1988). Redesigning education. In Far West Laboratory for Educational Research and Development, *The redesign of education: A collection of papers concerned with comprehensive educational reform* (Vol. 1, pp. 73-78). San Francisco: Far West Laboratory.

Imber, M. (1983, April). Increased decision making involvement for teachers. Ethical and practical implications. *Journal of Educational Thought, 17*(1), 36-42.

Imber, M., & Duke, D. L. (1984, Winter). Teacher participation in school decision making: A framework for research. *Journal of Educational Administration, 22*(1), 24-34.

Jacobson, S. L., & Woodworth, B. (1991, October). *Comparing administrators' perceptions of SBM.* Paper presented at the annual meeting of the University Council for Educational Administration, Baltimore, MD.

Jenni, R. W. (1990, April). *Application of the school based management process development general model.* Paper presented at the annual meeting of the American Educational Research Association, Boston.

Jenni, R. W., & Mauriel, J. J. (1990, April). *An examination of the factors affecting stakeholders' assessment of school decentralization.* Paper presented at the annual meeting of the American Educational Research Association, Boston.

Jewell, K. E., & Rosen, J. L. (1993, April). *School-based management/shared decision-making: A study of school reform in New York City.* Paper presented at the annual meeting of the American Educational Research Association, Atlanta, GA.

Jezer, M. (1982). *The dark ages: Life in the United States 1945-1960.* Boston: South End.

Johnson, M. M. (1993). *Restructuring schools: New roles and responsibilities of principals.* Unpublished doctoral dissertation, Vanderbilt University, Nashville, TN.

Johnson, P. (1991). *Modern times: The world from the twenties to the nineties* (rev. ed). New York: HarperCollins. (Original work published 1983)

Kandel, I. L. (1939). The practice of democracy in educational administration. *Phi Delta Kappan, 21*, 412-413.

Kearnes, D. L. (1988a). A business perspective on American schooling. *Education Week, 7*(30), 34, 32.

Kearnes, D. L. (1988b, April). An education recovery plan for America. *Phi Delta Kappan, 69*(8), 565-570.

Kerr, C. (1991, February 27). Is education really all that guilty? *Education Week, 10*(23), 30.

King, J. A., & Ericson, C. J. (1992). School renewal in Chaska, Minnesota, Independent District #112. In C. Glickman (Ed.), *Supervision in transition* (pp. 113-125). Alexandria, VA: Association for Supervision and Curriculum Development.

Kingdon, J. W. (1984). *Agendas, alternatives, and public policies.* New York: HarperCollins.

Kirst, M. W., McLaughlin, M., & Massell, D. (1989). *Rethinking children's policy: Implications for educational administration.* Stanford University, College of Education, Center for Educational Research at Stanford, Stanford, CA.

Koopman, G. R., Miel, A., & Misner, P. J. (1943). *Democracy in school administration.* New York: Appleton-Century.

Krug, E. A. (1966). *Salient dates in American education: 1635-1964.* New York: Harper & Row.

Krug, E. A. (1972). *The shaping of the American high school: Vol. 2. 1920-1941.* Madison: University of Wisconsin Press.

La Noue, G. R., & Smith, B. L. R. (1973). *The politics of school decentralization.* Lexington, MA: Lexington.

Lawton, M. (1991). Teenage males said more apt to die from gunshots than natural causes. *Education Week, 10*(26), 4.

Lawton, S. B. (1991, September). *Why restructure?* Revision of paper presented at the annual meeting of the American Educational Research Association, Chicago.

Levine, D. U., & Eubanks, E. E. (1992). Site-based management: Engine for reform or pipedream? Problems, prospects, pitfalls, and prerequisites for success. In J. J. Lane and E. G. Epps (Eds.), *Restructuring the schools: Problems and prospects* (pp. 61-82). Berkeley, CA: McCutchan.

Lewis, D. A. (1993). Deinstitutionalization and school decentralization: Making the same mistake twice. In J. Hannaway & M. Carnoy (Eds.), *Decentralization and school improvement* (pp. 84-101). San Francisco: Jossey-Bass.

Liebow, E. (1967). *Tally's corner: A study of Negro street corner men.* Boston: Little, Brown.

Lindelow, J. (1981). School-based management. In S. C. Smith, J. A. Mazzarella, & P. K. Piele (Eds.), *School leadership: Handbook for survival* (pp. 94-129). Eugene: University of Oregon, ERIC Clearing House on Educational Management.

Lindquist, K. M., & Mauriel, J. J. (1989, August). School-based management: Doomed to failure? *Education and Urban Society, 21*(4), 403-416.

Lortie, D. C. (1975). *Schoolteacher.* Chicago: University of Chicago Press.

Louis, K. S., & Miles, M. B. (1990). *Improving the urban high school.* New York: Teachers College Press.

Louis, K. S., & Murphy, J. (1994). The evolving role of the principal: Some concluding thoughts. In J. Murphy & K. S. Louis (Eds.), *Reshaping the principalship: Insights from transformational reform efforts* (pp. 265-281). Thousand Oaks, CA: Corwin.

Maccoby, M. (1989, December). *Looking for leadership now.* Paper presented at the National Center for Educational Leadership conference, Harvard University, Cambridge, MA.

Malen, B., & Ogawa, R. T. (1988, Winter). Professional-patron influence on site-based governance councils: A confounding case study. *Educational Evaluation and Policy Analysis, 10*(4), 251-270.

Malen, B., Ogawa, R. T., & Kranz, J. (1989, May). *What do we know about school based management? A case study of the literature—a call for research.* Paper presented at the conference on choice and control in American education, University of Wisconsin-Madison.

March, J. G., & Olson, J. P. (1983, June). What administrative reorganization tells us about governing. *American Political Science Review, 77*(2), 281-296.

Marsh, D. O. (1992, November). *Change in schools.* (ERIC Document Reproduction Service No. ED 353-673)

Marshall, H. H. (Ed.). (1992). *Supporting student learning: Roots of educational change.* Norwood, NJ: Ablex.

McCarthey, S. J., & Peterson, P. L. (1989, March). *Teacher roles: Weaving new patterns in classroom practice and school organization.* Paper presented at the annual meeting of the American Educational Research Association, San Francisco.

McConnell, R., & Jeffries, R. (1991). *Monitoring today's schools: The first year.* Hamilton, New Zealand: University of Waikato.

McNeil, L. M. (1988, January). Contradictions of control: 1. Administrators and teachers. *Phi Delta Kappan, 69*(5), 333-339.

McPherson, R. B., & Crowson, R. L. (1992, November). *Creating schools that "work" under Chicago reform: The adaptations of building principals.* Paper presented at the annual meeting of the University Council for Educational Administration, Minneapolis, MN.

Meyer, J. W., & Rowan, B. (1975). *Notes on the structure of educational organizations: Revised version.* Paper presented at the annual meeting of the American Sociological Association, San Francisco.

Miles, M. B. (1969). Planned change and organizational health: Figure and ground. In F. D. Carter & T. J. Sergiovanni (Eds.), *Organizations and human behavior: Focus on schools* (pp. 375-391). New York: McGraw-Hill.

Miller, W. I. (1942). *Democracy in educational administration: An analysis of principles and practices.* New York: Columbia University, Teachers College, Bureau of Publications.

Mills, G. E. (1992, April). *Participative decision making in public schools: Site-level description and cross-site analyses.* Paper presented at the annual meeting of the American Educational Research Association, San Francisco.

Mirel, J. (1990, August). What history can teach us about school decentralization. *Network News and Views, 9*(8), 40-47.

Mitchell, D. E., & Beach, S. A. (1993, May). School restructuring: The superintendent's view. *Educational Administration Quarterly, 29*(2), 249-274.

Mojkowski, C., & Fleming, D. (1988). *School-site management: Concepts and approaches.* Andover, MA: Regional Laboratory for the Educational Improvement of the Northeast and Islands.

Moore-Johnson, S. (1989, May). *Teachers, power, and school change.* Paper presented at the conference on choice and control in American education, University of Wisconsin-Madison.

Morgan, D. S. (1939). Difficulties inherent in the development of democratic procedures in city school administration. In W. C. Reavis (Ed.), *Democratic practices in school administration: Proceedings of the eighth annual conference for administrative officers of public and private schools: 1939* (pp. 29-40). Chicago: University of Chicago Press.

Moyle, C. (1989, January). *Implementation mechanisms for facilitating community participation in school management in Victoria, Australia:*

An overview case study. (ERIC Document Reproduction Service No. ED 322 590)

Mulkeen, T. A. (1990). *Reinventing school leadership* [Working memo prepared for the Reinventing School Leadership Conference]. Cambridge, MA: National Center for Educational Leadership.

Murphy, J. (1988, Summer). Methodological, measurement, and conceptual problems in the study of administrator instructional leadership. *Educational Evaluation and Policy Analysis, 10*(2), 117-139.

Murphy, J. (1989a, Fall). Educational reform and equity: A re-examination of prevailing thought. *Planning and Changing, 20*(3), 172-179.

Murphy, J. (1989b, Fall). Educational reform in the 1980s: Explaining some surprising success. *Educational Evaluation and Policy Analysis, 11*(3), 209-223.

Murphy, J. (1989c, February). Is there equity in educational reform? *Educational Leadership, 46*(5), 32-33.

Murphy, J. (1990). The educational reform movement of the 1980s: A comprehensive analysis. In J. Murphy (Ed.), *The reform of American public education in the 1980s: Perspectives and cases* (pp. 3-55). Berkeley, CA: McCutchan.

Murphy, J. (1991). *Restructuring schools: Capturing and assessing the phenomena.* New York: Teachers College Press.

Murphy, J. (1992a). School effectiveness and school restructuring: Contributions to educational improvement. *School Effectiveness and School Improvement, 3*(2), 90-109.

Murphy, J. (1992b). *The landscape of leadership preparation: Reframing the education of school administrators.* Newbury Park, CA: Corwin.

Murphy, J. (1993a). Restructuring: In search of a movement. In J. Murphy & P. Hallinger (Eds.), *Restructuring schooling: Learning from ongoing efforts* (pp. 1-31). Newbury Park, CA: Corwin.

Murphy, J. (1993b, May). Restructuring schooling: The equity infrastructure. *School Effectiveness and School Improvement, 4*(2), 111-130.

Murphy, J. (1994a). *Principles of school-based management.* Chapel Hill: North Carolina Educational Policy Research Center.

Murphy, J. (1994b). Transformational change and the evolving role of the principalship: Early empirical evidence. In J. Murphy & K. S. Louis (Eds.), *Reshaping the principalship: Insights from transformational reform efforts* (pp. 20-53). Thousand Oaks, CA: Corwin.

Murphy, J. (in press a). Restructuring in Kentucky: The changing role of the superintendent and district office. In K. A. Leithwood (Ed.), *Effective school district leadership: Transforming politics into education.* Albany: State University Press of New York.

Murphy, J. (in press b). Restructuring schools in Kentucky: Insights from superintendents. *Planning and Changing.*

Murphy, J. (in press c). The changing role of the superintendency in restructuring districts in Kentucky. *School Effectiveness and School Improvement.*

Murphy, J. (in press d). The changing role of the teacher. In M. J. O'Hair & S. J. Odell (Eds.), *Educating teachers for leadership and change* (Teacher Education Yearbook 3). Thousand Oaks, CA: Corwin.

Murphy, J., & Beck, L. G. (in press). *Reshaping school-based management for school improvement.* Thousand Oaks, CA: Corwin.

Murphy, J., Evertson, C., & Radnofsky, M. (1991, November). Restructuring schools: Fourteen elementary and secondary teachers' proposals for reform. *Elementary School Journal, 92*(2), 135-148.

Murphy, J., & Hallinger, P. (1989, March-April). Equity as access to learning: Curricular and instructional treatment differences. *Journal of Curriculum Studies, 21*(2), 129-149.

Murphy, J., & Hallinger, P. (1993). Restructuring schooling: Learning from ongoing efforts. In J. Murphy & P. Hallinger (Eds.), *Restructuring schooling: Learning from ongoing efforts* (pp. 251-271). Newbury Park, CA: Corwin.

Murphy, J., Hallinger, P., & Mesa, R. P. (1985, Summer). School effectiveness: Checking progress and assumptions and developing a role for state and federal government. *Teachers College Record, 86*(4), 615-641.

Murphy, J., Weil, M., Hallinger, P., & Mitman, A. (1982, December). Academic press: Translating high expectations into school policies and classroom practices. *Educational Leadership, 40*(3), 22-26.

Mutchler, S. E. (1990a, March). Eight barriers to changing traditional behavior: Part 1. *Insights on Educational Policy and Practice,* (18), 1-4.

Mutchler, S. E. (1990b, April). Eight barriers to changing tradition-al behavior: Part 2. *Insights on Educational Policy and Practice*, (19), 1-4.

Mutchler, S. E., & Duttweiler, P. C. (1990, April). *Implementing shared decision making in school-based management: Barriers to chang-ing traditional behavior*. Paper presented at the annual meeting of the American Educational Research Association, Boston.

National Commission on Excellence in Education. (1983, April). *A nation at risk: The imperative of educational reform*. Washington, DC: U.S. Government Printing Office.

National Governors' Association. (1986). *The governors' 1991 report on education—time for results*. Washington, DC: Author.

National Science Board. (1983). *Educating Americans for the 21st century*. Washington, DC: Author.

Newlon, J. H. (1939). *Education for democracy in our time*. New York: McGraw-Hill.

Notes from the Field. (1991). *Special feature: School-based decision-making* (Vol. 1, No. 2). Charleston, SC: Appalachia Educational Laboratory.

Oakes, J. (1985). *Keeping track: How schools structure inequality*. New Haven, CT: Yale University Press.

Oates, W. E. (1972). *Fiscal federation*. New York: Harcourt Brace Jovanovich.

Ogawa, R. T. (1992, April). *The institutional sources of educational reform: The case of school-based management*. Paper presented at the Thirteenth National Graduate Student Research Seminar in Educational Administration, San Francisco.

Olson, L. (1990). Milwaukee's choice program enlists 391 volun-teers. *Education Week, 10*(2), 1, 14-15.

Olson, L. (1991a). Dallas schools seek to streamline decisionmak-ing. *Education Week, 10*(16), 9.

Olson, L. (1991b). Effort to cut back D.C.'s bureaucracy proves nettlesome. *Education Week, 11*(12), 1, 18-19.

Olson, L. (1992a). A matter of choice: Minnesota puts "charter schools" idea to test. *Education Week, 12*(12), 1, 10-11.

Olson, L. (1992b). Chubb, Moe urge look at lessons of British reforms. *Education Week, 11*(27), 11.

Olson, L. (1992c). Detroit Board set to vote on plan "to empower" schools. *Education Week, 11*(26), 5.

Ornstein, A. C. (1983). Administrative decentralization and community policy: Review and outlook. *Urban Review, 15*(1), 3-10.

Ortman, E. J. (1923). *Teacher councils: The organized means for securing the co-operation of all workers in the school.* Montpelier, VT: Capital City Press.

O'Shea, D. W. (1975, August). School district decentralization: The case of Los Angeles. *Education and Urban Society, 7*(4), 377-392.

Ovando, M. N. (1993, October). *Effects of site-based management on the instructional program.* Paper presented at the annual meeting of the University Council for Educational Administration, Houston, TX.

Pacific Region Educational Laboratory. (1992, August). *Evaluation of implementation of school/community management: Final report.* Honolulu, HI: Author.

Passow, A. H. (1984, April). *Reforming schools in the 1980s: A critical review of the national reports.* New York: Columbia University, Teachers College, Institute for Urban and Minority Education.

Perry, N. J. (1988, July 4). The education crisis: What business can do. *Fortune,* pp. 38-41.

Peterson, P. E. (1975, August). Afterward: The politics of school decentralization. *Education and Urban Society, 7*(4), 464-479.

Petrie, H. G. (1990). Reflecting on the second wave of reform: Restructuring the teaching profession. In S. L. Jacobson & J. A. Conway (Eds.), *Educational leadership in an age of reform* (pp. 14-29). New York: Longman.

Porter, S. (1989). *Wisdom's passing: The decline of American public education in the post-World War II era and what we can really do about it.* New York: Barclay.

Portner, J. (1994). School violence up over past 5 years, 82% in survey say. *Education Week, 13*(16), 9.

Prestine, N. A. (1991, October). *Shared decision making in restructuring essential schools: The role of the principal.* Paper presented at the annual conference of the University Council for Educational Administration, Baltimore, MD.

Prickett, R. L., Flanigan, J. L., Richardson, M. D., & Petrie, G. F. (1990, October). *Who knows what?: Site-based management.* Paper presented at the annual meeting of the University Council for Educational Administration, Pittsburgh.

Prilleltensky, I. (1989). Psychology and the status quo. *American Psychology, 44,* 795-802.

Purkey, S. D., & Smith, M. S. (1983). Effective schools: A review. *Elementary School Journal, 83*(4), 427-452.

Quality Education for Minorities Project. (1990). *Education that works: An action plan for the education of minorities.* Cambridge: MIT Press.

Rallis, S. F. (1990). Professional teachers and restructured schools: Leadership challenges. In B. Mitchell & L. L. Cunningham (Eds.), *Educational leadership and changing contexts of families, communities, and schools* (89th NSSE Yearbook, Part 2, pp. 184-209). Chicago: University of Chicago Press.

Reed, A. W., Prickett, R. L., Richardson, M. D., & Flanigan, J. L. (1990, November). *Site-based management: Knowledge base of Kentucky superintendents.* Paper presented at the annual meeting of the Mid-South Educational Research Association, New Orleans, LA.

Reed, C. J. (1992, April). *Political basis of teacher response to opportunities for involvement in school site policy and curriculum decision.* Paper presented at the annual meeting of the American Educational Research Association, San Francisco.

Reeves, F. W. (1939). Principles of democratic administration. In W. C. Reavis (Ed.), *Democratic practices in school administration: Proceedings of the eighth annual conference for administrative officers of public and private schools: 1939* (pp. 16-28). Chicago: University of Chicago Press.

Reyes, P., & Laible, J. (1993, October). *Building commitment to school restructuring.* Paper presented at the annual meeting of the University Council for Educational Administration, Houston, TX.

Rice, E. M., & Schneider, G. T. (1992, April). *A decade of teacher empowerment: An empirical analysis of teacher involvement in decision making.* Paper presented at the annual meeting of the American Educational Research Association, San Francisco.

Riley, D. (1984, Winter). Teacher utilization of avenues for participatory decision-making. *Journal of Educational Administration, 22*(1), 35-46.

Robertson, P. J., & Buffett, T. M. (1991, April). *The move to decentralize: Predictors of early success.* Paper presented at the annual meeting of the American Educational Research Association, Chicago.

Rogers, D. (1973). Foreword. In J. M. Cronin, *The control of urban schools: Perspectives on the power of educational reformers* (pp. xiii-xx). New York: Free Press.

Rogers, D. (1981, July). *School decentralization in New York City.* (ERIC Document Reproduction Service No. ED 219 466)

Rogers, D., & Chung, N. H. (1983). *110 Livingston Street revisited: Decentralization in action.* New York: New York University Press.

Rothstein, R. (1990, November). *Shared decision making—the first year.* Los Angeles: Los Angeles Unified School District, Independent Analysis Unit.

Rowley, S. R. (1992, April). *School district restructuring and the search for coherence: A case study of adaptive realignment and organizational change.* Paper presented at the annual meeting of the American Educational Research Association, San Francisco.

Rumbaut, M. (1992). *Project A+: School improvement in AISD.* Austin, TX: Austin Independent School District, Office of Research and Evaluation.

Rungeling, B., & Glover, R. W. (1991, January). Educational restructuring—the process for change? *Urban Education, 25*(4), 415-427.

Rutherford, B. (1991, April). *School-based management and school improvement: How it happened in three school districts.* Paper presented at the annual meeting of the American Educational Research Association, Chicago.

Sackney, L. E., & Dibski, D. J. (1992, August). *School-based management: A critical perspective.* Paper presented at the Seventh Regional Conference of the Commonwealth Council for Educational Administration, Hong Kong.

Schlechty, P. C. (1990). *Schools for the 21st century: Leadership imperatives for educational reform.* San Francisco: Jossey-Bass.

Schmidt, P. (1992). Census data find more are falling behind in school. *Education Week, 11*(38), 1, 9.

Schmidt, P. (1993). Hispanic poverty said linked to lack of education. *Education Week, 13*(1), 22.

Schmidt, P. (1994, January). Fraud marred N.Y.C. elections, report says. *Education Week, 13*(16), 11.

School Administration and Teachers. (1918). *School and Society, 8,* 740-741.

Sedlak, M. W., Wheeler, C. W., Pullin, D. C., & Cusick, P. A. (1986). *Selling students short: Classroom bargains and academic reform in the American high school.* New York: Teachers College Press.

Seeley, D. (1988, February). A new vision for public education. *Youth Policy, 10*(2), 34-36.

Seeley, D. S. (1980, February). *The bankruptcy of service delivery.* Presentation delivered before the Foundation Lunch Group: Panel on Children at the Edwin Gould Foundation for Children, New York.

Seeley, D. S. (1981). *Education through partnership.* Washington, DC: American Enterprise Institute for Public Policy Research.

Sergiovanni, T. J. (1991). *The principalship: A reflective practice perspective* (2nd ed.). Boston: Allyn & Bacon.

Shafritz, J. M., & Ott, J. S. (Eds.). (1992). *Classics of organization theory* (3rd ed., pp. 143-149). Pacific Grove, CA: Brooks/Cole.

Short, P. M., & Greer, J. T. (1989, March). *Increasing teacher autonomy through shared governance: Effects on policy making and student outcomes.* Paper presented at the annual meeting of the American Educational Research Association, San Francisco.

Sickler, J. L. (1988, January). Teachers in charge: Empowering the professionals. *Phi Delta Kappan, 69*(5), 354-356, 375-376.

Sirotnik, K. A., & Clark, R. W. (1988, May). School-centered decision making and renewal. *Phi Delta Kappan, 69*(9), 660-664.

Sizer, T. R. (1984). *Horace's compromise: The dilemma of the American high school.* Boston: Houghton Mifflin.

Sizer, T. R. (1992). *Horace's school: Redesigning the American high school.* Boston: Houghton Mifflin.

Slater, R. (1994, February). Symbolic educational leadership and democracy in America. *Educational Administration Quarterly, 30*(1), 97-101.

Smith, W. E. (1993, April). *Teachers' perceptions of role change through shared decision making: A two-year case study.* Paper presented at the annual meeting of the American Educational Research Association, Atlanta, GA.

Smylie, M. A. (1991, October). *Participatory decision making at the district level: Interactions between teacher work redesign and administrators' work roles.* Paper presented at the annual meeting of the University Council for Educational Administration, Baltimore, MD.

Smylie, M. A., & Denny, J. W. (1989, March). *Teacher leadership: Tension and ambiguities in organizational perspective.* Paper presented at the annual meeting of the American Educational Leadership Association, San Francisco.

Smyth, J. (Ed.). (1993a). *A socially critical view of the self-managing school*. London: Taylor & Francis.

Smyth, J. (1993b). Introduction. In J. Smyth (Ed.), *A socially critical view of the self-managing school*. (pp. 1-9). London: Taylor & Francis.

Snauwaert, D. T. (1993). *Democracy, education, and governance: A developmental conception*. Albany: State University of New York Press.

Sokoloff, H., & Fagan, J. (1991, February). *Restructuring for collaboration: A case study of school-based/university-based collaboration*. Paper presented at the annual meeting of the American Association of School Administrators, San Diego, CA.

Sommerfeld, M. (1992a). RJR Nabisco lays 30-million bet on "bottom up" reform strategy. *Education Week, 11*(38), 10-11.

Sommerfeld, M. (1992b). Survey charts rise in health problems among pupils. *Education Week, 12*(3), 8.

Spring, J. (1986). *The American school 1642-1985: Varieties of historical interpretation of the foundations and development of American education*. New York: Longman.

Spring, J. (1988). *Conflict of interests: The politics of American education*. New York: Longman.

Steffy, B. E. (1993). *The Kentucky education reform: Lessons for America*. Lancaster, PA: Technomic.

Stevenson, K. R., & Pellicer, L. O. (1992). School-based management in South Carolina: Balancing state-directed reform with local decision making. In J. J. Lane & E. G. Epps (Eds.), *Restructuring the schools: Problems and prospects* (pp. 123-139). Berkeley, CA: McCutchan.

Stevenson, Z. (1990, September). *Local school-based management in the District of Columbia Public Schools: First impressions of pilot sites*. Washington, DC: District of Columbia Public Schools. (ERIC Document Reproduction Service No. ED 331 188)

Stoll, L., & Fink, D. (1992). Effecting school change: The Halton approach. *School Effectiveness and School Improvement, 3*(1), 19-41.

Strusinski, M. (1991, April). *The continuing development of shared decision making in school-based management*. Dade County, FL: Dade County Public Schools.

Sykes, G., & Elmore, R. F. (1989). Making schools manageable: Policy and administration for tomorrow's schools. In J. Hannaway &

R. Crowson (Eds.), *The politics of reforming school administration* (pp. 77-94). New York: Falmer.

Taylor, D. L. (1992). *Restructuring in an urban setting: How one elementary school got started.* Paper presented at the annual meeting of the Association for Supervision and Curriculum Development, New Orleans, LA.

Taylor, D. L., & Bogotch, I. E. (1992, January). *Teacher decisional participation: Rhetoric or reality?* Paper presented at the annual meeting of the Southwest Educational Research Association, Houston, TX.

Taylor, F. W. (1992). The principles of scientific management. In J. M. Shafritz & J. S. Ott (Eds.), *Classics of organization theory* (3rd ed., pp. 69-80). Pacific Grove, CA: Brooks/Cole. (Original work published in 1916)

Thompson, J. A. (1988). The second wave of educational reform: Implications for school leadership, administration, and organization. In F. C. Wendel & M. T. Bryant (Eds.), *New directions for administrator preparation* (pp. 9-24). Tempe, AZ: University Council for Educational Administration.

Trestrail, C. (1992, July). *Devolution: Evolution or revolution.* Paper presented at the annual meeting of the Australian Council for Educational Administration, Darwin, Northern Territory.

Twentieth Century Fund. (1983). *Making the grade.* New York: Author.

Tyack, D. (1990, Winter). "Restructuring" in historical perspective: Tinkering toward utopia. *Teachers College Record, 92*(2), 170-191.

Tyack, D. (1993). School governance in the United States: Historical puzzles and anomalies. In J. Hannaway & M. Carnoy (Eds.), *Decentralization and school improvement* (pp. 1-32). San Francisco: Jossey-Bass.

Tyack, D. B. (1974). *The one best system: A history of American urban education.* Cambridge, MA: Harvard University Press.

Urban, W. J. (1978). Preface. In G. S. Counts, *Dare the schools build a new social order?* (pp. v-xiv). Carbondale and Edwardsville: Southern Illinois University Press. (Original work published 1932)

U.S. Bureau of the Census. (1960). *Historical statistics of the United States: Colonial times to 1957.* Washington, DC: Author.

Viadero, D. (1993). Majority of education workforce found to be non-teachers. *Education Week, 13*(14), 3.

Viadero, D. (1994). Impact of reform said to be spotty and not systemic. *Education Week, 13*(20), 1, 12.

Wagstaff, L. H., & Gallagher, K. S. (1990). Schools, families, and communities: Idealized images and new realities. In B. Mitchell & L. L. Cunningham (Eds.), *Educational leadership and changing contexts of families, communities, and schools* (pp. 91-117). Chicago: University of Chicago Press.

Wagstaff, L. H., & Reyes, P. (1993, August). *School site-based management* (Report presented to the Educational Economic Policy Center). Austin: University of Texas, College of Education.

Wallace, J., & Wildy, H. (1993, April). *Pioneering school change: Lessons from a case study of school site restructuring.* Paper presented at the annual meeting of the American Educational Research Association, Atlanta, GA.

Wardzala, E. (1993). *School-based management and the role of the superintendent.* Unpublished doctoral dissertation, Vanderbilt University, Nashville, TN.

Warren, D. (1990). Passage of rites: On the history of educational reform in the United States. In J. Murphy (Ed.), *The educational reform movement of the 1980s: Perspectives and cases* (pp. 57-81). Berkeley, CA: McCutchan.

Watkins, J. M., & Lusi, S. F. (1989, March). *Facing the essential tensions: Restructuring from where you are.* Paper presented at the annual meeting of the American Educational Research Association, San Francisco.

Watt, J. (1989). The devolution of power: The ideological meaning. *Journal of Educational Administration, 27*(1), 19-28.

Wayson, W. W. (1966, March). The political revolution in education, 1965. *Phi Delta Kappan, 47*(7), 333-339.

Weick, K. E., & McDaniel, R. R. (1989). How professional organizations work: Implications for school organization and management. In T. J. Sergiovanni & J. H. Moore (Eds.), *Schooling for tomorrow: Directing reforms to issues that count* (pp. 330-355). Boston: Allyn & Bacon.

Weiss, C. H. (1993, February). *Interests and ideologies in educational reform: Changing the venue of decision making in the high school* (Occasional Paper #19). Cambridge, MA: National Center for Educational Leadership.

Weiss, C. H., & Cambone, J. (1993, August). *Principals' roles in shared decision making: Managing skepticism and frustration* (Occasional

Paper #24). Cambridge: National Center for Educational Leadership.

Weiss, C. H., Cambone, J., & Wyeth, A. (1991, April). *Trouble in paradise: Teacher conflicts in shared decision making* (Occasional Paper #8). Cambridge, MA: National Center for Educational Leadership.

Wise, A. E. (1978, February). The hyper-rationalization of American education. *Educational Leadership, 35*(5), 354-361.

Wise, A. E. (1989). Professional teaching: A new paradigm for the management of education. In T. J. Sergiovanni & J. H. Moore (Eds.), *Schooling for tomorrow: Directing reforms to issues that count* (pp. 301-310). Boston: Allyn & Bacon.

Wissler, D. F., & Ortiz, F. I. (1988). *The superintendent's leadership in school reform.* Philadelphia, PA: Falmer.

Wohlstetter, P. (1990, April). *Experimenting with decentralization: The politics of change.* (ERIC Document Reproduction Service No. ED 337 861)

Wohlstetter, P., & Buffett, T. (1991, March). *School-based management in big city districts: Are dollars decentralized too?* Paper presented at the annual meeting of the American Educational Research Association, Chicago.

Wohlstetter, P., & McCurdy, K. (1991, January). The link between school decentralization and school politics. *Urban Education, 25*(4), 391-414.

Wohlstetter, P., & Mohrman, S. A. (1993, January). *School-based management: Strategies for success.* New Brunswick, NJ: CPRE Finance Briefs.

Wohlstetter, P., & Odden, A. (1992, November). Rethinking school-based management policy and research. Paper presented at the annual meeting of the American Educational Research Association, New Orleans, LA. Also in *Educational Administration Quarterly, 28*(4), 529-549.

Wood, C. J. (1984, Fall). Participatory decision making: Why doesn't it seem to work? *Educational Forum, 49*(1), 55-64.

Yauch, W. A. (1949). *Improving human relations in school administration.* New York: Harper & Brothers.

Zuckerman, D. W. (1992, April). *Shared decision making teams and school restructuring in NYC: Problems of management and leadership.* Paper presented at the annual meeting of the American Educational Research Association, San Francisco.

Zwyine, J., Stoll, L., Adam, E., Fullan, M., & Bennett, B. (1991, April). *Leadership effectiveness and school development: Putting reform in perspective.* Paper presented at the annual meeting of the American Educational Research Association, Chicago.

Index